CW00820397

SELECTED LETTERS

BOOKS BY CESARE PAVESE

Fiction

Among Women Only
The Beach and A Great Fire
The Comrade
The Devil in the Hills
Festival Night and Other Stories
The Harvesters
The House on the Hill
The Political Prisoner and The Beautiful Summer
Summer Storm and Other Stories

Non-Fiction

Dialogues with Leucò
A Mania for Solitude: Selected Poems
This Business of Living: A Diary, 1935-1950

Cesare Pavese

SELECTED LETTERS

1924 - 1950

Edited, translated from the Italian
and with an Introduction by
A. E. MURCH

PETER OWEN · LONDON

SBN 7206 1520 8

PETER OWEN LIMITED
12 Kendrick Mews Kendrick Place London SW7

First British Commonwealth edition 1969

Printed in Great Britain by
Bristol Typesetting Co Ltd
Barton Manor St Philips Bristol

Contents

Introduction

Almost immediately after Cesare Pavese's death by suicide in August 1950, the publishing firm of Giulio Einaudi, in Turin, who employed him as an editor and had published his poems, short stories and novels, began collecting his letters with a view to publication. They had three main sources : notes found among his papers, letters preserved by the people to whom they were written, and the files of the firm itself, which contained copies of Pavese's letters to would-be writers, translators and contributors to the various literary reviews published by Einaudi.

This task took some years to complete. Many letters had not been preserved by their recipients, particularly during the troubled war period. Pavese's friend and colleague, Italo Calvino, succeeded in recovering from America the letters Pavese had written in English to his contacts in the United States. Eventually, in 1966, Messrs Einaudi published in two large volumes more than thirteen hundred letters written by Pavese. Sometimes they were able to clarify the correspondence by giving in full the letters to which Pavese was replying. The whole collection has been meticulously edited by the publishers, even in such detail as adding a footnote when a word or two of Pavese's 'surrealist handwriting' defied all attempts to decipher it.

From this mass of material I have selected, for translation into English, those of his letters that shed the clearest light upon Pavese's own personality, his passion for literature, his views on life in general and people in particular. I have provided footnotes to clarify certain details for English-speaking readers.

Ideally, his letters should be read in conjunction with his personal diary, *Il mestiere di vivere,*[1] in which he recorded his fears and hopes, his successes and his all too frequent disappointments. His diary, however, dates from 1935, when he was fast becoming disillusioned and cynical, an introvert much given to self-analysis. His letters, on the other hand, began in November 1924, and so cover the important period of his adolescence, when he still felt a boyish zest for life and literature, an eager conviction that he would become a poet and a successful writer of fiction.

[1] *This Business of Living: A Diary 1935-1950,* ed and trans A. E. Murch (Peter Owen, 1961).

During his student years at the University of Turin he made a special study of English language and literature, but felt increasingly drawn towards America. The subject he chose for his thesis (against the advice of his tutor) was *The Poetry of Walt Whitman,* which won him his degree. He was already planning to translate works by American novelists—Sinclair Lewis, Herman Melville and Sherwood Anderson.[2]

Pavese's keen interest in American literature was fostered by his contact with an American student, Antony Chiuminatto, who spent the summer of 1929 in Turin and became acquainted with Pavese and some of his friends. When Chiuminatto returned to the United States, the two young men began a correspondence that continued for three or four years. Pavese was eager to learn all he could about current colloquial American terms, including slang, and the traditional phrases used to give orders to the crew aboard ship, to help him in translating *Moby Dick.* Pavese wrote to this friend in English, or, rather, in what he believed to be colloquial 'American', and, apart from a few excisions, I have left these letters unchanged. The youthful exuberance of this correspondence, its gay humour and optimism, is in sharp contrast to the sardonic, pessimistic or introspective tone he so often adopted in letters to Italian friends and in his fiction. Pavese also wrote in English, but more formally, to some of his English-speaking friends, notably Gertrude Stein and the sisters Constance and Doris Dowling. The letters he penned in English are indicated by an asterisk in the headnote.

Pavese longed for the love of a wife, but in vain. His shyness, his moods of depression, his asthma and the thick glasses he had to wear, made him diffident about approaching any girl. He dreaded being made to look foolish, for by nature he was a proud man and extremely sensitive. Apart from casual acquaintances, the only girl with whom he enjoyed a long-term friendship was Fernanda Pivano, and examples of his letters to her have been included in this selection. They first met when Pavese was teaching for a few months at the school she attended as a pupil. Later they met again and during holiday periods they enjoyed walking or cycling through the countryside near their homes. For her, their friendship was purely platonic, but Pavese fell more and

[2] At this period there was no embargo on translating foreign novels into Italian, but during the war a strict censorship came into operation, under the Minister for Popular Culture. No translation could even be started until the Minister's office had given permission. In several of his letters Pavese goes into detail about the restrictions he had to face.

more in love with her. On several occasions he begged her to marry him. She refused, but their friendship continued pleasantly enough until she married someone else. Thereafter his contact with her was limited to encouraging her to continue working as a translator.

Another figure shines out from this period, that of Pavese's sister Maria. Their mother, who died soon after Cesare obtained his degree, had been an austere disciplinarian, rarely showing her children any affection or sympathetic understanding. Maria was undemonstrative but considered it her duty to help her brother, who was six years younger than herself. She and her husband had two little daughters and their house was not large, but nevertheless they contrived to give Cesare a room in their home. For the rest of his life he used it as a study, a bedroom and a place where he could receive his friends.

When Pavese was sent to prison in 1935 for 'subversive activities' he was allowed to write to one member of his family, but to no one else. He wisely chose Maria. His letters show how staunchly she carried out his wishes, bringing him books he asked for, conveying messages to his friends, doing her best to buy items he wanted, with hardly a word of appreciation. (He exclaimed in a later letter : 'At least I realise the value of family ties.')

After his release, Pavese continued translating the work of English and American novelists—Dos Passos, Gertrude Stein, Dickens, Defoe, Melville and Faulkner among others. His employment as an editor brought him in touch with would-be translators, among them his old friend Fernanda Pivano, to whom he gave encouragement and sound professional advice from his own first-hand experience. He stressed the truism that a word-by-word rendering is not a translation. It is essential to recreate the atmosphere of the original, remembering that every language has its own characteristic pattern for shaping sentences. Even the punctuation may need alteration if the true meaning is to be conveyed to the reader.

From 1945 onwards Pavese was gaining increased recognition as one of the most outstanding figures in contemporary Italian literature. In 1950 he won the Strega Prize for his novel *Tra donne sole*.[3] His career seemed at its peak and great things were expected of him. Those hopes were to remain frustrated, destroyed by a personal grief.

While staying with friends in Rome, Pavese met two young

[3] *Among Women Only*, trans D. D. Paige (Peter Owen, 1953).

American girls who had come to Italy with a film unit, working on location, Constance Dowling and her elder sister Doris. Pavese was captivated by their beauty, their freedom of speech and action, their typical American frankness. He fell in love with Constance—some of his letters to her are included in this selection, dated March, April and May 1950.[4] At first he tended to regard Doris as 'the practical one' and discussed with her his ideas for a scenario to be called *The Two Sisters*. They were good friends: Doris accompanied him when he was presented with the Strega Prize and did her best to reassure him when Constance, who had returned to America, failed to keep her promise to write to him and to come back to Italy. For months Pavese was buoyed up with hope that both sisters would return to him, that one of them might agree to marry him, but at last he accepted the truth that this wish would remain unfulfilled.

In August his colleague Mario Motta wrote to raise a query about correcting certain proof-sheets, adding that 'the American girl is back in Rome'. Pavese replied: 'Who has "returned"? the American girl? I've something else to think of now.'

Indeed he had. Ever since boyhood he had been obsessed by the idea of suicide. Now his disappointments with life had become unbearable. On the evening of 26th August, 1950 he left home, nodding as usual to his sister but saying nothing. In the street he boarded a tram, then wandered about for a while and finally entered a hotel where he was not known. He asked for a room with a telephone, and was given one on the third floor. He made three or four calls to friends, the last being to Fernanda. The following morning he was found dead from an overdose of sleeping tablets.

A. E. Murch

[4] Ten poems (eight in Italian and two in English) for Constance Dowling, written by Pavese (probably in Turin) between 11th March and 11th April 1950, were found in Pavese's office at Einaudi's after his death. Published by Einaudi in 1951, they are included in the collection in English translation, *A Mania for Solitude: Selected Poems, 1930-1950,* trans Margaret Crosland (Peter Owen, 1969), published concurrently with the present volume.

1924 - 1925

To Mario Sturani, Monza[1]

Turin [in reply to a letter
dated 4th November 1924]

My thanks to you, good friend! Your warmth and fervour
Almost convince me, even against my will.
From you I learn that joy bursts into bloom
Along the path you tread for that sole purpose.
Creative fire is blazing in you now,
Dispelling any hope that you'll find time
To study Nature's self. Do you not see
The universe as one unending act
Of new creation for the greater glory
Of its own God, indeed for that alone?

I've always thought that all one needs to do is to mount the creative muse like a horse and control it by the reins, but my trouble is that I'm convinced my muse is like one of those bony, worn-out cab horses in the market square. Believing this, how can I summon up enough nerve to seize the reins?

However, since I'm writing, I'll let my pen run on and tell you my thoughts. A stanza by Tagore keeps running through my mind. Here it is:

Languor is upon your heart and the slumber is still in your eyes.
Has the word not come to you that the flower is reigning in splendour
Among thorns? Wake, oh awake! Let not time pass in vain. At the
End of the stony path, in the country of virgin solitude, my friend
Is sitting all alone. Deceive him not. Wake, oh waken!

[1] Written when Pavese was sixteen. Sturani was one of his few close friends at the Liceo D'Azeglio. After three years at that school, Sturani left it in the summer of 1924 and went to Monza to study decorative art.

What if the sky pants and trembles in the heat of the midday sun?
What if the burning sand spreads its mantle of thirst? Is there no
Joy in the deep of your heart? At every footfall of yours, will not
The harp of the road break out in the sweet music of pain?[2]

That describes me absolutely, don't you think? I shall make it my rule in life. Tell me, don't you agree that there's no joy greater than the joy of suffering? Don't laugh. Please tell me exactly what you think. Don't forget I've told you that some of your poems 'aren't much good'. Now do the same for me. It would be the greatest proof of friendship you could give me. I hope to send you plenty of work to keep you busy. Would you like a word of advice? When considering my verses, forget it was I who wrote them.

I'm counting on finding fresh inspiration, one of these days, and reviving my poetic fire (fires of straw) by taking another look at the *Vita nuova*, trying not to let my own thoughts intrude.

I notice, and am not too pleased about it, that you're getting to be a real highbrow. Quotations from here, quotations from there. In this field, I assure you, you are well ahead of me.

Some day I'll manage to write you (not that I'm sure you'll understand it) an outpouring of all my boyhood. Oh, my memories of my early studies of the *Vita nuova*! I don't understand it completely, even now, but don't let that trouble you. It's not for lack of intelligence. I'm talking about the innermost depth of my soul.

Meanwhile, going on to philosophy, you say: 'Poetry is the awareness of beauty.' It is more than that. It's an awareness of everything, beauty and ugliness, good and evil, truth and falsehood, *that clash of good and bad that is life itself*. There can be poetry in a painting, too. Poetry is everywhere. The ability to perceive it is a divine gift, the only thing we can truly call our own, since science is, in a way, a reality outside ourselves, belonging to everyone and to no one. Even so, if a man turns to science, it is because he is attracted to it by his personal preference. The fact that you are enjoying life so much, stems from your own attitude towards it. Poetry is queen of the world for everyone who can feel it. You could call it God (though I'm speaking of it in respect of man).

Your verses seem to me too detailed, too minutely contrived, to be discussed in full. For the rest, you have a surprising command

[2] Rabindranath Tagore, *Gitanjali*, Stanza LV.

of vocabulary, a freshness of phrasing that is all your own, and keen powers of observation.

C. Pavese

(The more unsure of himself a man feels, the larger his signature becomes.)

To Mario Sturani, Monza

Turin, 21st February 1925

I'm writing to you because it is a long time since I did, but I've nothing new to tell you.

I have seen good reviews of your free verse—a real triumph for you. You are quite right to say: 'As you see, they are in free verse because that is how I feel them.' I myself can no longer manage to restrict my own ideas within a network of rhyme. The utmost I can do is to hammer out blank verse. As always, these verses of yours are delightfully gay and have in my opinion a keen descriptive quality. Your ingeniously worked out allegory is not too bad, but all those subtle, inner meanings tend in my view to detract from the effectiveness of your poetry. Take for example the lines: 'Flock after flock the little grey sheep go by', and 'The wind delights in ruffling their fleece'. Let me enjoy them for their own sake, enjoying the impression they immediately make on me, without intruding glimpses of so many other things. Nevertheless, you have a happy touch when revealing your true purpose, and your spring morning was well chosen. That season is dawning at this very moment, and I feel myself gradually coming to life. My spirit glows with fresh inspiration, I feel gay and I laugh at misfortune. I'm trying my utmost to restore myself and enjoy all these good things. More and more I realise how much I hate science and love every kind of art.

I shall enjoy the spring, rambling in the country with Baraldi and

Barale,[3] revisiting of course those cliffs by the Sangone. All I need is the baptism of love (as others talk about the baptism of fire). Then I shall be content. When I look at the lovely faces and beautiful bodies I see around me, I have the feeling I am missing something. Some time or other, tell me in detail your own feeling on this subject.

I can't tell you how pleased I was with your review of those few verses I wrote for Luty.[4] For a whole day I did nothing but laugh and day-dream, looking down on other men from my superior height or embracing them as a brother. You inspired me with a greater pride than Dante ever knew. Not that I have any desire to set myself above Dante. I appreciate, much more than I did at one time, how great, how exalted, Dante is. We must strive to follow him. No doubt you, too, realise more and more each day the greatness of Leopardi and his contemporaries.

About painting, I have at last succeeded in understanding one of Botticelli's pictures, his Madonna and Child with a pomegranate. It is sublime. The canvas is discoloured, the technique somewhat unsure, the faces have imperfections and the background is insignificant, but if you gaze at it long enough you will see what depth of expression there is in the face of the Madonna, so childlike, so thin and pale, so reddened by her tears.

To me, the distinctive features of Botticelli's art lie in the sweeping clarity of his lines and, even more, his colours, his typical introduction of slight irregularity in his faces to make them more interesting. You know about such things. Tell me if I'm right. I know very little about the painters of that period, but it seems to me that the one who comes nearest to Botticelli, in technique at least, is Fra Filippo Lippi.

So much for the artistic-literary point of view. Between ourselves, I consider that your own power of description comes very close to Botticelli's.

My mind is stagnating. Once a man becomes tied up with materialism, he can go no further with art. Everything is ruined. There's nothing left for him but to seek pleasure for its own sake,

[3] Baraldi and Barale were classmates of Pavese's for some years, first at the *ginnasio,* later at the *liceo*. A year after this letter was written, Erico Baraldi killed himself with a revolver following an unhappy love-affair. This act had a tremendous effect on Pavese, as did the suicide of another of his school friends shortly afterwards—namely, Carlo Predella, son of the mathematics teacher at the school both boys attended. Pavese's obsession with suicide stemmed in part from these tragic events.

[4] The real or fictitious name of the girl to whom Pavese dedicated his first poems.

and that I cannot bring myself to do. I try to pull myself out of this mood, but more and more I'm convinced there's nothing I can do about it.

I hope you'll catch the fever (of creation),
Pavese

To Mario Sturani, Monza

Turin [in reply to a letter
dated 23rd February 1925]

Dear Sturani,

At this moment, as I write to you, I'm fairly well satisfied with myself, but there are times when I feel my life isn't worth tuppence.

I've gone a long way this past year. Though I feel more and more convinced that I'm still not worth much, deep in my heart, in some rare moment of perfect happiness, I catch a glimpse of strong power in the future. My ideas are growing clearer, broader. I'm getting to know my own personality. Many vague intuitions that came to me last year now present themselves much more clearly and take their proper place in the broad picture of my ego. I'm always in a ferment, even when I'm in despair, as I now am, more than ever, but I'm certain I've already done some good work, and shall do more. . . .

So now you're tackling a study of myself (with what tedium I can well imagine. Nothing is more shattering than listening to other people talking about themselves). What do you want me to tell you? You won't expect me, I hope, to describe the rebirth of spring? In any case, fair nature springs to life more lovely than ever in the paintings of Fra Lippo Lippi and Botticelli!

During the Easter holidays, from 28th March to 7th April, I shall be on a walking tour through Tuscany and Umbria.[5] Try to stay in Turin a little longer, so that I can see you when I get back.

C. Pavese

[5] Two of Pavese's school friends, Carlo Predella and Tullio Pinelli, were his companions on this trip. Pinelli took a photograph of Pavese and Predella standing beside the River Sangone, a snapshot reproduced by Davide Lajolo in his *Il vizio assurdo* (facing p. 113).

To Cesare Meano,[6] *Turin*

Turin, May-June 1925

I have just been reading your recent publication and know nothing about your 'brotherhood', though I believe I understand your ideals. Young, unknown beginner as I am, I am writing to offer you my collaboration in helping forward this work by young writers.

Here is a suggestion. I think it would be a good idea to circulate copies of the *Ricerca* among critics of good standing who would be willing to discuss with us the work under review. Then we could all learn to improve and look forward to having our work published in periodicals produced by one or other of your colleagues. Thus, instead of being a shop window as it has been so far, it could become a fertile field, a contest from which someone, even if only one, would emerge more finely tempered. Everyone would feel the touch of a spur in his flanks, and would derive vital energy from your periodical, not merely contemplative pleasures. A journal of young writers, a journal of life and of battle.

But you may object that this has already been considered, by the establishment of competitive examinations, but this seems to me inadequate; above all because there is no discussion, simply a decision that leaves the tempo unchanged, furthermore because the competition is an annual event and too specialised: so the *Ricerca* would lose nothing of its character if it were modified as I suggest.

The reform, as I should like it to be, would involve materially only an almost negligible addition, but on the other hand it could alter the whole nature of the journal. In short, as I have already said, instead of being a museum showcase full of still life, it could become a little world palpitating with vitality. Who knows? It could serve as a hotbed to bring out poetic powers in the future. That is what the title *Ricerca di poesia* should mean.

As a beginning I enclose a few of my own verses and shall have great pleasure in hearing your opinion of them. I am prepared to defend them well, but above all to recognise the truth.

C. Pavese

[6] Cesare Meano (1899-1957), a playwright, founded in 1925 a magazine called *Ricerca di poesia*. Young contemporary Italian poets who contributed to it sometimes referred to themselves as a 'brotherhood'. In addition to poetry, the magazine contained short translations from works by Tagore, Gorky, Yeats and Poe. The publication was short-lived.

To Mario Sturani, Monza

[Turin, in reply to a letter
postmarked 23rd November 1925]

Dear Sturani,

Each of us is fully intent on himself, and that's quite natural. As I write to you my teeth are clenched because I am more and more convinced that your genius is a strong conscious unity, wholly devoted to its ideal, while I'm only a poor little versifier afraid to open his eyes wide in bright sunshine lest the light should hurt him. Yet I hope that you, and all those who do something out of the ordinary, may to some extent share my endless uncertainty. But, I assure you, my trouble is no longer the depression I used to feel at school: it is a battle I have to fight every day, every hour, against inertia, dejection and fear; a conflict of opposing ideas that should, I think, refine and temper my spirit as metal is smelted and hardened by fire.

This struggle, this pain that I find so harrowing yet so very sweet, keeps me on my toes, always ready and eager, and is, in short, what drags my works from my spirit.

It seems to me I have already done a good deal and shall, I hope, do much more.

Well now, you can claim to be the main cause of this transformation of mine from schoolboy depression to constructive pain. If ever I complete a great work, I shan't forget that your strength has been a great stimulus.

'It's been a pleasure', you'll say, but bear in mind that however wretched I may feel, I am a proud man and glad to be so; remember that nothing thrills me more than thinking of the splendid isolation all men of genius know. I tell you now that, notwithstanding my love of working alone, I bow my head before you and acknowledge you have been my master. I should shout for joy if you were to write the same about me.

Leaving aside compliments, conventions and all the sugary things one says to friends, in all frankness I tell you that in my opinion you have powerful talents. I have thought so for three years. But don't believe I write this so that you should say the same about me. No, treat me as severely as you can. That will give me an incentive.

C. Pavese

To Mario Sturani, Monza

[Turin] 10th December 1925

Dear Mario,

This is extraordinary. Each of us feels inferior to the other and takes a sour kind of pleasure in declaring himself feeble and paltry. But note that we both feel our individuality. Not for anything in the world would you want to change into me, just as I would never like to change into you. We are both dissatisfied with ourselves, that's all, and this is the best possible sign that, but for the urge to keep up with one another, we should neither of us do any more work at all. Cheer up! It is also a sign that we are both destined for great things.

Meanwhile, your comment comparing your smile with those in Leonardo's paintings made me think of the term, 'a smile of resignation'. But on the lips of Leonardo's faces there is more than resignation. A whole world lies below those smiles and your own face bears, it seems to me, the mark of all that world.

Leaving aside the consideration of our respective talents, which serves no useful purpose (people alive in thirty years' time will see for themselves), I want to tell you that your letter gave me a whole day of complete happiness, free-flowing and (let us hope) productive.

Listen. I need to unburden myself of a thought that continually torments me and is the pivot round which all my inner world revolves.

In life, in our every action, even in our sacrifices, we are really seeking our own pleasure and gratification, material or spiritual. Which raises this point for consideration: 'Why should I despise and condemn (as certain futuristic thinkers do) all that is past?' I say: 'The past is gone, its customs, institutions, languages, history, all have fallen and are dead for ever. But the sentiments, the ideas, that disturbed men of the past, still live eternally in the art they created. Why consider them dead? A thought, a feeling, when you have one, is a living thing. And what is Art but a means whereby a feeling, a conception, lives for ever and can be brought actively to light by other men?'

Why should I deny myself the pleasure, the exaltation, of reviving a life that, idealised in its own art-form, can lift me out of myself and fill my breast with a surge of burning poetry? If I compose anything it is with the hope that it will last, a hope that men who, in due time, will consider this present period as the past, will be moved and exalted by it.

To enjoy this pleasure, this satisfaction of finding exaltation in the work of others, one must experience it as one does any other pleasure, and find satisfaction in reviving the dormant life within it. But when dealing with one's own art one must not say: 'Such and such a great poet did this or that, so I must therefore do the same, otherwise I shall fail as an artist.' Such stagnation is absurd, since every time one is looking at oneself and nothing else. I enjoy, find exaltation as much as I can, and seek to understand works of the past, but then, when starting my own work, all I try to do is to express as clearly as possible my own exaltation, my own feeling. In my view, this is not a worship of the past, for my feelings, my exaltation, are modern, expressing my own spirit.

All this I have expressed to you in rambling fashion, for this is the first time I have tried to explain fully my conception of Art. Try to understand it if it interests you. If not, go straight on to my review.

Critical Review

I must tell you that the first of your two poetic compositions is, as you say yourself, not worth much. Ideas are set out starkly and crudely, and the feelings you have about them in your mind are not expressed in such a way as to convey those ideas and feelings to the mind of the reader. But there are a few verses, especially towards the beginning (and don't think I'm telling you this just to sweeten the dose), that move the soul. The thought behind them is good and says things I think myself.

Don't imagine that by saying this I am running counter to those earlier lines of my own that you praised so warmly. When I wrote them I was simply working off the terror and anxiety that seizes me at the thought of a slow, conscious death agony, and I long instead for a quick death 'with no regret', a death that gathers me up in an instant of exaltation, of joy for evermore.

Your second composition is better, poetically, because it conveys more clearly the sentiment you wished to express. It would be pointless to analyse the verses one by one. They are all clear, tender, full of the vision and emotion that tormented you as you wrote them.

In all your poetry there persists an air of submission, of longing, that I can hardly explain to you. It is a new thing. Speaking pictorially, the colour of these verses, the interplay of black and white, is wonderful; so is your light touch with swiftly flying thoughts; and the serene, ecstatic flow of those verses that have no metre but are linked together by their words and accents. There is a sustained harmony flowing smoothly through the whole poem, 'a gentle murmur from beyond the tomb', as you yourself describe it. There is, too, the thought you have admirably condensed in the final line, '. . . the thousand offspring of a single love'.

I have told you all I feel. It is not flattery and you can believe it. I should have been pleased to find you inferior, but no. It seems to me that in poetry, too, you surpass me, and I tremble at the thought. Since poetry is not your personal choice of art, you treat it merely as an amateur, yet you achieve success. What then am I to do, since I have made poetry the ideal of my whole life?

Finally, here is something I knocked up two months ago, one evening on my way home from a cinema:

Within my soul there struggles hopelessly
The longing to possess a living girl,
Her spirit and her body, so that I
Could clasp her tight with no restraint, excite her,
And feel her trembling body close to mine.
But then on other, quieter days to stay
Gently beside her, with no carnal thought,
And gaze upon her soft and childlike face
All unaware, as though absorbed in grief,
And listen as her light and gentle voice
Talks to me slowly, as it does in dreams.

1926

To Mario Sturani, Monza

Turin, 4th February 1926

Dear Sturani,

It is not I myself but my sister writing to you because I am in bed. Let's hope I'll get over it. I shan't write you much for a while because I do not like disclosing my thoughts to strangers, and in this respect my sister is a stranger.

I cannot give you any sound assessment of your verses because there is something too modern in them for me to understand, something I do not feel (it must be my temperament), something, in fact, I'm afraid to understand. For the rest, I compliment you on them.

That famous work I told you about a year or two ago, I've now finished, with much weary effort, but I've done it. For the moment I'm not telling you any more about it, but you shall be the first to know it. I have exhausted all my reserves of poetic feeling and have nothing more to send you. Here in bed I would rather sleep than think. You can work, so get on with it. As for me, my will to work gets feebler every day, but if I were to lose it completely, I should kill myself. Then you will write my funeral panegyric, and I assure you that's nothing to laugh about.

Greetings,
C. Pavese

To Mario Sturani, Monza

Turin, 10th May 1926

Cheer up! You're not the only man to feel lazy. At the moment, with exams just ahead, I have to study (or seem to be studying) desperately hard, never allowing myself to slack off for a minute.

All my inner life has ossified into an absolutely dull, purely mechanical, utterly stupid effort of memory. I shall make up for it in the summer. As soon as my exams are over I'll let you know when and how to reach Reaglie.[1]

I've heard nothing more, so far, about the *Ricerca di poesia.*[2] I feel somewhat consoled by your appreciation of my little poems. The one and only thing in the world that sustains me is the hope that, now or later, I can do something really worth-while with my pen. When I stop to think about it, even that seems an empty dream.

I like these verses of yours perhaps more than all your earlier ones. The thoughts you express in them I can grasp as they fly, because they are my thoughts too. There is nothing pretentious about them, just the simple, warm-hearted expression of your spirit. The one or two flights of fancy come so naturally that they no longer strike me as intrusive, discordant trimmings. They are so expressive! The best part is from '. . . how much I cherish' to the end. The first two verses do not please me much. They give nothing new, and the presentation of the Madonna and Child seems laboured. Furthermore, I find the almost brutal words 'love born dead' so terse and so unexpected in their present context as to be rather shocking.

But I'm not going to analyse this work of yours in greater detail. What I tell you now will be worth more to you than any erudite review, supposing I could write one: I read it as if it were my own—that is, finding nothing to hurt me and living to the full all that it expresses.

Cesare Pavese

[1] A village on the hills behind Turin, where Pavese's mother had a small villa with a garden, set in open country. Cesare spent his summer vacations there, and often invited a few close friends to join him.

[2] Pavese had sent a few of his poems to Meano, hoping for publication in the *Ricerca,* but Meano had come to the conclusion that 'there's no great hope for Italian poetry at present'. From a letter (dated 16th April 1926), from Giuseppe Vaudagna to Mario Sturani, we learn that Meano had nevertheless been well impressed by Pavese's quality as an artistic personality.

To Augusto Monti,[3] *Giaveno*

Reaglie, August 1926

I have received your letter and one of these days I will call at your house, hoping to be luckier than I was last time. I shall persevere, as your letter encourages me to do. In it I found, expressed in a few words, all that I have for a long time wanted to say to you. 'This summer, after I leave school, I want to make a friend of Professor Monti.' That is what I had in mind to say, and I have already been practising a certain blunt way of saying it. If this seems to you too outspoken, remember it expresses precisely what I felt and still feel. It would run counter to the principles you taught me to dress it up in a flowery, but less straightforward, literary style. It looks as though our letters may well tend towards provincial candour, rather than to a polished elegance of phrase.

If I may, I should like to tell you how I'm occupying my time, here in the country. I scribble and study all the blessed day until, mad with frustration, I rush out of the house. There, all around me rises a ridge of wooded hills, a marvellous place for a ramble. At this point I rather expect, presumptuously perhaps, some fatherly advice from you—I should have more fun in life, sow my wild oats while I'm still young, not wait till my hair is grey, that books alone won't tell me all there is to know of the world—all the things people tell me all the time.

But you, who till now have known me only at school, can say such things to me, and with good reason. As for other people who share my daily life and are forever telling me what to do, I should almost pity them if they hadn't the excuse that my personality is too reserved for them to fathom. Just imagine! There is not one single member of my family who, over the past four years, has managed to read anything I have written without secretly trying to 'persuade me out of it'. They must understand me about as much as I understand higher mathematics. Fancy calling me 'highbrow' just because, every year, even when circumstances make it difficult for me, I spend a month or two studying intensively the things that I like best!

To counter their first suggestion I reply that if a man feels no

[3] Augusto Monti was Professor of Italian and Latin at the Liceo D'Azeglio in Turin, where Pavese was for three years one of his pupils. Monti usually spent his holidays at Giaveno, within walking distance of Pavese's home at Reaglie.

need for amusement there's no point in seeking it. As for 'wild oats', I assure you I was worse than any German soldier. Three years ago—I was only a schoolboy then—I scarcely broke out at all, content to live inside my shell, but, as the years passed by, my ideas and aspirations broadened, your teaching had its effect, everything fused together and I began to live. At first I had a craving, boundless as the sea, for knowing and doing. If I mixed with all sorts of people it was to find out how they lived and to try it for myself, to broaden my own experience. After I was twelve, I remember having a score or so of professional prostitutes over the next few years. Every time it seemed to be a seduction. I was timid and reserved by nature, but in spite of that I managed to gain a footing in the modern way of life. Every day I learned something more by living in the midst of it, always conscious of my own tenseness, but glad that my mind could feel, understand and treasure up all this experience. I got to the stage of frequenting the sort of brothels that Cato recommended. I found it a hard struggle, but I got over it and a whole new world opened out for me.

This goes to show I was not living only in books or through books. Yet I think books did a great deal to show me what life is like. Not grammar books or dictionaries, but all books in which some feeling came to life. At first dazzled by great names, I settled for Homer's poems, the *Divina Commedia,* Shakespeare and Hugo. Four years ago I started getting to grips with their works and felt a confused sense of exaltation without understanding why. Now, after four years of hard work, and after you taught me how to read, I think that little by little I have reached the stage of understanding their magic.

What poetry does is to bring immortality to life. Consequently, works of poetry are an epitome of centuries of thought, preserved while actually alive. Living thought! That's the great message I discovered after weary effort and not a few discouragements.

As, little by little, I discovered this truth for myself, and, little by little, I learned from books what life was like in bygone centuries, so grew my fervour to understand life as it is today. The reason why is obvious, but is also something to be proud of, as I'll leave you to find out for yourself.[4]

So you see, I'm absolutely wrapped up in books. Indeed, some

[4] In his original draft, Pavese added here: 'I will write the poetry of my own century, as those great men did of theirs. This is my dream, to succeed in this or lose my life in the attempt.' In the actual letter sent to Monti this sentence was deleted and replaced by: 'I'll leave you to find out'.

of those I have on my shelves send a quiver of enthusiasm down my spine if I so much as glance at them.

At this point, if I'm not boring you, I'll give you a summary of the work I'm doing now. I have started to learn Greek,[5] so that one day I can really understand the civilisation of Homer's time, the century of Pericles and the whole world of Greece. I'm reading Horace and Ovid in turn, discovering imperial Rome, and am also studying *Faust* (the first modern poetry) in German. I devour Shakespeare, read Boiardo and Boccaccio alternately, thus covering all Renaissance Italy, and finally Walt Whitman's *Leaves of Grass,* the greatest of them all. By covering all this ground, helped by my own knowledge of contemporary thought (not much as yet, but growing all the time), exploring ancient civilisations that now live only in poetry, I feel exalted by their ideals and see in them our own way ahead. In brief, I am studying modern trends in living.

I have ventured to tell you all this in defence of the way I spend the summer, also to break the ice and begin that spiritual communion I have wanted for so long. Now, to my great delight, you yourself have offered it to me.

As you see, I have without ceremony served all my experiences up to you on a plate, if indeed I can use that name for what may be merely the gilded illusions of an inexperienced young man. But I console myself with the thought that you were young once and no doubt have had illusions of your own. And I believe (I have not actually experienced this, but imagine it must be so) that in later life the best moments are when one relives those days. Am I wrong, perhaps?

Talking of admiration, I assure you I esteem you more than any other professor in the world. I don't know what you will make of this paltry declaration of mine, but I tell you that at least half of my companions, those I know well, hold precisely the same opinions as myself, if not more so. Finally I may add without fear of contradiction that I am considered a good violinist.

That is enough for now. You must have something else to do. I venture to hope for your reply when you have leisure. 'Treat me severely, since the more solid obstacles seem, the more pleasure there is in battering them down.' That is what I used to write, with that impertinent self-assurance I never managed to get rid of even in my three years under you. It shows even in this letter and I doubt whether it will ever leave me. Perhaps it may be a great

[5] At school, Pavese took the 'Modern Syllabus' which did not include Greek. He began studying this language for himself, during the long vacation.

asset. You, imperturbable as always, will alter my 'solid' to 'hard' or 'difficult'. I can just see you doing it! From now on, my warm feeling for you is something beyond my regard for you as a teacher.

Your
Cesare Pavese

To Tullio Pinelli, Loano

Turin, 1st August 1926

My telegram will have already relieved most of your anxiety.[6] Now I will use the ordinary postal service to send you a list of your successes, or, more precisely, the *numerical equivalent* awarded to you by the examiners. (Just think! You're hearing those words for the very last time!) Italian, 7; Latin, 7; Greek, 7; History, 6; Philosophy and Economics, 7; Natural History, 6; History of Art, 7; Physical Training, 'Highly Commended'. My own assessment for gym is only 'Good'. Congratulations! Good lad!

The examiners docked me a mark for my Italian because I dared to contradict their 'correction' of my composition, but I'm not complaining. I appreciate the power of progress. In the seventeenth century I should at least have been burned alive, but now, in their middle-class way, they just deducted a mark from my average. You may well ask how I got involved in such a historical-philosophic digression. It was quite intentional. My last chance to cock a snook at school, that stuffy fattening coop for capons, and my first opportunity as a free man to hurl a challenge at the whole way of life as it is today. I shall put a bit of devilry into it, that's certain.

I hear you are producing a comedy by Goldoni.[7] I, here in these

[6] Pinelli, holidaying in the country at Loano, had asked Pavese to let him know the results of the school-leaving examination.

[7] Pinelli did in fact stage a performance of Goldoni's *I rusteghi* (The Misanthropes) in the parish hall at Alpignano, followed by a comedy of his own written in the Piedmontese dialect.

woods, am enthusing over Walt Whitman. You have my address if you want to write (Reaglie, Villa Pavese), and if you will let me know when, I will come and applaud your Goldoni.

Be good, and don't let all those profiteers eat you up,

Cesare Pavese

To Mario Sturani, Celle Ligure

[Reaglie, in reply to a letter dated 8th August 1926]

'Write me a long letter,' you say. What do you want me to write? One of my usual gossipy dissertations? The monotony of my life, now, makes that even more impossible. Never a breath of inspiration. Nothing. That one word is enough for my reply.

No poetry to send you, no ideas to offer you, no adventures to tell you, no trip to the sea, nothing, nothing. I am a nihilist. Any day now I shall rush out of the house and go to the Pole.

The only people I have here want me to play cards all day long. But that doesn't appeal to me. I would rather stroll through places I see every day, and study, study, fill my mind with other men's poetry, since it seems impossible to fill it with my own. Do something for me. Fill my mind with yours. Give Vaudagna[8] my good wishes,

Pavese

To Mario Sturani, Celle Ligure

Reaglie, [end of] August 1926

Here in peace and quiet I have read the verses you sent me. Since we shall meet at school on Monday, I think it better to write and tell you I understand your poetry much more clearly

[8] Giuseppe Vaudagna, a year older than Pavese, was a classmate of his for three years. At this time he was spending his summer holidays by the sea as a guest of the Sturani family.

now. I'm not sure I could discuss them with you when we are together.

Your girl-friend has an unusual, mysterious face, not like the typical *femme fatale,* but yet with something of the same look because of her eyes, very serious, good and highly intelligent. I have met her only briefly, but I really feel there is something about her far superior to the common run of her companions. I can quite understand how you came to make her your ideal.

Don't be alarmed by all this enthusiasm. As you know, I wander about like a man in despair. Whenever I meet a feminine face that appeals to the better side of my nature, I fall in love. That's how it was when I fell for ——,[9] the same for that little American actress you know about **,[10] and, more recently, for Wilma Banky[11] and for ***.[12]

But I was wrong to say 'I fall in love'. Not quite! What I feel when I think of those faces again is a terribly shy admiration mixed with purely platonic affection, an ending as ridiculous to others as it is to me. (I take comfort in thinking you are not one of those 'others'.)

Most of those women I dreamed of so—shall we say 'romantically'?—turned out to be no good at all, riff-raff, strumpets, in short very different from what I had thought.

There is no point in discussing *. You've told me too much about her already. As for the 'little American actress', just when I was getting fond of her I came across her photograph in the pages of a review. A lovely photograph, as far as that went, but underneath was written: 'Soubrette M.B. in one of her most roguish poses.' She was wearing plenty of clothes. That wasn't what put me off. As for W. Banky, I can't give chapter and verse but I think an actress who knows how to embrace a man so impetuously, so passionately, when playing a part, can hardly be having her first brush with life. Yet how divinely sweet her face is! It draws one's very soul!

I've learned by now that appearances are very different from reality. At the time I felt that reality could perhaps be corrected by art, but art, especially the art of the cinema, may be simply pretence, wholly composed of imaginary elements whose only value consists in the emotion they manage to evoke in our minds.

[9] This unnamed girl was probably a school friend.

[10] Probably Mae Bush, who appeared in Stroheim's film presentation *Mad Women* (1922).

[11] A star of the silent screen who appeared with Rudolph Valentino in *Daughter of the Sheikh.*

[12] The identity of this lady has not yet been established.

Since life is nothing more than the pursuit of pleasure, or, rather, of pleasurable sensations, art becomes (for me at least) the ultimate purpose of life. It can give my spirit the keenest possible pleasure, sensations that in actual life are not, and never can be, realised. So let me nurture in silence a little flame of love, a reflection of your own love for this girl. Pretence? I am so used to pretence in art that it doesn't much matter to me whether the lucky one is myself or some other fellow, as long as, now and then in life, I can feel that my highest aspirations have been achieved. I remember her mysterious eyes and the warm smile she has for you. I've seen them a thousand times in my dreams. It's better that you're the one to have it all, rather than some other man. You are worthy of it.

Cesare

To Tullio Pinelli,[13] *Alpignano*

Reaglie [in reply to a letter dated 19th September 1926]

You've picked a fine one to ask for advice! That calls for an impartial mind and cool judgment, qualities I wouldn't recognise if I saw them! I have no sense of moderation whatever. I am capable, for example, of spending a whole year praising American civilisation in literature, art and educational institutions, even having my eye on an American actress. Then, if that actress turns out to be a woman like all the others, I should despair over America and all the world, weeping, howling, planning to do myself an injury. It's the way I'm made, so you see what fine advice I'm likely to give you.

Having made that plain, I'll quote to you what I replied to Baraldi Monti, one day when that fine fellow was trying his hardest to get me to give up the study of belles-lettres: 'In matters concerning marriage or the choice of a profession I would never undertake to advise. I should leave every man to decide for him-

[13] After passing his school-leaving examination, Pinelli wrote asking Pavese's advice on whether to study law, as his family wished, or whether to try to earn his living as a poet and playwright.

self what he wants to do in life.' But the best of it was that Monti gave his advice just the same. That temptation is always too strong to resist. So I will tell you what I think. Listen to what I say and then please yourself.

Dedicated to writing as you are, following that first success of yours, tormented as I think you have always been by that poetic muse which is eternal youth and which, unlike earthly loves, grows ever more lovely and more perfect, I feel you would not want to throw away so suddenly all those hopes and those dreams. But, unless you are prepared to value those things more than anything else in the whole world, it is a sign that you are not born to be a poet. (I preach pretty well, don't you think?)

Pursuing the idea of 'eternal youth', can you call your feeling for poetry true, sincere love if you are willing to discuss it, make capital of it, consider it in terms of a contract? If you really love the theatre, that should be your ultimate goal and everything you do should bear upon that objective.

Examining, then, on these lines the cross-roads you have reached, I myself (note that I'm advising objectively), I say you should choose law. What do you want? You say you prefer working in the country, because you would like to devote yourself to bringing to the theatre 'the rugged life of the fields'. You say it would help you 'a great deal, while the strict dry-as-dust practices of the law would blow all your best projects sky high'. Note again what I said just now, that unless you are willing to give your life to art, it would be difficult to make a success of it.

Art is a very jealous mistress who demands everything for herself, like one of those women of antiquity you admire so much, even the life of the man who loves her. I do not deny that one can manage to get along with some other occupation on lines linked in some way with one's artistic work, but such an occupation must be only a means of gaining time or money, in short a stopgap. Never, *never,* can you make art a secondary consideration. Far better bury yourself in something else and grow into a mathematics master.

I, then, would choose law because, leaving on one side the point that legal qualifications can very easily lead to a hundred other occupations, among which you could certainly find one that would allow you leisure to devote to your writing, there is the important consideration that as a lawyer you would meet and be able to study many different people, characters to give you the basic material for playwriting. Agriculture, on the other hand, is a very limited occupation, a closed world shut in upon itself, far more dull than what you call 'dull legal practices'. Besides, agriculture would probably limit you to living in the country, while law would allow you to live in town.

I myself (I don't know if it's due to the influence of Walt Whitman) wouldn't exchange a city like Turin for a couple of dozen country estates. The country is all right for a short break, to rest one's mind and admire the view, but then get away as quickly as possible in an electric train. But life, the real, modern life, as I dream of it and fear it, is a great city, full of noise, factories, houses, great palaces and silly, pretty women (though I don't manage to get near them).

And now I've sweated blood to write all this, you must take your own road. All that's left for me to do is to apologise for keeping you waiting for my reply. I should add that when your letter reached me I was in the country, in the very house where I was born, where I would choose to die. Perhaps in a hundred years or so it will be a national monument!

You've been working, this last month. Best wishes. Send me that farce of yours to read. I'm very curious about it! I've been working, too, but day by day my longing grows to kick it all away, rush out of the house without a sou and travel the world. That's how to learn what life is! Not puzzling over books and building castles in the air! But that takes courage, and I have so little that I've never yet dared say two words to a woman about what's in my mind.

Cesare Pavese

To Giorgio Curti,[14] Bra

Turin, 6th October 1926

I haven't ever written to you because I didn't know just what to say: 'Dear friend . . . how are you? . . . how are things going? . . . what about your career? . . .' As you well know, that's not my

[14] Giorgio Curti, a native of Sardinia, became one of Pavese's classmates for two or three years at the *liceo*. He graduated in jurisprudence, with a thesis on the rights of an author whose work is used in cinema films. He became an actor and appeared in one of the earliest Italian talking films, but his main interest was producing and directing. Later he left Italy for France and then went to America.

way. In the end I felt shamed into starting this letter, but you can be sure I shall only write of things that strike me as out of the ordinary, ideas that interest me in particular.

First of all, then, how are you getting along with all your girl-friends? That's a subject I'm never tired of, so write and tell me in detail how you get to know them, how you work up a flirtation. Send me some photographs too, if you like, so that I can always follow you in spirit.

Girls are my weakness, and the worst of it is that I've never had a girl-friend of my own. Worse still, almost all the women who come anywhere near me make my head turn and my heart begin to throb. I turn into a wild beast! Women! I'm only a plaything in their hands! Just think, I've not yet known a single one of them. Who knows whether I ever shall! Yet I am more and more convinced that I'm just not made for social life. I'm too overbearing, too much of an individualist! If a woman really loved me (heaven help her!), I should drive her mad in three months!

I advise you not to abuse your fatal charm. Now Rudolph Valentino is dead you have no rival! The girls at Bra must all be warming themselves at a single flame, but think of your fellow-citizens and your health (more important than your fellow-citizens). Think of me, too, and leave one girl out of the whole world for me. As yet, I haven't been troubled very much by women (and always at a distance, though, always at a distance!). It would be torture for me to know one of them intimately. I don't mean bodily. There are Greek statues and whores for that. But the mind, the mind, a little kindness of spirit to tell me it's not true that I am a nothingness in the world, but that I'm worth a little affection or, at least, a little interest. But what the hell! I remind myself I don't know how to dance and I have no manners. Should I try to acquire that sort of thing, for God's sake? I've said enough. Let's leave it at that.

When you were here at Reaglie, you suggested we should correspond with each other. Apart from our friendship we shared a love of the arts, so you wrote to me . . . I wrote to you. Listen. A day or two ago I wrote to Pinelli, who was proposing to cultivate the theatre in his spare time. He would 'take care not to make art a secondary occupation'. 'It's all or nothing in that field,' I thundered. 'Give it your whole life, or leave it completely alone.'

But now I realise this is not absolutely true. Those few moments of joy and exultation that lift you above everything around you, moments of artistic creation, will always be a wonderful memory, even if they do not lead to anything more.

I used to believe one could devote one's life to art, but I begin to see that I'm too small, too paltry, for this mistress. I must devote my effort to the other thing—earning a living, that terrible 'other thing' which may well absorb all my powers. Yet my lost hopes have not spoiled the joys I knew when writing those little scraps of mine, even now I believe that every time my spirit swells with inspiration I shall have the keenest pleasure in expressing it in words.

In conclusion, then, if you are not already completely given over to that other 'horrible thing', go on writing, write a lot, whenever you have something to say. I shall be very happy to read it and tell you my impressions.

To Tullio Pinelli, Alpignano

Reaglie, 12th October 1926

I hear you are going round complaining that I replied to your letter with one word—'Work', and nothing more. Isn't that sublime word enough for you? Don't you know that work ennobles a man, raising him to the level of a beast?

In any case, if this is what you want, here's the extent of my own aspiration towards bestiality. I have been studying:

(1) *Poesie Latine* by Francesco Berni (16th century)
(2) Fourteenth Canto, Part II of the *Orlando Innamorato* by Matteo Maria Boiardo (15th century)
(3) Half-way through the *Legende des Siècles* by Victor Hugo (19th century)
(4) The opening pages of *Faust* by Wolfgang Goethe (18th century)
(5) The final pages of *On Heroes and Hero-worship and the Heroic in History* by Thomas Carlyle (19th century)
(6) *Leviticus* of Moses (? century)
(7) The Preface to the *Stimmen der Völker in Liedern* by Johann Gottfried von Herder (18th century)

Every now and again I take a quick glance at:

(8-9) *Grammatica Greca* with an Italian vocabulary

(10) *Laudi del cielo del mare della terra e degli eroi* by Gabriele d'Annunzio
(11) *Leaves of Grass* by Walt Whitman
(12) I have finished reading *Othello* by William Shakespeare (16th century)
(13) The *Decameron* of Giovanni Boccaccio (14th century)
(14) The *Poems* of Ossian (4th century)
(15) *Carmina* by Quintus Horatius Flaccus (1st century)

Are you still conscious? . . . Then I'll go on.

Almost all my work boils down to understanding these writers and placing them in their correct historical perspective, a study I thoroughly enjoy. It is like creating a drama, in fact it actually *is* a drama of stupendous grandeur. I am continually discovering new things about it, *living* it more fully, this drama of the whole history of mankind. My own work is paltry, I often think, and I feel ashamed to go on with it. I don't seem to have the power to create anything original. I still have bits and pieces of all my earlier efforts, but they look to me more like relics of the past than material for some future construction. I'm just a weakling, full of aspirations I am not capable of achieving, a flaccid mass of unhealthy sensitivity. I'm like many of the sons our country produced in the nineteenth century—who could no longer believe in their own ideals, but could not bring themselves to look for new ones. I tell you, they were *afraid* of finding new ones. I am the same.

Not for nothing did I once have in mind (though I hardly ever think of it now) the idea of writing a play against the background of the Russian Revolution. In it a family, completely imbued with those new ideas, is horrified and disillusioned by the first results of that upheaval. They suffer as I am suffering now, for I believe the Russian Revolution was the final attempt to carry out the nineteenth-century ideal of *Liberté, Egalité, Fraternité*.

I have seen only too well its measure of success. I can no longer believe in those ideals, nor can I find others my mind will accept. I don't really know what I want, or, rather, I do know but cannot see how to attain it. In fact, my mind is a faithful copy of what the world would be, with nineteenth-century ideals realised to the full, without the counteraction of the twentieth.

I could go on writing about this all night, but you would hardly want to spend all tomorrow reading it. I should very much like to hear you holding forth about my 'lack of courage with women'. Talking of women, I'm happy to hear you're not thinking of the little American girl any more, and have an Italian girl instead. Was it a question of singling out a national product? You could have told me a lot more about it than you did. Write me a long letter (twelve pages, like this one) all about yourself (and her, naturally), and love.

Cesare P.

To Giorgio Curti, Bra

Turin, 22nd October 1926

In spirit, I feel like a beggar. I keep on telling everyone about my inner suffering, just as beggars parade their sores and filth. Why do I do it? In the hope of finding comfort? Am I simply boasting? Trying to get out of it enough material for a page of good writing? Who knows? Even this uncertainty is part, and a very large part, of my own misery.

Hence the fact that, for the past two months, I've been making myself a nuisance to everybody, even to people I hardly know, so they never stop complaining. A good many people here in Turin could tell you a thing or two about it. Here's your ration of the same thing.

Meanwhile, I should tell you I've seen Monti again (he's always bright and gay), and have come across Monferini, too; I've also been contemplating suicide, but that's enough of that. Whoever lives longest will see most. Thank you for your advice about pre-military training, but I shan't do anything. I've become a fatalist and haven't enough initiative to lift a finger, come what may.

You too, I feel, are bored and fed up. You can't be bothered to write. Listen, I'm telling you from my heart, if it's not too late for you, get out of trying to follow the path of Art. If a man is not born to that road, he'll find it too painful even to skirt the edge of it. I'm only one of many to discover that. Don't kid yourself as I have done, poor creature that I am, reduced to playing the part of a misunderstood genius.

From this you'll note that what I say now is inconsistent with the first letter I wrote you, urging you to keep up your art as a comfort, a divine consolation in life. But what do you expect? At this moment I think as I have said. I've reached such a point of spiritual putrefaction that inconsistency no longer makes me go hot and cold. Perhaps I shall turn into a fervent Christian, or kill myself, or go mad, or adapt myself to this wretched life. That's the sort of dance I'm led in my present state of mind. I no longer believe in anything at all, I'm good for nothing, abject, contemptible.

This is why I'm always bemoaning the fact that I have no woman to love. But think about it a moment. How could I venture to think seriously about an intelligent beauty when I have nothing to offer her but these lovely thoughts of mine? You'll tell me that men even more stupid than I am have been lucky in love. I agree, but those men don't know they are stupid. I do, that's my trouble. *I know I have nothing of my own that is in the least worth having.*

My first hopes of becoming a colossus were too high for me to be able to adapt myself now to stark reality, without doing something beastly. But that's enough. Let's leave it at that.

So you have a love of your own. What can one do when one hears that a friend has a girl, worse still, a fiancée? His pals will say: 'Poor chump, he must have slipped a bit, to get himself tied up like that at nineteen.' My mother would say: 'As long as she's a good housewife, that's enough.' My instinctive reply is: 'It must be marvellous to love a woman as much as that, and be loved in return.' You can take that as you like, but say two or three paternosters for this poor fool and his troubled spirit.

1927

To Mario Sturani, Monza

[Turin, February 1927]

The moment I received your letter I dashed off a reply you'll have had by now. That was three weeks ago, and after going over your MS. several times I decided to make a fresh copy. I'm feeling rather lazy, and couldn't be bothered to insert all the necessary amendments on the rough copy.

Here is the document. At one time I was inclined to indulge in an affectation of melancholy, and you lectured me against it on the score of dignity. It seems it's now my turn to assist a wavering friend. But cheer up. I don't know how to be persuasive, so I shall never write to you with that purpose in mind.

The way you are feeling now, I have felt on countless occasions, yet I'm still alive, as you see, and I've written things that you've told me were not too bad. Remind yourself that your arts are painting and sculpture, and you can give to poetry only the odds and ends of your time. I, on the other hand, am compelled to give my whole life to poetry.

But then, of course, to each of us our own things seem poor and pretentious, while the work of other men strikes us as highly original, simply because it is easier to be impressed by what someone else has said, something we haven't said ourselves. In short, there's no point in dwelling upon an impression that in my opinion is merely transient.

My own position at the moment is very odd. I'm trying to cheer up someone who is ill in bed, and I'm dashing off gay little poems like shots from a gun. Keep cheerful, and when you least expect it you will see with your mind's eye a fine poem full of all your usual highly decorative ideas and characters: 'Archangels in the darkness of my dream', and so on. But who knows? While I'm rambling on like this, you may already have produced for me some triumphant act of faith!

Cesare P.

To Milly,[1] *Rome*

[Turin, March 1927]

Signorina,

You will certainly be very surprised, if no worse, to receive this letter from someone you, in fact, do not know. Perhaps you may be more inclined to forgive me for writing if I tell you that though you do not know me, I know you. I have often seen you, if only briefly, in passing. I have followed you often. Sometimes I have watched you for quite a long time, but have never dared to approach you. I know your face and figure, Signorina, I have watched several moments of your life and have especially enjoyed that hint of animation in your face that can reveal so much to an attentive observer. But that is very little, Signorina, compared with the immensity of what I should like to know about you.

I'm just a very ordinary, nineteen-year-old student and you are far away, so very far. But how could I ever have come anywhere near you, here in Turin? Whenever I found you, there were others with you and it would have been *ridiculous*. Besides, even if I had managed to meet you alone, I should have been confused with all the other fellows who were chasing you, and that would have been the end of it. I was terrified of this and I did not dare. So, for fear of spoiling the image of you that I have before my eyes, I have perhaps lost you irrevocably.

But when you had gone away I couldn't forget you. I searched through all the papers and eventually found you in Rome.

If all I've said has merely made you laugh, throw me into a corner and it will all be over. But if I've managed to express even a tiny bit of what I feel, and you have understood, then do not leave me in this uncertainty. It's a wild hope, I know, but I should be overjoyed to have a kind reply from you. I should have so many things to tell you if you would listen to me. Will you, Signorina?

[1] This lady was almost certainly the 'ballerina Milly' whom Pavese mentioned several times in his letters to Pinelli during this period.

To Mario Sturani, Monza

[Turin] 8th April 1927

I haven't written to you lately because I had nothing to send you, and so much to tell you that I didn't know where to begin. Eventually, tonight, when spring has inspired me, I have managed to put down on paper some account of the way I'm 'truly living'.

First I should tell you I shall not write any more. I'm practically sure I shan't. I no longer have the power, and besides, I have nothing to say. For the past three months I've lived in an agony of uncertainty. I try to write, then tear it up. This softening of the brain is dreadful, terrifying.

In this latest love-affair, the one with the ballerina, I thought I had definitely brought myself to the point, but I hadn't the courage. Now I'm going along passively, amusing myself, forgetting myself, studying '*for the exams*', not for my own pleasure, for my longing for higher things is dead.

Recent events have definitely taught me a lot about myself. I am incompetent, timid, lazy, uncertain, a weakling and half-mad. Never, never shall I be able to settle into a permanent job or make what is called a success in life. Never, never.

I no longer have the energy to cope with such an achievement or make the necessary effort, for I know so well it would be useless. I should not succeed. Even if I did, would it be worth the trouble? From now on, I mean to make the least possible effort in life. It won't last, of course. It cannot last. Too many wild thoughts torment my brain. I shall never manage to control them. See what a state I'm in! It's no use to keep drinking and sink lower still. I should never get out of it. I'm just a fool. As for cocaine or morphia, heaven knows what they cost!

That way I should at least have the exaltation of a spectacular end. But I haven't the nerve! Even as a baby I was a cretin, a *poseur*. No doubt I shall knife myself one of these days. I'm behaving like a man in the depths of despair. It's lucky that no woman has ever accepted me. With the fine personality I've got now we should both have been in trouble!

Write and tell me what you've done and what you're doing now. I still enjoy talking about such things. Don't imagine you've got to send me a consoling letter. I know how boring that can be. Don't even try to cheer me up. Let me enjoy my depression in peace.

Cesare Pavese

To Mario Sturani, Monza

[Turin, in reply to a letter
dated 5th July 1927]

My dear fellow,

I am tormented by doubts. Let's assume their ultimate object is matrimony, dull, stolid, suffocating, horrible matrimony. The very word sounds sickening! We expect women to be chaste as ice, and yet reserve for ourselves the right to talk filth and even, alone or with others, to indulge in it.

Don't talk to me about a membrane called Hymen, a difference in age, the possible consequences and other things of that sort. If morality is to be something quite apart from economic interests, its standards must apply impartially to both sexes.

In fact I have decided I must either give up my own filthy habits or stop pretending that women don't indulge in them too. Naturally I shan't manage to carry out either of these good intentions, because I'm such a swine myself, and because atavistic feelings inherited from past centuries impel me to cling to that belief, choking or overmastering any thoughts of my own on the matter.

Thus I can at least suffer in silence and put this problem aside with all the others that keep me in my present state of mind. No longer will I fight against 'dishonesty'. I'll say no more and do no more, unless perhaps to undertake mechanical work such as translations or studies of bitter irony. Only every now and then I shall lose my patience and go round muttering to myself about a search for *truth*.

Yet the truth means nothing to me. Nothing at all. If now and then I seek it, that's just a relic of my atavistic instincts.

I've something more to tell you. My ballet dancer has come back. That's why I'm a little late in replying to your letter. At first I just wanted to see her again. Then I made myself wander about all night over these hills of mine and caught a frightful cold. She's lovely, yes. Young, marvellous, everything she is said to be, but between her and me there seemed to be a line of chairs where a lot of men sat waiting. This gave me a good deal to think about and, little by little, that lovely, divine creature, whose legs move so wonderfully in the dance of Venus, had vanished from my mind, leaving me with hardly a single regret. Now my fire of love has sunk to ashes, and I shall certainly not try to relight it. My spirit is too tired, too sluggish for that. To feel my mind inflamed with inspiration or love (the effect is the same), is terribly wearisome.

She disappeared, as she had every right to do. What else could she have done? Even if she had come to find me, as during this past winter I had tried to find her; if she had said to me all that I meant to say to her, but did not dare to in the end, what would have been the use? If the loveliest of all the women I brush shoulders with in the street were to want me, love me for myself alone, what could I do about it? There seems to be a curse laid upon me. I don't know what it is, but it prevents me from loving anyone or anything in peace.

Perhaps it's only egotism, an unwillingness to make sacrifices in the hope of finding happiness. But what need is there for happiness? Why should it be considered manly to enjoy happiness, but unmanly to use face powder? Who cares, anyway, whether a thing is considered manly or not?

To Tullio Pinelli, Chiavari

Reaglie, 12th July 1927

My ballet dancer's back again, lovelier, younger, more marvellous than ever. At last I've found out the secret of her unique fascination when she's dancing on the stage. There is a sweetness, a childlike delicacy of movement, a terrifying grace in every gesture. Never, never in my whole life have I known anything like it.

Yet with all that I'm utterly weary, worn out. Weary of noble thoughts, tired of thinking about her, sick of it all. All I have left are feeble spurts of energy to tackle daring but wearisome works I shall never manage to finish. At the base of every exaltation of mine is the supreme exaltation of thoughts of suicide. Oh that, one of these days, I shall have the nerve to do it. Hour after hour, trembling, I long for it, my final consolation. Write me something. I am too much alone, too lost and bewildered.

Even at the very moment when I see how lovely she is, it bores me to think of her! Listen: I have discovered this refined instrument of torture. Every time that my confused spirit longs for something I ask myself: 'What could I do about it?' and my peace of mind has gone.

Oh! To live, to live! I'm beginning to understand what that means.

N.B. I beg you not to show this letter to anyone in the family.

Cesare Pavese

PS. Last night, coming out of the theatre where I had seen her again, I went back to Reaglie and wandered all night among the bushes and country lanes almost as far as Chieri, restless as a wolf. (I'm going mad, if I'm not mad already!) Reversion to barbarism. That's what I wanted. But it's heavenly to feel so exalted!

To Tullio Pinelli, Chiavari

[Reaglie, in reply to a letter dated 24th July 1927]

I am very pleased by your letter, not so much for the usual reasons—renewing friendship, hearts beating as one in spite of the distance between them—but because it reached me at a time when I was suffering from deadly boredom. Now I can spend an hour, or half an hour, writing to you in reply. Recently Sturani wrote me, saying that my letters are real literary masterpieces, lyric poems. Quite pointless!

You know, better than anyone, that summer just kills me. I never finish anything. I'm dead, simply dead. All those bright ideas I had last winter never occur to me now. Winter stimulates my spirit, renews and warms it to compensate for the cold outside. I should live in a great modern city, not in an outdated, primitive state of nature, as here. It really does kill me. Worse, it makes me soft, sluggish, a mere dabbler in literary pursuits.

But none of this really matters to you. You want to know about my ballerina. Even if you don't, it matters to me, gives me a chance to write one of those literary-lyric epistles. I'll go straight to the point and tell you without more ado that my ballerina (if mine she is!) . . . is still dancing.

(What did you expect? I intended to write you something lyrical about her, but a mocking mood has just come over me and nothing's sacred.) Yes, she still dances, her face has the same wonderful air of youth, she's even more splendid, more eye-catching than before. You know what the stage is like at the Michelotti, with the front stalls only a yard or two away from the footlights. There is one seat far over to the side, almost on the stage itself. That's where I sat, quite apart from the main audience. I could hear their heavy breathing behind me. I watched her dancing, always with other performers, but to me she seemed alone, expressing her own joy of life. I had no right at all to wonder, as I left the theatre, 'Who knows who's with her now?'

It's not exactly true that I'm in love with her. I don't suppose I shall ever fall in love. I don't really know what the term means.

So my ballerina disappeared. All night I wandered through the woods and finally realised how artificial it all was. Now for hours I've been walking round the streets in a kind of daze, thinking of something quite different.

Suddenly I saw in the street a lost cat, yowling with hunger and thin as a skeleton. She ran between my legs and would not leave me, so at last I picked her up and decided to take her home. I would call her 'Bambola' and keep her as a symbol of my sleepless night and the one who had caused it. In the end, the little cat realised I had nothing to give her and ran off to attach herself to a more substantial citizen who happened to pass by. So much for my 'symbol'.

That's enough. I'll end this letter now, while I feel a sweetly sentimental impulse in my heart.

To Tullio Pinelli, Chiavari

[Reaglie] 18th August [1927]

Dear Pinelli

What a beast you are! Even if you've managed to understand that my work is good, you're a beast just the same. So you consider my play has 'quite the wrong setting', and you ask 'Didn't you notice you were committing two frightful mistakes?'[2]

Just so. . . . These were your own two batteries, turned to fire at you. It all happened in that blessed century before gunpowder was invented (by Roger Bacon, or by Schwarz, whoever he may be, but not by an Italian. God forbid).

The first thing you turn up your nose at is that the setting is Paradise. Quite the wrong place, you think. (But I'm the one who wrote it, and I have the right to choose any setting I like. Why shouldn't I soar to heaven on the wings of art? Not that it was worth the trouble.) Your first objection is not worth a fig.

Your second is that I show pride where humility would be more suitable. Here again I decide such things for myself. Anything wrong in that?

When I examine the dogmas of Christianity I realise that, in spite of all their claims about infinity and eternity, they leave life itself to sort out the dark problems and contradictions that face us day by day. I myself, with all due respect, don't believe a word of their stupid fables. If, over the centuries, living men have been content to accept them as truth, as a path to heavenly bliss, good luck to them! I not only have the right, but a precise duty as an artist or philosopher, to decide the setting of my work. This time I made it Paradise, the place where things are settled for all time in accordance with the stern laws of those dogmas. Not even the immense force exerted by centuries of thinkers has succeeded in reaching a conclusion that can satisfy a clear-thinking, pious man. If he lives in the shadow of factory chimneys he must now and then withdraw to a church, but more often to a casino, to sort out his problems for himself.

[2] Pavese had sent to Pinelli his MS. of a kind of parable or morality play entitled *Crepuscolo di Dio* (Twilight of God). The blessed saints in heaven are unhappy, their peace destroyed by the cursing and groaning ascending to them from hell. They fear their own salvation is in jeopardy. To set their minds at rest, God deprives them of free will, but in the end, dissatisfied with the mechanical creatures he created, he destroys them all, good and bad together.

I am deeply moved by your lecturing me about 'evangelical humility', and I hasten to assure you that for years I have been, and still am, far far humbler and more angelic than you realise. Listen, you well-meaning, good-hearted man who can sense the truth as a rheumatic sufferer can sense the approach of bad weather. I exist, possibly as a spirit but certainly as a body. I have never dreamed of denying that, as a certain feeble-minded English philosopher has done, and he a tonsured bishop, Berkeley by name.[3] I have hands, feet, a stomach, sight (short) and tongue (long). Finally I have a brain that can think and is aware of certain laws that it can choose to obey or disregard if it so decides. I generally follow them, but when that would be inconvenient I silence their voice for the time being.

Outside myself there exists a whole universe that my brain tries in vain to explain. In the end it can only cry: 'That's enough! I don't understand it in the least and so will not venture to express an opinion.' Mine is a very humble brain, very sensitive and unsophisticated, rather unpredictable and moody, with a core of pure gold. It worries over my aspirations that it can neither explain nor interpret. It is my ego, the centre of my whole being.

This brain of mine is also equipped with a pair of dainty little ears that I carefully wash every day, though they always look dirty. They hear a great deal and instantly pass on every bit of information like the gossips they are. A day or two ago they listened to a solemn-looking man with a noble face, talking about 'the significance of dogma'. Now my brain has its own opinion of my personality and prospects. 'Obviously this fine young fellow is too simple-minded, too gullible. He claims to have in his own hands a panacea that could set the whole world to rights, yet he describes himself as "humble". He can "sense" various conditions and has his own aspirations, thinks he knows his own future. Let him be. He is simply ingenuous, that's all. Life will have a great deal to teach him.'

If, my dear Pinelli, you consider I was guilty of presumption in regarding my brain as the ruling power, you are just as bad, for you place brain and heart together on that throne. They will always be quarrelling, contradicting and fighting each other. Twenty centuries of Roman Christianity have so far failed to end this conflict and bring peace to the heart of the world.

Not that it greatly matters. All you fellows wouldn't hesitate to

[3] Pavese is referring to the Irish (not English) bishop, George Berkeley (1685-1753), a distinguished philosopher whose works on metaphysics dealt with his teaching that 'no object exists apart from the mind'.

murder your fathers and mothers if that would forward your own beloved aspirations. You know how to by-pass the awkward frictions that occur when the brain comes up against old-fashioned sentimentalities—a belief in justice, for example. Brain and heart do not function together as smoothly as clockwork, but at least you have the courage to say aloud, as I do, 'I don't understand it at all, so I just go ahead as I think fit, enjoying myself whenever I can and suffering as little as possible.'

At least you have the good sense to leave your problems 'open and pending', but you long to solve them at all costs, establish your position in the world and know beyond question that your ambitions will be fulfilled. If you find it more convenient to attain that end by practising 'Christian humility', believing that 'He that humbles himself shall be exalted', that's up to you. In my opinion it makes no difference. The whole thing is a matter of calculation —you do me a favour and I'll do the same for you.

I'm much more modest. In all humility I try to understand the world, using the only tools I have at hand, my brain and my heart, but I confess I have failed. I've tried to find ways of amusing myself, hoping to forget, but I am always aware of the unending struggle between common sense and ambition. I make no pretence to have solved the problems that we agree are there. You haven't solved them either.

To show me that freedom of choice is still the finest thing God could have given to men, you point out that what we consider wrong may in fact be good. As if I believe what I say when I talk about divine justice or mercy, or believe in paradise when I describe it! These are simply shafts of satire, essential to the position I'm taking up : criticising your dogmas and pointing out the contradictions they contain.

Tell me. Which of us is the more closely in touch with contemporary literature? I who love living among buildings and studying life in action, or you who prefer Gothic ruins, belles-lettres and ancient stones crumbling to dust? What if I do live among books? I have at least one great advantage that you lack. If any uneasy restlessness begins to affect the man in the street I can sense it at once. It is a living thing, not to be found in books. You live like a fish in water, and never dream there can be anything different! Disabuse yourself of all such ideas. Your argument that, according to your rubric, an appeal should be made not only to the brain but to the heart as well, is worth less than all your other theories, and they aren't worth much anyway.

I'm as bucolic as Petrarch; but I'm also an individualist, don't forget. My feeling for nature is like Darwin's, a matter for the brain. For its appeal to the heart I look to poets such as W. Whitman who knew Darwin personally, but above all to my own heart, which counts for a good deal. You must remember that, before I became a sceptic, I was blown up like a football by my aspirations, even more troublesome then than they are now.

I must reply to you as best I can. It cannot be denied that I am a literary man and that I write letters to you. But possibly you may have given my words an interpretation very different from their literal meaning. A 'literary man' is one who lives only among books, sees nothing but books, can no longer live apart from books, reasons through books, feels and loves, even sleeps with books. That describes Cesare Pavese, a bookish man.

With all your talk about St Francis, you say nothing about suffering animals, and seem to have no feeling for them at all. Over the years I have often shuddered for them and have devoted my life to helping their cause, a life bounded by living things and the horror of death, by my appreciation of all feelings, all passions, factory buildings and churches, gamblers and poets, scientists, hospital doctors and suicides.

I strive to live through it all with a zest that slackens only to gain fresh enthusiasm and I suffer intensely for my most shattering desires, my darkest fits of despair. If I love books, too, it is because books are a part of the world, like women, trees, animals, flowers, poets, fine buildings and the very stars themselves.

To an unnamed girl in Turin

[Turin] 7th September 1927

Yesterday Sturani remarked to me, 'What a very seductive face that girl has!' I was trembling between confusion and hope. Reading over the pages you have written I am filled with joy and with wild despair, torn between acute physical pain in my heart and spirit, and joy to know that you have found something great in me to love. What unexpected and delightful tenderness! You had no intention of arousing any passionate response in me just to amuse yourself, so I will reply in all sincerity, without reserve.

I suspected something of the sort from your kisses, sometimes hoping for them, sometimes shivering in disgust at the very thought. Now I am resigned, I feel much happier. All you mean to me now is a vision of tenderness and ideal beauty. If, now and then when my mind is unbalanced and overtired, I feel a momentary twinge of disappointment or regret, I am comforted by the dazzling thought that I love and am loved in return by an ethereal creature, golden-haired and equally fair in spirit. I think, too, of the sadness deep in your heart. It shows in your lovely face, revealing that poetry means more to you than reality.

Yet when you tell me so frankly of your great love for another man, I tremble with desire and despair. Never yet have I known to the full what love can mean. The first pang brings me to a halt and I shut myself away in a mood of deep depression, wallowing in the luxury of suffering.

It grieves me terribly to realise you now belong to someone else who has won your love and the right to keep you for himself. I try not to think about it. It is too dreadful, but I cannot control my thoughts and I try to deaden the pain by weeping over my misery and doing my best to keep alive the flickering flame of my poetry. This evening, hoping to drown my sufferings, I've been sitting drinking and inhaling the smoke of my cigarette, day-dreaming of you and wondering if I could use the theme of your love to create a great masterpiece of art, full of all good things, written with inexpressible tenderness.

As the light smoke-clouds drifted round my head, my whole body seemed enfolded in a mist of love. My thoughts were painful, but no more so than the obsessions I used to have about becoming a poet. Was that merely an illusion? Another even sadder thought was that I should have grown tired of you in a few weeks, no matter what you did. Everlasting love is no more than a tedious convention dreamed up by literary people.

So, engulfed by this wave of trembling sweetness, I forget all else, letting my thoughts follow the trailing smoke, happy in the great surge of poetic inspiration I find in you and in the world you have brought to light again for me. Already I must be quite resigned, since I can compare your love for me with smoke from the cigarettes I've lit this evening to fill my heart with dreams and to forget.

Yet I'm unhappy, baby, so unhappy I could weep. I long for your caress, for any contact with you, for one of your laughing smiles. I can never forget how you smiled and kissed me when I ventured to ask if I might address you as '*tu*'. That was the sweetest thrill of my life. I love you so much, you know. You may well have given me a new and higher inspiration for divine poetry, and for that alone I shall adore you in silence for ever. You've done nothing wrong, baby. Don't blame yourself, and forgive me if I sometimes forget you.

Do you know what terrifies me most of all? A dread that your inspiration may fail me, one day.

To the same girl

[Turin, September 1927 (?)]

My greatest grief is that I have no more poetry to give you. Indeed, any impulse to write seems further and further away from me. For the sake of all those passionate days when I dreamed of you so much, do not desert me now. Come back to me, if only for a moment. I shall not ask you for what I once believed you might give me. I can well understand you might think it would be wrong, now, but if only I could be near you for a minute or two you would give me fresh inspiration. I'm sick of life, weary of it all. Even my memories of you seem stale and lifeless.

As you see, I'm being frank. Only, out of all this great disaster, I am still fired by indescribably lovely things that give me a sense of intoxication and forgetfulness. These moments of exhilaration are all that is left to me now. Our friendship was born of poetry, and if you no longer love me, you must at least give me poetry. Come to me, then, come often, you who alone can fill my heart.

To the same girl

[Turin] 9th September 1927
(written at night)

Forgive me if in my egotistical, unbalanced way, incapable of living normally, I cause you displeasure, grief and annoyance. Nowadays I cannot find peace and relaxation. I feel forced to behave as I'm doing now, pretending to be gay, keeping well away from you and, in short, hiding. My only way of being any different would be to kill myself, and a deed like that at this stage would be too much. Besides, I shouldn't have enough physical courage. I feel humiliated, and tremble at the sad disillusion, the fears I have inflicted upon you, but I could not act in any other way.

I beg you, show me some charity, at least. Do not consider me unsympathetically; do not treat me unkindly or laugh at me heartily as you do when others are with you, as if I had never existed. Perhaps you may find me quite unbearable—and after all our dreams, our passionate reality, that would be shattering, baby—but I don't know, I'm not in control and cannot see anything that lies ahead—I am suffering and trembling more than ever, I am conscious of dreadful darkness where my heart shudders endlessly, as though with fever.

I am being punished, Signorina, for all the harm I did you. You gave me so much. For me you have been the only feminine influence for good I have ever known in all my life. Yesterday you caressed me, but today you have told me all is over between us, and my heart is broken.

For the last year I've been thinking too much about suicide. If I suffer the slightest rebuff in life, that thought fills my soul and robs me of all strength, leaving me limp and exhausted, as I am now. But if I ever do find the courage to kill myself it will be a long way from here and from you. You need not feel the slightest remorse. It will be due, not to you, but to the delusions of life itself.

To the same girl

[Turin] 10th September [1927]

Last night I wrote you a long letter, full of despair, but reading it through again this morning I found it too dismal, too cruel. Not for me, because in the last few days I've suffered infinitely more than I expressed in that letter, but for you. What happened was no fault of yours, but it must have caused you pain and fear. (You can be sure, Signorina, that I shall bring you nothing but suffering.)

This morning I got up early. The freshness of the dawn, the trees, the sky and the shining clouds cleared all sorrow from my heart. I thought longingly of those lovely mornings when we walked through those green paths together, talking about the sweetness of love and of poetry. Never again, never again.

I really am sorry that I caused you such suffering. Oh baby, if you'll forgive me I will do my utmost to put things right and 'welcome you in my heart as a symbol'. Your letter and your rose are two sacred things that I shall treasure. I will become a poet again, for your sake.

To the same girl

Santo Stefano Belbo, 17th September 1927
(written at night)

All the way here I've been thinking only of you, your face, your figure. More than that, caught up in a cloud of secret sweetness, I've been weaving fantasies, finding fresh intoxication as I recall the exquisite, indescribable gift you gave me yesterday, so much more than I had ever dared to hope for. In days now passed you had already bewildered me with lovely things, simple, wonderful gifts, but yesterday your intimacy taught me the sweet, sad culmination of life itself. Your passionate yet submissive responses showed me that you are a creature of the noblest nature, living in dreams and in sorrow. Yet in your kisses, your caresses, you brought me to a culmination of joy and also convinced my heart of the need for resignation. For me you became something hitherto concealed by the jealousy of others and the worthlessness of my own spirit—a delicate, ineffable flower of poetry, full of sweetness and sadness, giver of agony and joy, a vision with the beauty of a dream.

You make me suffer, and in all probability will make me suffer more when I think of you, your past and your future, but now I understand better than ever before how much you sacrificed to give this poor, inept versifier such poetic sweetness, just for love of giving something good to a being as unhappy and childlike as I am.

You have made me determined to be a poet. Before you came, my pages were forced and timorous, dwelling too much upon my own long periods of suffering. But when you appeared like a grand melody, with your gay blonde hair, your dreamlike fragility, the deep sadness in your eyes and your smiling face, your sweet voice . . . . You see, baby, that I'm lost when I think or dream of you.

To me you are something superhuman, baby. You are poetry and life, the poetry of life. You see how grateful I must be to you. And yesterday you gave yourself to me with kisses, caresses and words of comfort that no one but you could speak. All this for me, out of charity and perhaps a little love, as much for my stricken look as for the way life itself, cold and hard, has turned me to ice. I've seen once more the hills where I was born, the smooth flow of the river, the gentle slope of the landscape, full of trees, where as a child I played and ran free. I have seen once again the outline of the hills, faint and distant, where I roamed in my childhood years. I loved the clouds in the sky when I was ten, and ever since then my heart has filled with joy whenever I have seen them, joy that has increased from year to year. You are like one of those clouds, baby, and I love you too, dreaming in my exile of your eyes, gleaming behind the curtain of your golden hair.

Yesterday you became mine for always, and are now my great poetic theme, born in me without my knowledge, in this vast tree-covered plain enclosed by dreaming hills, poetry that now, after long years of seeking, I have found again in you. My grief may well be greater than yours, for you must remember how tenderly, how gently I tried to be near you, get to know you and become a friend of yours. I could weep with shame and grief if you were to suffer because of our friendship, for I love you, adore you with a hopeless passion, and I know how terrible such a breach would be. Perhaps you may say, with a smile, 'Bah! Poets are always like that, so impetuous, but they soon get tired of everything.' I know how unhappy I am, how contemptible, but believe me, all I've told you is the truth, the real truth.

To Tullio Pinelli, Alpignano

[Turin,
postmarked 26th September 1927]

No, I'm not dead. I've just been finding how to express those 'words from the soul' we need so much. I've been silent all this time because great revelations of the spirit can be discovered only in solitude, in the wilderness, as the prophets did. I never dreamed I could live like this, but I really have.

Do you remember the lovely face weeping among the flowers in that illustration of the *Vita nuova*? That's how my girl-friend looks, but I think our affair will soon be over.

Pavese

To Milly [?], *Turin*

Turin, 25th December 1927
(written at night)

It is extremely bold of me to write you like this, since you do not know me. Yet, Signorina, for a long time I have loved you in secret and felt like writing to you. I doubt, though, that I shall ever finish this letter. After the first few words I shall probably tear it up and toss it in a corner.

What can I say to you, Signorina? Early in this year, when you were in Turin, I saw you for the first time. Ever since then I've felt as if I were caught up in a wonderful dream, and all that time the thought of you has left me no peace. Your face has always been before my eyes. I hesitated for a long time, even being mad enough to hope, sometimes, but more often I felt bewildered, conscious of making myself ridiculous to no purpose, though clinging desperately to my dream.

I followed you, at a distance, but never dared to speak to you. That would have been crazy, and besides, I never saw you alone. So forgive me if I write to tell you all this. You may well find it boring, but do please listen to me a moment longer.

At the beginning of March you went away. I suffered terribly, but I soon learned you were in Rome. Now, this very evening, I saw you again, under another name, with different friends, but you yourself the same as ever, except that you are lovelier, more fascinating. Such a tempest rages in my heart that you'd be terrified if you only knew what it means.

I can no longer resist the impulse to finish this letter and so end, once and for all, the long agony that has tortured me ever since I first saw you. Today has made it worse. I beg you to send me one word in reply.

I have nothing to offer you. I'm not like those admirers I imagine must always be flocking round you in your own world. I'm just a poor student of nineteen, but I'm as different from other students as you differ from your companions.

You love your art. That is obvious in every movement you make. Hence you must be keenly sensitive. I, too, am striving desperately to achieve art with this pen of mine, and so I feel somewhat akin to you. I can understand several things about you that no one else would see. One evening in February, on your way home by tram, you were reading *Mimi bluette*. If you have read that book, and if you really are as I have imagined you to be, you must realise the humility and the immensity of what I'm offering you now.

I beg you, Signorina, to send me one word, one good word, in reply.

Cesare Pavese

1928

To Milly [?], *Turin*

[Turin] 5th-6th January 1928

A day or two ago I wrote you a letter, and so far I have had no reply. Perhaps it did not reach you, or you may have moved from that address. I realise now how ridiculous, how crazy, it was of me to write to you at all. You do not even know my name or anything about me. I ought at least to have come and talked to you myself, instead of writing from a distance like a coward, but I couldn't possibly come and see you now. I don't think I could even try, and if I did I should never find you alone.

What I asked of you in my letters wasn't much, just a kind word in reply. It wouldn't have cost you anything, and I can't ask for anything more. You yourself are so different from the people around you, your gestures in the limpid movements of your dancing, in your way of living. Surely you will not deny me this favour?

Perhaps my letter was boring and irritating to you. If so, I'm very sorry, but how else can I relieve the dreadful tremor I've had in my heart ever since I first saw you, a year ago? As I told you, I'm only a nineteen-year-old student with nothing at all to offer you, other than my desperate, hopeless affection, yet I'm not really a stranger to you. I love you and all your artistry, because I, too, am striving to achieve art with my pen.

One word from you, if no more, is as essential to me as music is to you in the performance of your art, to create a waking dream.

For pity's sake, Signorina, give me your answer.

To Augusto Monti, Turin

[Turin] 18th May 1928

Dear Master,

I'm a man who knows so little, and finds it difficult to reason clearly, while you are precise, limpid, enriched with vital experience of life, so that when you speak I pause to listen with the same assurance I feel when I am confronted by nature itself. Yet on this subject, the work of artistic creation, my view at the moment is the exact opposite of yours.

You say that to achieve a great work of art, all one needs is to live as intensely and profoundly as possible. If a man's spirit has within itself the qualities for creating a masterpiece, they will emerge by themselves, naturally and soundly, as happens with all vital phenomena. In short, you regard art as a natural product, a normal activity of the spirit, with clear-thinking as its essential characteristic.

I don't agree. In my view almost all the qualities you mention, especially the last, have no real significance. To me, art is achieved only after long travail and maceration of spirit, a never-ending crucifixion of the attempts one has made, most of them failures, before a man can get anywhere near the level of a masterpiece. So much so that efforts of this kind could very well be classified among man's anti-natural activities.

A really good work of art is sound in itself. In essence it is simply an organic structure palpitating with life. No matter what form it may take, it has a life of its own, just as trees and rocks have. Its soundness, i.e. the perfect co-ordination and activity of its various parts, is an essential condition. The subject of the work and the mind of the creator must be equally in harmony.

If that mind is not distorted, troubled or anaemic; if it has not passed through a long series of experiences that have now become completely absorbed; if, in short, it has not already worn itself out by the trials of individual contacts and attitudes outside the normal scope; then this mind will never create a masterpiece.

Because of this, art is the highest activity of all, and can carry a man nearer to divinity than any other occupation; it permits him to create characters that live and breathe. With this wild hope I can never bring myself to 'think of the other fellow first' while waiting for the birth of my own masterpiece in the near future. Meanwhile I shall go on wearing myself out with worry and enriching myself with more experiences of life.

To Carlo Pinelli, Alpignano

[Turin] 14th July 1928

Carlo, you great oaf,

I should think you've had as much holiday as you want by now. All sorts of concessions may be granted to a budding artist, but he can't be allowed to shut himself away with his nose in the air, idly watching life pass him by. Not that a man should be for ever reading or writing, that might drive him mad, but he should observe all that is going on around him and study his own reactions, continually striving to interpret his conclusions in terms of his own art. No wonder I'm certain you've had enough of doing nothing.

Drop me a line at my usual address (I look in there every other day), telling me all about your mental preoccupations or your criminal tendencies. (I say 'criminal' because if you go on doing nothing you'll be robbing Italy and the world of a great composer.)

You're a fine man. So am I, a conviction I have reached after five years of endless torment. Take a tip from me. Read and think about the books I recommended (or any others), compose a song or two or write a few stories. Send me something, no matter what.

To Carlo Pinelli, Alpignano

[Turin] 29th July 1928

Joking apart, all this week I've been expecting a letter from you, an important one at that, but now it seems it will never come (nor will the woman of my dreams). Were you perhaps trying to pull my leg? If so, watch out! I'm almost bound to retaliate!

When I do get this famous letter, I hope the handwriting will be rather more orthodox than in your last. What's this I hear? You 'don't trust me', 'don't understand me' and so on?

Is it myself you do not trust, or the postal service? If the latter,

I assure you it would be very wrong to show a lack of confidence in the State. Personally, I've never yet found any cause to complain about the postal services. If, however, I'm the one you distrust, I would remind you that I am your tutor, and that should be enough.

So far, the manuscripts cancel one another out. As far as music is concerned, I grant you I do not understand it, but if you had kept me informed, from the literary point of view, about your symphonies, what you intended to express, what effect other men's music has had upon you; if you had only sent some of your scores that I could have got someone to play to me, without telling him who had composed them, or could have tried them over on my piccolo myself, then I could have formed an opinion about them.

Imagine how people will talk!

'Have you heard Pinelli's latest?'

'Magnificent!'

'Remember when he conducted the Royal Orchestra?'

'Quite spectacular!'

'Yes, but I wouldn't consider his *Chorus of Raging Madmen* fit to compare with other orchestral scores I've heard.'

'It's true he seems to introduce notes one has never heard before. Just imagine! He's a classic where his art is concerned!'

'Now you're exaggerating. He's typical of all *avant-garde* composers.'

'Don't talk rot! His melodic line has such purity. Can't you hear it?'

'That's true, but it's also highly complicated.'

'You're right there!'

My dear little Carlo, if you want to hear people talking about you like that, you'll have to start discussing it with someone. Why not me? I'll be your first convert, your first apostle. I know very little about music, but as you are well aware, the apostles didn't know anything about their job either.

So get to work, bend your head, clench your teeth and stop talking. You'll find that's the only way to bear fruit, on my word of honour.

At one time I used to study madly at my desk, but now I make no special effort even though I'm preparing for a biennial exam. Every now and then I toss off a poem or a story, otherwise I get too tense. So take my advice and set about carving your future. (I assure you, it's harder than granite.)

To Carlo Pinelli, Alpignano

[Turin] 4th-5th August 1928

So the lordly young gentleman has taken offence at finding himself described by one of those vulgar terms borrowed from popular idiom! Such language is bracing, uplifting to the spirit. Even babies are quick to learn slang as soon as they can say 'Papa', 'Mamma' and 'no'. Apropos of this I'll remind you of a bit of fun Monferini and I had last winter.

It struck us that many words in common use are prohibited in polite society, and that it's fatally easy for anyone to fall into the trap now and then. So we had the idea of compiling a list of such improper terms and sticking it up wherever we could on walls where people could see them, street walls for preference, but also in classrooms, cafés, assembly halls and public conveniences so that everyone could see at a glance what was allowed and what was not. (Don't you agree that a study of the common idiom ought to be included in any school curriculum?)

The stilted phraseology of your letter (*basso profundo,* with pedal) makes it obvious to the naked eye that you have no intention of taking my advice. Just as you'd say to your confessor 'I won't do it again', so that his absolution would give you *carte blanche* to do something worse next time.

In everything I tell you, I shall strive to be as little as possible a 'literary critic', though I think that is my real province.

To begin with, then, you have a characteristic 'personality'. The whole atmosphere of your family is so dominating (not in any offensive way), that I myself, though an outsider and country-bred, almost succumbed to it. Yours is a charming home, and everything about it is well organised: kitchen routine and questions of education; religious observances and postal services; artistic pleasures and electrical installations. Individuality disappears in your family. I'll bet even their sins are traditional.

I've always thought your family could produce intelligent Pinellis, even artistic ones if you like, but first and foremost they are Pinellis. Your brother Tullio is a clear instance of this, and you yourself have shown me that your family may well include halfwits, cretins, morons and swindlers, all free (as free as anyone can be nowadays) to follow their own way of life. In short, to do anything worth-while you should emerge as Carlo, not merely as a Pinelli.

A typical member of such a family derives from it only aristocratic manners, a lordly air and a dignified reserve. For the rest he is entirely absorbed in himself, cultivating an 'artistic temperament' that has nothing to do with culture. These 'impressions' you sent me have little or no real value. They are disjointed, ill-considered and slovenly, with no regard for the reader or anything else. Yet, partly because of this and partly because they are so intimate and revealing, they tell me a great deal.

Quite unconsciously you have shown me a truth that has cheered me considerably. When we discussed it, last winter, you were all against free verse, while I told you that, life being as it is now, a man can no more write in rhyme than he can go about wearing a wig and carrying a sword or even a dagger.

Now you yourself, writing without any pretension to literary style but simply to satisfy a whim of your own (and that's the only way to be sincere and reflect the spirit of our own times), you never even thought of casting your ideas into metrical form. Instead, you have allowed your words to create a rhythm of their own. Remember, metre had every right to exist when poetry was sung to a musical accompaniment, but rhyme was never anything more than a specious device typical of decadence.

I don't advise you to write poetry as yet, because some people consider it an incitement to corruption. But, in view of my own opinion, I tell you only to think of yourself and start working, do something, anything at all, any work you have the ability and the guts to tackle. Write what you like to me, but remember you should be reading widely and keeping me informed about the books you choose.

To Augusto Monti, Giaveno

[Turin] 23rd August [1928]

This year I have not paid you my customary recuperative visit because I gathered from friends that you have other things on your mind and I did not wish to intrude or bore you. However, I'm now completely at a standstill and feel I must clear my ideas by writing you a letter you may not have time to read. If so, don't bother to reply or even to read it. Anyway, it's just my usual fit of depression.

It's a completely pointless letter, really, because any advice you might give me now would be the same as you've given me before, with complete sincerity, but it didn't change me.

I'm a young fellow with nothing whatever to do and am leading a thoroughly wretched existence. My mind is bogged down and I cannot see how to get it free again. Now and then there comes along some tedious literary job that I cannot take seriously. I've reached a point when I must either find fresh inspiration or die. I know just what you would tell me—enjoy being alive, give up literature, learn to be a man, become a child again, organise a few committees and all the rest of it.

But literature has already worn me down, reduced me to seeing the world simply as a conflict between romantics and futurists. As for enjoying life, throwing myself into various new activities, I simply can't do it. To live, one must have power and understanding, knowing how to choose. That's something I've never managed to do, just as I've never understood politics or any of the other complicated things of life.

I scribble a bit, spew out odd scraps of poetry, all to give me a place where I can make a stand and say 'I am myself', just to prove I'm not a mere nothing.

Nowadays only the futurists are doing creative work, but I can't understand them. They're too intellectual!

Monferini laughs and tells me that even if I kill myself I shall always be 'good old Pavese', a scholar with a craze for getting away from school. Sturani watches me with those dead-looking eyes of his (who knows what new romance lies hidden behind them!), and Giacchero sings me little songs.

Sometimes even that woman irritates me, for I see now that she's nothing but another Madame Bovary without any element of tragedy. All the humorous novels I read seem to be poking fun at me. Ginzburg just studies me.

Now that I've come to the end of this letter, I see only too well it is no reply to yours. It's merely an impertinence, a kick in the pants. Take it as a human document from one of your former pupils and don't think any more about it. It's not worth the trouble. Forgive me.

Pavese

To Carlo Pinelli, Alpignano

[Turin] 3rd September 1928

I've been keeping quiet for quite a long time, giving you a chance to breathe the country air, also because you had work to prepare. Now, here I am, popping up like a jack-in-the-box to startle you and to tell you I'll be visiting you soon. Meanwhile I am forwarding to you a good bundle of manuscripts to keep you happily occupied.

A little while ago I started reading the new draft of your free verses and have found them even more satisfying than when I read them first. After their period of incubation, a certain roughness of style that was criticised earlier now seems to me to have almost disappeared.

Your two compositions titled *The Nightingale* and *Rain* are not basically as slipshod as they seem. They show a certain approximation to a style of their own, doubtless because you felt that your material demanded that particular treatment and no other would do. See how familiar I am with your personality! I'll return these manuscripts to you very soon, in Turin.

Well now, what are you doing? It grieves me deeply that I cannot respond to your comment about Tolstoy's story, *The Godson.*[1] I haven't read it, nor can I get hold of a copy just now. I know very little of Tolstoy's work: one or two stories, a critical review and part of his *Resurrection*. The only book of his I have read in full is *The Kreutzer Sonata,* in which he takes one of Beethoven's sonatas as a symbol of perverted and useless art and makes it the theme of a romance.

Your comment that Tolstoy knew nothing whatever about music is thoroughly justified. The same could be said of his literary construction, for although he takes the trouble to clothe his subjects in bright, strong colours, true to nature, he is really setting out his own ideas, that's all. Actually he cares nothing for elegance in his writing, and most critics agree that his style is 'contemplative'. He takes ideas, mulls them over, repeats them and clinches the argument to his own satisfaction. In my opinion his claim to 'greatness' lies wholly in his profoundly true portrayals of passion, his sensitive treatment of pyschology and his very interesting way of subjugating everything to his own conscience. But, as I say, I do not

[1] One of the less well-known 'legends' recorded by Tolstoy.

yet know his major works and must therefore reserve judgment. So far I have never gone into Russian literature or given it any serious thought.

To change the subject, I've been skipping through some of Heine's work and have read his *Intermezzo* and *Nordsee*. Have you perhaps been covering the same ground? If so, write and tell me your views so that we can discuss it.

Let me remind you that this summer you should have been studying some of Shakespeare's plays and sonnets. He is at the very root of all romanticism. It is vitally important to take into account the historical perspective of any work we are studying. What do you know of Goethe or Leopardi, Manzoni, Victor Hugo or Carducci? If you and I are to work together again this year, we simply must have everything about them at our finger-tips.

What of Poe? Remember that the two or three hours devoted in class to studying a writer are of some importance. We must get to know him, make him a part of our lives. Only so can we discuss him seriously.

Kipling, too, and Jack London? You have some of their works at home and must have formed your own opinion about them. You should know everything about them, so that should you hear their name mentioned it will instantly change your train of thought and a brief summary of the writer and his work will run through your mind. I know only too well how infamous it would be to try to inject 'culture' into other people's minds. That is something every man must do for himself. This is why this year, rather than filling your head with aids to memory learned by heart, I've been trying to inculcate in you a love of books, *my* books, bringing them before you as I keep them before me. You must create for yourself a world of books, a world of poetry written by men who in life have lived their lives much as we do ours, and are still remembered only because they had the power to leave behind them books of great worth. We should love their spirit, discuss their ideas, dream their dreams, and so build up our own spirit on the foundations they have already prepared for us, formulating our own ideas by discussing theirs, hoping our own dreams, our aspirations, will be worthy of theirs. Here is the highest proof of the brotherhood of man.

To Tullio Pinelli, Pinerolo

[Turin] 27th September 1928

Dear Pinelli,

How much, how very much, I miss you![2] With all these devils of free-thinkers about, I go home with my brain (and my bones!) stiff with boredom and exhaustion, having settled nothing. With you, I could at least discuss all that's going on. Now I feel myself drying up and shrivelling like a rabbit-skin on a frosty night. But that's nothing new. If everyone else was away and you were here in Turin, I should probably tell you that your mantle lies heavily upon my shoulders. Your brain, I know, is stuffed like a mattress with brilliant gems of literary style. As things are, I find the world has changed. I'm even tempted to join the futurists! You see how inconsistent I am! It's a pity, but it goes to show what I am and always shall be.

Actually I've got less to complain about, this year, than I've had in earlier autumns. It seems to me (write and tell me if it's true) that I'm managing to organise and control my art. (For a man like me, whose only hope lies in doing just that, it would be salvation. But who can tell?) Out of my innermost instincts I have found how to deal with the world outside me, my own flights of fancy, my personality, whatever it may be. Little by little, laboriously, I have discovered from my own sensibility that I'm on the verge of writing really fine poems. In other words, my verses will no longer be fragmentary. That was due solely to my inadequate vision, my lack of imagination. All I have to do henceforth is to set about living in real earnest.

You will recall that in June I said I would either come back to Reaglie as a great poet or I would not return at all. I may still be in time to make good those day-dreams.

You should know that your brother is not the feckless young fellow we took him for, free-thinkers as we were. In twenty years or so we may well be basking in his reflected glory. He's something like Sturani, but more virile. He knows what course to take and has the guts to follow it.

[2] Tullio Pinelli had been called up for military service and was being trained as an officer-cadet at the Cavalry Academy in Pinerolo.

1929

To Tullio Pinelli, Pinerolo

[Turin] 1st May 1929

The sight of the yellow and blue quarterings on your coat of arms makes me feel all medieval. In preparation for my Italian exam, I'm bogged down, just now, studying poems about the Age of Chivalry, and feel like a paladin myself. The make believe entertains me for a while, but leaves me dazed and sick all next day.

So when I leave the library after working on those eight-line stanzas, I find myself back in the same sea of tears, with the usual broken bones and my skin hot with fever, full of remorse and a sense of futility.

I meant to write you a long letter full of strange confessions, which, unlikely though it seems, might also be a work of art, but that impulse has left me and I've nothing more to say.

Crackpot

To Carlo Pinelli, Arenzano

[Bibiana] 4th August 1929

I'm writing to tell you I'm here at Bibiana to coach a silly young fool who has to sit for an exam.[1] I'm beginning to take my work seriously and am finding it not nearly as boring as I expected. I say 'seriously' because our lectures had a rather different atmosphere.

[1] At this period Carlo Pinelli was spending his vacation at the seaside. Pavese was a guest at the home of the Bibiana family, at the mouth of the Pellice. Augusto Monti had introduced Pavese to this family and recommended him as a private tutor for their son, Manolo.

If you have any qualms of conscience, intellectual curiosity, unpublished works and so on, ask me about them. And meanwhile read Ibsen, just to please me.

Some time or other in September I'll come and see you, if my pupil's father, a punctilious gentleman, will agree to give me and his son a day off.

Do the opposite of all you've been doing so far and you'll be great.

Greetings

To Augusto Monti, Giaveno

[Bibiana] 5th August 1929

Things here are not as bad as I was expecting. I arrived on the 2nd and already feel quite at home. All the family are very friendly, especially the daughter who drives the car like a Valkyrie and took me for a tour of the valleys without being asked. They all call me 'Signor Professor'. The manservant tells me he'll be spending the coming winter in Turin and would like me to go out with him sometimes for a bit of fun. We must cultivate him.

I'm working like a horse, rereading all the Grecian myths, ready to stuff my pupil with them while trying to teach him bits of grammar. I already have a stock of interesting details of morphology that I bring out now and then, while the lad eyes me suspiciously and asks me to explain what I mean. We do two hours of Greek every morning and two of Latin in the afternoon. It takes me at least an hour to prepare all this. Any time I have left is spent in reading Walt Whitman,[2] writing home, flirting with the Signorina, playing tennis, taking coffee with the family, playing billiards or chess and sometimes persuading the Commander to tell me the highlights of his family history. I even find time to rest. I no longer think about poetry or going to a cinema, but, as I say, it's all going well.

[2] Pavese had already started working on his thesis on Walt Whitman's poetry.

I must thank you warmly, Professor, for your recommendation. Except for the social visits, which bore me, I'm enjoying it all. I've even lost my asthma.

As yet, my salary hasn't been settled, since the arrangement was made through you. When I stressed the point that I'm not a qualified teacher, the Count replied, 'We'll refer the matter to Professor Monti', so you can expect to be consulted any day now.

To Leone Ginzburg, Turin

[Bibiana] 20th August 1929

Dear Leone (you gay young dog),

I'm writing this with a great blue quill that must have come from an ostrich, and if I were to ring the bell a chambermaid would appear, always one I haven't seen before.

What news have you got to tell me? Here Casalini is being killed off and the Concordat making headway in perfect freedom. We have a commander who belches, a waiter who joins in our conversation at table, my unmannerly pupil, slumping in his chair like a sack of potatoes; a countess, always nursing her dog on her lap, even in the drawing-room; and the second eldest son, whose only subjects of conversation are manure and chamber-pots. *He actually eats his fish with a knife!!* They all treat one another like half-wits, in the most brotherly way. We are extremely religious and go off to mass all together, to set the villagers a good example.

The youngest boy regards me as a model of correct behaviour. There he sits in the drawing-room clasping his feet and mouthing foul obscenities. The Countess reproves him for what she calls his 'lack of delicacy' and goes on to compare his manners with mine, paying me all sorts of compliments.

This Countess is a fine *grande dame*. I was talking to her one evening when, across the room, I nodded to Buzano Monferrato and mentioned to the Countess that my brother-in-law's family lived not far away, at Serralunga. Instantly the social atmosphere became much more cordial! When I first arrived here, I did not kiss her hand as she greeted me. Then I noticed that everyone else did, so I wondered what to do. To start making such a gesture point-blank at this stage would be ridiculous. Fortunately she did not take offence.

Going back to the question of kissing hands, on my first Sunday here we came upon a flock of titled ladies in the open square in front of the church. (I ought to have expected this, for the Count had told me that Piedmont is much favoured by the aristocracy.) I was formally presented to these noble dames one by one: 'Lady this . . . the Marchioness of that . . . Madame Pompadour . . . Lucrezia Borgia . . . allow me to introduce Professor Pavese, who is with us to safeguard our son, Manolo, against the searching thrusts of his next examination.'

Imagine that! 'Professor Pavese', no less!! Just think of it! So I duly kissed the hand of every lady there, except one. She was a bad-tempered little old woman who told us she had the honour to be a lady in waiting, now retired, in the service of Her Majesty the Queen of Italy. 'Professor Pavese' raised her hand to kiss it, but she withdrew it and turned away, leaving me thoroughly snubbed.

I'm quite sure that I was sent here to broaden my experience of life and reshape my own existence. Observing some of the most illustrious families in the land is teaching me as much about humanity as I learned from watching people in my own walk of life. I've made myself quite indispensable to my patron and his family, helping them with all sorts of problems.

This pupil of mine is reasonably intelligent, but lazy. He has a habit, poor lad, of reading Greek in a sing-song voice, sometimes imitating the speech of a country bumpkin, or a drunk, or a eunuch, ending with a great burst of laughter. I just let him get on with it, and when he has finished I say, sternly, 'Now translate it'. Sooner or later he nearly always does. What can you do about it, anyway?

His parents discuss him with me, in his presence, during the long evenings we spend sitting on cushions strewn over the steps leading down to the garden. (Very chic, no doubt, but awfully hard on the spine.) His mother maintains that it's hardly true to say her son takes no interest at all in his studies. His blasé, apathetic manner is just a pose, and any attempt to correct him might break his heart.

'He'll get over it himself, don't you think, Professor?' she asks me.

'I would say, Contessa, that his character is hardly likely to change now. Manolo will carry it to his grave.'

'Good God! Do you really think so? Surely it's only a pose? He won't be like that all his life?'

'That's just the point, Contessa. If such a lack of interest were due to youthful exuberance and inexperience, it might well correct itself, but when it is deliberate, even malicious, there must be a prior, powerful antipathy, and to bring about any improvement would be very difficult.' After a pause, I added, 'I have a friend, your ladyship, who is a qualified psychologist. He might be able to help. . . .'

Manolo, sprawling in a deck-chair, started singing 'What a lot of fools you are!'

'I don't like you talking like that,' the Count snapped at him.

'If you don't understand the poetry of beautiful things, that's no reason for finding fault with others who do,' the lad's mother complained.

'Especially when those "others" are ourselves,' his sister remarked.

That kind of bickering went on all the time. The family always had a current catch-phrase (lasting sometimes for a week or two, sometimes for only a few hours) that they would use between each other whenever circumstances offered the slightest opportunity, the phrase being greeted with uproarious bursts of laughter.

During my first day or two here I found it quite amazing. The Count would make some comment over dinner, for instance: 'Manolo, sit up properly! You look like an old man!' His son and heir would retort, 'Nobody gets older at table', and the others would shriek with laughter. The Countess explained to me: 'You seem surprised, Pavese, to see the children laugh so much at these improprieties. It's just a family joke.' So I even invented one or two catch-phrases myself that proved very popular, but I quickly grew bored by the repetition and wished I hadn't.

But the Commander is by no means a fool, nor is he unfriendly. He has travelled widely, and was once our consul in Siam. Now he is a fine example of a country squire, a much respected member of the aristocracy. I could write many pages about his family and my period with them all, but my letter is already too long. I will tell you more about them later.

To Augusto Monti, Giaveno

[Bibiana] 24th August 1929

Here's a piece of cake for you, a bit of good news I must tell you at once. I've been organising a grand publicity campaign for your forthcoming book.[3] The Count and his daughter are both eagerly waiting to read it, fired with enthusiasm by my warm praises.

By this time, the Count has told me the history and amazing achievements of all the noble families living nearby, and has explained the meaning of their coats of arms. It has become a regular thing for him to take me for a walk before supper. We stroll through the fields, discussing history, heraldry, education and agriculture. He quotes Latin, any countryfolk we happen to meet greet him with friendly respect and we come back to the house in high spirits. There could not be a more pleasant companion than this high-born country gentleman.

Once home again, though, my usual problems have to be tackled. It is not easy to enter a new world and have to change all one's habits. I know I'm living in the lap of luxury, but I have to watch and listen, school myself and be careful not to make any mistakes. For the first couple of days the glamour of it all impressed me very much and I had no time to feel bored, but soon I began to notice periods when life seemed empty. What at first seemed marvellous became commonplace, then monotonous and finally pitiable.

Talking of practical matters, you advised giving up Greek as a bad job and concentrating on Latin. The trouble is that our young Manolo is keen to take the exam, yet will not take his studies in real earnest. He'll crack a couple of dozen jokes in the course of a single lesson. We have now finished working on grammar and have started on the writers themselves—Homer, Livy, Horace and Tacitus.

Everyone in the family seems confident that Manolo will pass, though his father speaks of your advice that he should continue attending classes until March, so it seems that he, at least, feels uncertain. I rather fancy that Manolo may have had to give his solemn promise to behave himself and study hard. I wouldn't say

[3] At this time Monti was checking the final proofs of his book, which was published towards the end of 1929 with the title *I Sansossi*.

I've no faith in the outcome, for he would be quite capable of passing the exam out of spite. I've given him plenty of tips on how to improve his memory and enlarge his vocabulary. That should help him. I don't know how he'll get on with his Greek orals, and if the examiners question him on grammatical analysis, that'll be the end of him.

In the twenty days he still has left, we'll be lucky to cover the prescribed writers, but then there's history, science and Italian literature. The nights are too short to give me time to prepare the next day's work.

Meanwhile we are living in the cream of society, familiar with names so illustrious they seem terrifying. The other day a prince called, and I was 'Professor Pavese' again (I shall end up by qualifying for it). Various barons come and go, spending the evenings discussing avidly such matters as family genealogy and quarterings, new designs of furniture, investitures and the vital importance of keeping the strain of blue blood free from any taint. I've already gained considerable prestige by identifying the subjects of a pair of sixteenth-century statues in the garden. They represent Hebe and Ganymede. This bit of erudition, plus the fact that I can drink my coffee practically boiling, has very much impressed the Count. While chatting with the Prince he described me as 'the expert who knew about Ganymede and the eagle'.

That manservant I mentioned in an earlier letter is now getting much too familiar. He claps me on the shoulder and refers to me as 'Signor Pavese, our personal professor'.

To Carlo Pinelli, Alpignano

[Bibiana] 31st August 1929

Why have I never heard of Joseph Balsamo until now?[4] I spent last winter rereading Salgari and the series of adventures enjoyed by the Three Musketeers. Being more intelligent than you, I understand Dumas, and Ibsen too, for that matter. You should set about

[4] This query is in response to a comment made by Carlo Pinelli in a letter to Pavese dated 7th August. After mentioning his study of Dumas and Ibsen, Pinelli remarked: 'If you haven't read Joseph Balsamo, you're missing something really good.'

reading Ibsen again and notice how he handles the development of his plots. If you have read *Hedda Gabler* without shuddering at its atmosphere and the kind of woman she is, then I can't have taught you as much as I thought I had. Read that work again, more attentively. You could do something else too. Set one of Ibsen's plays to music, any one you like. Then we'll get Ponina[5] to play it and Giacchero[6] to sing.

At present I'm still here in the country, working with a student who seems a complete blockhead, but I'll be free by the fifteenth. Then I'll contact you again to arrange where and when we can meet. Let me know how your brother is getting on, and when he will be back at Alpignano. Meanwhile, if you have any musical scores, verses or meditations, send them on to me here and I'll swallow them whole.

Give my kindest regards to Ponina

To Ponina Tallone, Alpignano[?]

[Turin] 3rd October 1929

Yesterday, with so many people about, once again I had to put off talking with you less formally. But the afternoon was not entirely wasted. I sent you a few pages, you replied with Debussy, not with any comparison in mind but because they each express our innermost thoughts. You did talk to me, but in the general confusion with everyone chattering I could hardly hear your words. All I remember is their sound and general purport. All I regret is my inability to write in your language—the language of music.

I'm beginning to understand it, though. Listening to the *Appassionata*, I felt myself engulfed in a world that was crashing in ruins. In the *Ninth*, I seemed caught up in a swift ascent from

[5] Ponina Tallone, whose real name was Giuditta Ciliberti Tallone, was a professional pianist, sister of the painter Guido Tallone and of Alberto Tallone, a printer.
[6] Remo Giacchero of Asti, a friend of Pavese's from boyhood; studying for his degree in medicine, he was an active member of an amateur operatic society.

star to star, while all around me was a harmony so remote, so high, that it seemed beyond human comprehension. All these things come to me only by fits and starts, like a lightning-flash. In between, I am conscious only of an irritating mental deafness.

I'm sure that if only I could listen to you more, talk with you at greater length, read you some of my poems while you played your music to me, we two, working together, might discover marvels. But life is sad and heavy, and you are far away, though even if you were near I should probably feel still more shut in and depressed. I'm like an out-of-tune piano—the nearer one gets to it the worse it sounds.

Who can say whether I shall ever manage to save myself? Just think, since June I haven't written a single verse. I'm beginning to convince myself that all my hopes of becoming a poet lead only to a blind alley. Now all I'm waiting for is death. The other day an old school friend of mine shot himself through the heart and 'gasped out his life in a pool of blood'.[7] Ah well, we shall all finish one way or another.

I'm very cheerful, don't you think?

Cesare Pavese

*To an English girl**

[Turin] 16th October 1929

Dear Miss,

I hope you will be remindful of that Italian student who, together with Mr Curti, got rowing with you on the Po. I was acquainted by our beautiful Georgie that you remembered my company and by him also I got your adress.

Would it not bother you, I should like to had some correspondance with you and to be kept knowing about your literary England, as, if you like, I will make with you for Italy.

Perhaps I will now also undertake the translation of some English or American books—novels—and I'll be glad to receive by

[7] This was Carlo Predella (see p. 14 *n*. 3).

* This letter, and subsequent letters thus marked with an asterisk (e.g. to Antony Chiuminatto), were written in English by Pavese and have been left unchanged except for a few minor cuts. See also p. 85 *n*. 3.

you a kind explanation of a lot of words and phrases—idioms, slang, americanisms—which no dictionary makes clear.

As you can see I am enough brazen faced, but I hope you will forgive for your similar wants' sake.

I'd be most pleased to help you in such cases, if, though, you have such needs, knowing you Italian certainly better'n I English. However, write freely me, whatever be the contents.

Besides, I pray you, send me back some notice of my greatest blunders in this letter and I'll be grateful.

Now, begging your pardon and waiting,

Yours respectfully

Cesare Pavese

To a student's mother, Turin

[Turin] 11th November [1929]

Dear and much-respected Countess,

Yesterday's meeting reminded me of the promise I gave you, to obtain for you a copy of that unedited fragment by Guido Gozzano we discussed at Bibiana.

It is a work of his final years, as you will see anyhow, and reflects the whole spirit of his *Signorina Felicità,* full of his conviction that death was imminent, full, too, of the sober pleasure he found in his solitude. One can even detect a controversial suggestion against D'Annunzio, already hinted at in the *Signorina Felicità*.

You will, I'm sure, treat this with the utmost discretion, since the writer has never given his consent to publication and is still proposing to polish it up.

The text, as I've already told you, has been recopied in a friendly way from the original manuscript now in the hands of Gozzano himself, who had no intention of having it published. However, this fragment seems to me one of the best things this poet has ever produced, and I think that you, loving his work as you do, will be pleased with it.

With my respectful greeting to the Commander and his daughter,

I kiss your hand,

Cesare Pavese

*To Antony Chiuminatto, Green Bay, Wisconsin**

Turin, 29th November 1929

I hope you will yet remember as great a borer as I was with you during your last Turinese year. I got your adress [sic] from Mr Mila, our witty friend who is now contributor in a whole row of musical reviews, has got a scream derby and surtout and walks as an equal together with your lovely Mr Della Corte (!). All the day long they are both in search of a concert, to write about.

By the by, I heard—or better read—of your own hit in Green Bay. I'll tell the world—as you taught me to say—! From the scraps I got it seemed you came back to your country as an hero and a conqueror. Using another of your teachings, I could say you are now shaking a wicked bow, can't I?

Good luck! I hope we'll soon—we, Maxim, the Misses Franchi, I, and in short all other Italian friends and acquaintances of yours —we'll, I say, hear and see you in some talkie as a fiddler and a sheik—an Al Jolson of the violin.

Do you remember our slang lessons? You see: I took advantages of you the most brazen-facedly, but as for you now the saddest thing is certainly whether I intend to go on.

Put your heart at ease: it was so kind of you to get wasting your time initiating me to the mysteries of your language and nation that I cannot forget it and make myself so bold as to write you all what follows.

I guess you remember yet how fond an admirer and a student of American things I was last year and such I have increased. You also know that here in Italy is almost impossible to find anything American a fellow is seeking for.

One month ago I discovered in Rome a certain 'Library for American Studies in Italy', but also this one is little acquainted with modern poetry—or novel—publications of America and only owns classics or non-literary works.

I succeeded barely in finding something I wanted for my degree's thesis about Walt Whitman. (You don't know, I'll be the first Italian to speak at some extent and critically of him. Look me over, I'll almost reveal him to Italy.)

What I am looking for now is some way of study, especially about

* As noted, this and other letters to Antony Chiuminatto were written in English by Pavese, whose spelling errors and idiosyncrasies have been retained.

your modern literature. There is a lot of contemporary poetry and fiction in the Union worthiest of note, but unattainable by us. Not even our booksellers can reach those works. In Italy there is only the Tauchnitz edition to supply them, but this one is too scanty.

I should like then to agree with you about a kind of business. Methinks you told me once you should have accepted such an agreement: each of us should have sent to the other the worthiest novelties of his own literature. But this is a little risky, one does not know enough the tastes of the other and, after all, I should require more wares than you, as it is my very profession to read books. We could then begin envoying each other a hint of the books required and—if it'll be possible and you'll agree—each of us will seek for and send them.

Meanwhile, as the most pressing thing, would you be so kind as to go fetching, whether there is in U.S.A. a book—a dictionary, a treatise, something—about modern American language, which can enable me to understand better your contemporary writers? They are full of slang, idioms, I don't know what, and so for an half incomprehensible. I want such a book as the air I am breathing. Can you fetch it?

Perhaps you don't even assume what usefulness had for me your little lessons of American spoken. Yet I keep those jottings carefully, and scanty as the expressions and words are I could put down, yet as I read modern American authors, I feel more assured, bolder in understanding them, more in touch with their mood of living and thought. And all comes from your lessons of language! Would it not bother you I should like to enclose in my letters a list of words and phrases picked out from contemporary writers and unexplained by our dictionaries and you should send it back to me with your wanted so interesting explanations. But only if you can and like it, I beseech you. You see, I am always the same bore. I beg your pardon. You have certainly other jobs to think about. But if you'll dedicate a little time, you'll do me a big, big gift. Think, 'tis for your own country's sake!

And even more. I make myself bold as to collect the first of these notes, from *Dark Laughter,* a wonderful (and the unique one as yet published by Tauchnitz) novel by Sherwood Anderson, whom I discovered some months ago and whose complete works I'll some day thoroughly read.

This book, if you don't as yet know, make yourself haste to seek for, for it is worth the while. Anderson is a true American writer—a poet—not only an imitator of European art, as many ones among your otherwise rank and luscious literature.

I enjoyed also in these days the most sportful biography in the world, the *Gentlemen Marry Brunettes,* which reminded me of our antique Anita Loos' *Blondes,* and the newer reading of *Babbitt* by Sinclair Lewis, a great humorist of yours, but a damned slang-tongued guy for any Italian reader to understand. I became acquainted with Carl Van Vechte's *Nigger Heaven. . . .*

But 'tis too much, to have abused you so. I must drop it out or I'll get your nanny. (These are your lessons which come back.) Don't you feel dejected after such teasing and impudence? And, after all, in such a preposterous English (I beg your pardon—American) as mine?

But be conforted, these are the evils of report, of stardom. . . . You have got to be a teacher beyond the Ocean, all the world round. 'Tis a fault of yours, you were too kind with me here in Italy.

Now recollect if you can do something for me, of what I wrote you here (my adress is Via Ponza 3, Turin, Italy) and, as you taught me, slip me the glove, with the best wishes of further success.

Yours sincerely

1930

To Ponina Tallone, Milan [?]

[Turin] 2nd January 1930

Would you believe this, Signorina? Of the twenty-one years of my life, twenty at least would be better forgotten. Only a few moments of the past seem to me worth remembering, and those simply because they are far away and widely scattered. Things of the past die away in the mind. That is why life is so frenzied, so filled with remorse and grief.

After so many failures that would cause only sorrow to remember, there comes an urge to shut one's eyes and mouth, to remain silent and to disappear. Have you never felt, when evening comes, a sense of shame and horror at having said something, laughed at something that day, even of being in the world at all?

I'm beginning to believe this may be an obsession peculiar to myself, for never a night goes by without my suffering this torment. Yet I'm cheerful enough, I go about and know people, I talk, I work. In short I'm alive. Don't you believe this?

Forgive my hysterical ramblings.

Your
Cesare Pavese

*To Antony Chiuminatto, Green Bay, Wisconsin**

[Turin] 12th January 1930

Dear Mr Chiuminatto,

I'm befuddled, all in a daze, with your titanic kindness. I'm now seeing the world only through a veil of pink sheets, all bristling with slang-phrases which are meddling together, re-echoing and staring at me from everywhere. I've got now I can no more take a pull out of a bottle together with my gang, without thinking

I'm going on the grand sneak. And how flip I get sometimes! My whole existence has got a slang drift now. You could almost say I'm a slang-slinger. (Ha!)

But I must, for the first thing, give utterance to a whole row of thanksgivings for your long-yearned, hard-hoped, fast-sent and all-surpassing answer to my letter, with all its flippancy and hard-boiled guyness. But you were so widely christian as to ship your hand to the poor sinner hearkening to him.

All your explanations are quite well, easy, clear, better than any would have dreamed of. I'm studying them by heart. Whence did you get the time to put them down? And more, being such a work intended for a fellow you remembered scarsely perhaps? There is something of witchcraft in it.

All is useful and masterful in your items, and so abundant is the treasure there one is almost dumbfoundered, not by lack of clearness but by dint of wealth.

You speak always of slang as of a special language or dialect, which exists by itself and is spoken only on certain occasions or places and so on. I think that slang is not a diversified language from English as, for instance, Piedmontese is from Tuscan, so that a word or a phrase can be told to belong to a class or another. . . . As slang is the living part of all languages, English has become American by it, that is the two languages have developed themselves separately by means of their respective slangs.

Now being in a literary turn I pass to my opinion on Sinclair Lewis. Meanwhile you can present my homages to the exceeding good-minded young lady-friend of yours, first as I like very much young ladies, especially American ones, and second, in order to excuse me if I'll come short of her good opinion which really seems a little flattering and hazarded.

I'm sorry to know S. Lewis only through *Babbitt*. I've not yet succeeded in getting at least his *Our Mr Wrenn* and *Arrowsmith*. In *Babbitt* the first thing that rises one's attention is its lack of plot: not of plot intended as a development of 'interesting' facts—a wooing, a murder, etc. (which things indeed there are)—but also the development of a spiritual adventure such as a research, an experience, a conversion. Whatever episode I read in *Babbitt* I can almost always enjoy it without knowing before or further. I think *Babbitt* can be well understood only if regarded as a suite of different pieces, each of them pent up in itself, nowhere attaining a climax, or at least each of them beginning, proceeding and concluding by itself alone.

I must add that I like *Babbitt* also for another reason. It is the most complete picture of contemporary America in its whole character: throughout manners, language, culture, doings, the whole life in short. And this refers itself to the powerful mind of Lewis himself, certainly one of your greatest living writers.

You'll kindly give me a sincere hint of my lecture here in your next letter. But I should also like, were it possible, to have something written down by the curious young lady-friend of yours, about American literature or whatever else there is of common interest. Would she be interested in it, I should gladly inform her about our modern Italian writers and culture.

And still there are scores of modern American books I should like. I found an American library in Rome very rich with American works such as historical and critical ones. Some classics also, such as Thoreau and Howells. I'm borrowing two volumes a fortnight by it. But as for modern, living productions, there is nothing. There is only your help there yonder. Let us begin with Frank and Hemingway.

I am sending you now a copy of *Nothing New in the West,* which you are wrong in believing a French book. It is by a German author, as you'll see by perusing it, for it is worth while. As I don't know whether you are conversant with German language, I don't send you the German text nor the Italian translation which does not exist by way of a legal prohibition. It seems that this book has the wrong to describe the war how it is really, an atrocious thing, and naturally we Italian babies are defended to know it by means of a direct translation. We could become too moody and refuse the next war. We also wonder how Fascism will fan out.

But I must leave off. I wind up my yarn with a final thanksgiving for the book you so kindly sent me. I'll read it notwithstanding my many scholarly occupations and I'll write you something about it.

Now I'll slip you the accustomed glove and am,

Yours sincerely

*To Antony Chiuminatto, Green Bay, Wisconsin**

[Turin] 22nd January 1930

Dear Mr Chiuminatto,

Your gift of such a book as *Sorrel and Son* caused me to think of an answer. Here it is, in this same package. When I perceived the wonderful plot of *Sorrel and Son,* I bethought of an Italian book—moreover, a Peidmontese one—written by a friend of ours, which is dealing with almost the same situation of a father trying to rear his son.

As you'll see, this book was issued only last year and really it is one of the worthiest contemporary books in Italy. I cannot speak of so wide a diffusion of it here, as of *Sorrel and Son* in America, for its very nature defends such a diffusion. Against Deeping's, which is a book of universal appeal for its—in a good sense—triviality of experience, its elemental semplicity, being the expression of a life among common wants and needs, a life without a weight of tradition or culture, save what is common to all middle men. In *Sanss-Sossi*[1] we have a world of extreme complication, breeded in a literary mood, old of ages by historical experiences and, more, bounded to a certain liking towards a definite region of the country—Turin and the Monferrato, the dialect-title—which thing can but keep aloof most Italian readers.

But the miracle of the book is that with such a dangerous foreground it has succeeded in shaping a human world where such foreground becomes poetry. Look only at this : these two books are the same fable related the former in America and the latter in Europe. Never the two continents reflected and diversified themselves better than in these two books.

I feel sure that you, who were so much in Turin, will like this fond description of the city since last century, of his hills and country such as you'll find here. And I close this note again renewing thanks.

[1] See p. 70 n. 3.

*To Antony Chiuminatto, Green Bay, Wisconsin**

[Turin] 1st March 1930

Dear Mr Chiuminatto,

I was just reading the *Spoon River Anthology* which I want you no more to trouble about as I found it here on loan from the Y.M.C.A. library, when I received the wonderful bunch about *Babbitt* you mailed me on February 11th. It's too awfully nice of you to behave so. I feel lost in your graciousness. When I begged of you the boon of some explanation I did not mean to overcharge you so. The best compliment I can pay you is to profit from your lessons. You bet I mean to be a go-getter, but to succeed!

As for your own opinion about *Babbitt,* I think the same. Those personae are really capital fellows and it is an endless carnival of fun to follow them throughout Lewis's slang-stunts of style. What you say of *Sorrel and Son* is quite true, and I don't know what you're complaining about the 'childish American spirit I seem to find in it'. What I said about its simplicity and triviality was, as I warned you, in a good sense. I certainly blundered in my English as I meant that its characters were common people, stripped of all the classical learning which underlies the pages of *Sans-sossi.* . . . And now I have taken advantages of you in all possible manners. I skulk away and on the bargain sting you in the rear: here's a list of some words from *Babbitt* I yet am puzzled about and some others gleaned from Van Velton, O. Henry and Anderson.

I guess you are muttering: 'Damned fool! I'm too late onto his intentions now. He has made a shipping clerk of me and, what's the worst, he teases me with the very words I taught him. Blow him!' Don't you, Mr Chiuminatto?

But think it out: ain't you enticing people with your unearthly serviceableness?

Always chums,

To the editor, Bemporad, Florence

[Turin] 12th March 1930

Dear Sir,

In the Appendix attached to a volume of very modern stories,

I read about the projects you have in mind for your series of translations of contemporary foreign works, especially those from North America.

I refer in particular to your plan to 'build up in Italy a group of enthusiastic translators whose taste and efficiency are beyond question'.

If your team of such translators is not already complete, or if the ever-increasing production of foreign literature makes it necessary to add to their number, I wish to inform you that I am available as a translator of North American novels, possessing a high degree of competence and the advantage of being able to obtain information direct from the United States.

If you would be so kind as to give consideration to this offer, and write to inform me of the terms and prospects, I could send you at once a specimen of my translation or a certificate confirming my studies, whichever you wish. Meanwhile I venture to draw your attention to the authors who have been my special study, Sherwood Anderson and Sinclair Lewis, the first of whom you yourself have mentioned in your list of projects. There is certainly no need for me to stress the importance of the second, who has been completely ignored, even in France, but who is so typically American that the success of his work is assured.

Naturally I am speaking of these two, but I would give favourable consideration to any other suggestion you may care to make within the field of North American contemporary literature.

Awaiting your kind reply I remain, yours respectfully

Cesare Pavese

*To Antony Chiuminatto, Green Bay, Wisconsin**

[Turin] 5th April 1930

Dear Tony,

Well, we have now got a fair bond of a friendship, a little bothersome perhaps on your part on account of the way I'm overworking you, but, out of this, I hope we get some usefulness from it. As, for instance, to receive letters with such strange stamps which cause janitors to stare a bit. It's grand to be addressed as Mr So and So from Green Bay, Wis!

I noticed what a waste of 'Golden Gates' and 'Liberty's statues' you are practising in your mailings of books. I know that a cent is part of a dollar, so I pray you to enclose henceforth with the bookseller's bill a note of the postal charges.

There's another complication, also. Giving vent to your righteous indignation, you used certain phrases you've now got to explain. What the devil were you meaning in such nonsensical words as 'I'll be pulling with you and not against you', and 'You tell the world, *I haven't the heart*!' and 'to rag someone'. You see, I also am 'right on the job'.

But, to stop kidding, I want to thank you infinitely for your troubles which never seem to come to an end, but always voluntarily to breed and multiplicate. I'm almost terrified with the awful kindness I've started.

Now I put Lewis' book aside to hurry on the library's ones. I began with *The Grandmothers*. There is no other living country in the world able to boast such a contemporary literature.

You Americans are the peach of the world! Not only in wealth and material life but really in liveliness and strength of art, which means thought and politics and religion and everything. You've got to predominate in this century all over the civilised world as before did Greece and Italy and France. Each of your worthy writers finds out a new field of existence and writes about it with such a downrightness and immediateness of spirit it's useless for us to match. A good modern European book is, generally speaking, only interesting and vital for the nation which produced it, whereas a good American one speaks to a larger crowd, springing as it does from deeper wants and really saying new things, not only queer ones, as we at our best are today doing.

The Grandmothers is another book about your history, one of your national books, which demonstrate a thing not yet generally known here in Europe: that you, as a nation, have already a tradition and a pride, a great thing which fills your last want. Now you can really go and conquer the earth.

To which let us come down.

Did you never fall in with the works of Mr Artemus Ward? If you didn't, you drop this sheet at once and stir about till you find out and read them. It's a capital fellow, a wonderfully American one, something of an Anita Loos in checkered trousers and Yankee spelling. It's a terrible knocker of great things and as for little ones he has a charming naive philosophy 'than which there is no whicher'. You must read the way he gets along with the 'show biznis', his war-correspondance and his letters to the

English Punch. Here is a half-page of his to sample the stuff.[2]

Ain't it really corking? And you can go on, he is always the same feller. I want to write something about these humorists, from A. Ward to A. Loos. They are an exceedingly interesting gang.

I wonder what has happened to the second package of books you mailed the same day with the library's I got already. However, hardly I'll have it, I'll write you something about.

Always yours,

*To a young English lady**

[Turin] 8th May 1930

Dear Miss Wilson,[3]

I want to beg your pardon for my long silence. I hope you'll yet remember me, as I had your kindest wishes on Christmas last year. I want yet to praise you for your surprising Italian, the wonderfullest letter I got from English or American people. I knew already you spoke it fluently, but you are also writing it exceedingly well. Best compliments!

I want to thank you for the nice list of my blunders, followed by so clear explanations. I cannot account for my long silence, else than alleging the essay I'm after for my degree, notwithstanding I hope you'll forgive me.

Say, Miss Wilson, I heard now from Mr Curti, who is running through France in order to get some appointment by a movie manager, you are asking him for an Italian comedy to teach your pupils about. If I can be of some usefulness I'll be glad to help you in selecting and getting your book. If you agree, write me about it and also about every want you could have here in Italy.

Now, you'll certainly have gone to the Italian Art Exhibition in London, and I should like you would write me something about. Will you?

[2] Pavese left a page blank in this letter, obviously meaning to fill it with a passage from Artemus Ward (pseud. of Charles Farrar Browne), but not in fact doing so.

[3] Pavese initially began this letter 'Dear Miss Nora', but changed the wording before despatch. This lady is almost certainly the one to whom Pavese wrote on 16th October 1929 (see pp. 73-4).

*To Antony Chiuminatto, Chicago**

[Turin] 17th May 1930

Dear Buddy,[3a]

I got somewhere, besides your tiny photograph for which I thank you, that the last of May is your birthday and so I hurried, as fast as I could, to have you honored and thanksgiven as you deserve. No, I blundered : not as you deserve, for it's impossible to overtake you in kindness, but as it is granted to me, poor fellow that I am.

So, you'll receive, in a few days since, there in Chicago, a little present I dare to make you, to sweeten—posthumously (it's my habit)—your birthday. It is some liquor-center chocolates you wrote me once you are so fond of.

Would the chocolates arrive in Chicago someway marred (the shopclerk assures me they become dried within, in a spell of time), you could then think that you are in Prohibition land. But the ditto clerk swore me the sweets had arrived the day before from the factory.

You have certainly rec'd now my two silly letters about the 'lost books', and you'll, I hope, excuse me for my flurry. If you intend to go on with your mailings of library books (and I'll be tickled to death if you will), send me only Lewis's books except *Babbitt, Arrowsmith* and *Our Mr Wrenn*, which I got here. The reason is I want to know him perfectly in order to write about him, an essay asked for by a certain literary review of Rome. The essay would be presented in the summer, so, if you can, give me a lift.

With best wishes,

[3a] Chiuminatto's letter to Pavese generally ended with this term.

*To Antony Chiuminatto, Chicago**

[Turin] 10th June 1930

Dear Tony,

I've a lot of things to write about.

Well, I got the whole bunch of 'them' books safely. Naturally I want to thank you infinitely, but this is too little. Did you not receive my suggestions about your wasteful expenses of mailing and my firm and businesslike proposition to pay for them? Absolutely you must, next time, enclose in your letter a bill of all your stamp expenses. Get me? I'm overflowing with merriment for the new books.

Say, I'm becoming a true authority about American literature. I begin to feel chesty with my fellow-students, and especially with co-eds. As for the funnies you sent me,[4] it's again an awfully kind idea. With these texts and your explanations, I'll not miss the target. You bet: in those cuttings there's slang galore. I'm fattening on it, day by day.

Now the blow-out: perhaps this winter I'll be in New York to teach (look me over) Italian literature or such similar things in Columbia University! I've been so admired on account of my smattering of America that a professor in my University has written about me to Columbia's Dean who was searching for Italian students 'to cross over'. I'm now waiting for a reply.

Yours,
C. Pav.

*To Frank D. Fackenthal, Columbia University, New York**

Turin, 13th June 1930

Dear Mr Fackenthal,

I got both your envelopes containing the printed material you spoke about in your kind note. The Record of Fellowships and Scholarships in 1930-31 and the Bulletin of Information of the University.

[4] Chiuminatto had sent Pavese cuttings from the *Chicago Daily News*, in particular the 'comic strip' of Mutt and Jeff.

I want to thank you infinitely. As for the further information about the precise conditions which are likely to be granted to me, I should pray you, if something is not yet on mail, to send me a kind notice of yours about.

I excuse myself for being so bold as to cause you a second trouble.

Very truly yours,
Cesare Pavese

*To Antony Chiuminatto, Chicago**

[Turin] 21st June 1930

Dear Tony,

Gosh all fish-hooks! It's my lot today to be lectured by all. I've been lectured by the Board of Teachers of the University about the fondness of slang I showed in my degree (which I got safely. I'm Ph.D., now!).[5] Late in the night, coming home a little tight I found both your letters of 5th and 7th and worried myself infinitely about your lecture on comparative Italian and American fastness. Going this morning to the office, to retire Lewis's goods, I got together with them some curt advice about the best manner to pack things: 'Write to the forwarder, let him know, his frequent mailings of "books" have been noticed, customs begins to feel obliged to open your packages, so let him pack them more loosely.'

Get me? My buddy, you go on packing them in your wonted accurate way, if they get damaged it is we must pay, no? Let custom-officers pry and ferret out—they are on the job for that.

All this turns out to cast the blues on me, and I feel the more worried as you also put down that your hurry and scurry gets you in wrong and you worry about it. Now that it is done, I've only to thank you a thousand times, but you must not go fetching you so much trouble and hustle so, and disturb so many persons (e.g. your landlady), for your ungrateful buddy's sake. Till now I've only answered to your kindest boons with always growing boldness.

[5] Pavese gained his degree on 20th June 1930, with 108 marks out of a possible 110.

Now I must stop absolutely, and for the first time I'll try to write you a letter without asking for something.

I'm now so overwrought I forget sometime to breathe. When you get the books back on 1st of October, you'll read a corking essay on Lewis. It will beat everything! I've something to say about slang, also. It will be grand and glorious. I'll teach a few fellers now overflowing Italy with vacuum-gabble about America, what people must say and how they must say it.

As for my coming to New York, till now I got no reply from the University, but the thing seems sure and I've only to wait somemore. I beg your pardon if this time I write you a comparatively short letter, but I want extremely to begin *Elmer Gantry*. Let me know something I can do here in Italy for you, otherwise I'll be too shameful to write you any more. Whatever thing, from buying you a Fiat to find out a bride for you. I'll be glad to do it for you, you have been too kind to me!

*To Antony Chiuminatto, Chicago**

[Turin] 20th July 1930

Dear me,

Now I'm writing. I've just finished my essay. Some amendment yet and it'll be ready. You see. I've not only already read the whole of the Lewis you sent me, but also criticised him. Look me over! I wonder if ever there was such a snappy eater of American language! As for your 'comment', I can only say that you are the slickest teacher I ever enjoyed.

As yet, I don't know anything sure from 'my' Columbia, but I'm in corrispondence with them and hope and dream. Would it not be a grand thing were it only for the frolick you and I would have in old Manhattan?

I thank you for the trouble you took typing that article by Ch. C. Baldwin. I found it very useful and interesting and should like the title of the newspaper or magazine in which it appeared, and its date. And now, with your kindly permission, I go 'to hit the hay' as I am ossified by a whole day of poling on the river Eridanus, commonly called the Po.

Good night old socks and keep remembering your

Cesare Pavese

To Dina, Turin

[Turin] 24th July 1930

My little poppet,

If you were one of those silly society girls who know nothing about life and pretend to be flirts, I should pretend to be madly in love with you. But you are a good girl, already quite capable of looking after yourself, having learned the hard way to recognise what is sincere and dependable.

We're not in love, Dina. We don't say we are, even to ourselves. What we are looking for is a certain community of interests that we think we've found in each other. In you I see a pretty little girl, intelligent and fond of kisses. When we're together we feel happy, but we aren't in love. You, Dina, are afraid that one day you may fall in love and that it may bring you suffering.

Dearest, don't you see that life is all the lovelier because between one day and the next we may lose it? Don't think about tomorrow. That is too sad, too pointless. Why not live every day with the thought that this miracle of love might blossom between us? You know how hard life can be. Then why not enjoy a moment that could be a precious memory to you for as long as you live?

I'm not saying this for myself, Dina. I don't know whether I love you. Certainly, if you were to leave me now, I shouldn't die of it. (You see, I'm sincere.) I'm fond of you, and the thought of never seeing you, never kissing you again, would be sad. Very sad.

Perhaps one day we shall forget each other, but why should that day be now? In a month's time we may be in tears, but why should we start weeping now? Sometimes I kiss the air and think of you, of your pretty little face. I don't hug you nearly enough. I do love you, Dina. Do you love me? Just a little?

Your devoted

To Arrigo Cajumi, Florence

[Turin] 25th July 1930

Illustrious Professor,

Enclosed herewith is the article on Sinclair Lewis I promised you some time ago. Composition has been delayed because I have had to obtain copies of this writer's early works from a public library in the United States. However, I have been able to see everything Lewis wrote, and my article embodies a study of the development and activity of this writer.

I have found it impossible to keep up to date with all the bibliography of the subject, for the material has been widely scattered and was in any case scanty. After some difficulty I have been able to see some reviews by French critics and some by American, but generally speaking I have not used these in my article. Instead I have tried to present the problem in my own personal way. I hope this article will conform to your wishes and to the exigencies of your publication, and that its length, necessitated by the subject, will not prove a bar to your acceptance.

Leone Ginzburg will have written you about Sherwood Anderson. I hope you have been able to give it your attention, and that in the very near future you will write to me about this proposition. Meanwhile I venture to beg you for a prompt and favourable reply to this letter of mine.

C.P.

PS. If you wish, I will naturally undertake the task of correcting the proofs.

To Dina, Turin

[Turin] July 1930

Meeting you so unexpectedly this evening gave me a great thrill. Maybe you were just as surprised, since all we had in mind was having to wait a long time before the appointed day came round.

I talked to you, kissed you and felt blissfully happy. Then you told me something that changed my joy to sadness. Perhaps you may not come back to Turin again.

A whim, you called it, just a fanciful idea. But doesn't every love-affair start with a fancy of that sort? I'm being frank with you, Dina, so frank that I run the risk of losing you. My feeling for you was at first no more than a fancy of that sort, but it is deeper and broader now. Every day you please me more, Dina. Every day I see you, my desire for you grows, so does my conviction that you belong to me. Why cut short the happiness that may be on the point of bursting into bloom between us? Is it love? Who can tell? But one thing we can be sure of. Everything in life ends with tears, yet it would be foolish to deny oneself a moment of love for fear of how it will end.

I make you no promises, Dina. I know your sincerity and your way of life well enough to be equally frank with you. Your body gives me pleasure, so does your mouth, but when we are together I'm beginning to discover so many other, even lovelier, things about you. You are a most unusual girl, Dina. If I were to lose you I should weep. You would weep, too. So what's the use of breaking away from each other now, to avoid suffering later on?

You'll come back, Dina. Otherwise it would be too tragic. I'm sure you'll be back. I'll be waiting for you.

Cesare

*To Antony Chiuminatto, Chicago**

31st July 1930

My dear Prof,

Here is at last another literary specimen of mine to enjoy yourself. (You seem to fancy them.)

I'll begin shrieking Haboy for your corking lingo—you are the most wonderful slanger (does it go?), nay, you are turning out a regular writer, a creator of speech. I think someday the manager of 'my' sheet will send me a 'best-seller' by Mr Chiuminatto-

Haliburton[6] to review. I won't fail then to point out my previous friendship with the 'Big boy'.

Do you know, Tony, that my essay (I beg y.p.: my and *your* essay), has done kind of a hit in the office of the manager and editor, etc.? It will appear on the issue of September—maybe we are not so slow in the Old Land, eh?—and, tear your hair, *they asked me for another of them criticisms on Sh. Anderson,* our good old Sh. Anderson, whose complete works you will now have to find out and borrow and send to me. Really, could you—which I think at this season of the year a little difficult—gather for me the works I want? I should be exceedingly grateful to your person.

I am expected to hand over my essay before New Year's Eve, so we have plenty of time to ferret out and mail and read the books.

Now we are arranged and you'll have to run about with a new pair of shoes. What do you think of your lil old flea-in-the-drawers of a friend? Make it snappy, Amuriccano.

You see my kidding is a little heavier than yours and his gist is always some unending trouble for the fellow. This sort is the renowned European kidding. How do you like it? Now I thank you another time for the gift of *The Big House*, which is truly a gold mine of slang, a thing to be studied by heart. My admiration for your wonderful new language has yet increased since the pleasure of your unforgettable conversation, and to my eyes you are now the hero, the saint, the representative of a new religion.

As for Columbia I don't yet know anything sure. Now pardon me my long silence and have a friendly wallop on the shoulder by your—

[6] Pavese is linking Chiuminatto with a 'best-selling' American writer, but it is not clear which of the two authors of that name he means. It may have been Thomas Chandler Haliburton (1824-1903), but was more probably Richard Halliburton, a popular author of travel books in humorous vein.

To Ponina Tallone, Milan

[Turin, in reply to a letter dated 18th August 1930]

I'm disappointed that I haven't managed to get in touch with you, and should be glad if you would write me something about your music and your thoughts as you compose it.

I have changed a good deal from what I used to be, but I still enjoy renewing my contacts with old friends. It's possible that I may not be able to visit Alpignano this year, but I can at least hope.

C.P.

*To Antony Chiuminatto, Chicago**

[Turin] 19th August 1930

Dear Tony,

I got your letter of 1st August and as I'm mailing back to you the other library books I take the occasion to unite here a few lines for you.

I shall be much gratified to receive other pieces of criticism about Lewis, but don't worry too much, because I cannot change anything on the drafts of my essay.

I'll write about the ideas of the several Rev. Critics[7] you quoted when I'll answer to your next letter. Now I'm in a hurry. Important: On the 1st of September my address will change, the new one being Via Lamarmora 35.

By the way, I pray you (but take it leisurely) to look after the association conditions of the following reviews: *Transition, The Scribner's, Harper's Magazine, This Quarter, Poetry,* a magazine of verse. And please don't cease to pull on me slang galore, I feed on it, do you know?

[7] With his letter to Pavese of 1st August, Chiuminatto enclosed cuttings reporting adverse criticism by the Jesuit Fathers of America, accusing Lewis and Hemingway of immorality in their novels.

I beg a hurried pardon and give you a last order: borrow or buy it, send me *Congo,* or *The Chinese Nightingale,* or better than all, *Collected Poems* (Macmillan 1923) by Vachel Lindsay.

Your always ashamed and never reformed friend,

To Leone Ginzburg, Viareggio

[Turin] 20th August 1930

This morning I received from Columbia a reply to my application.[8] They ask me to send them the certificates required for my admission to the University. I may then be allowed to enter a Graduate Faculty as a non-classified student. If, after a trial period of one year, my work is considered satisfactory, I may put in a request to become a full member of that Faculty (which I take to be a Degree course).

Such certificates as I have aren't worth a red cent. One of them, from the Director of a shorthand typing class, testifies that, as from 5th September, I shall know sufficient English to be able to follow lectures in that language. Beyond that, my passport will be adequate identification.

Not a word about salary or terms of appointment. Can it be that in America such things are regarded as too delicate to discuss? Can one safely entrust it to them? It's hardly likely, I think, that when I get to the director he will tell me, in a language I don't understand: 'Here's £50,000 for you. Wait while I hand it over.'

Surely they don't expect me to go to America and enrol for such a course at my own expense? Let me have Farinelli's address.[9] I'll write and tell him this isn't the way to do things. He'll have to pay me damages!

[8] On the advice of influential people whom Pavese met while at Bibiana, he had applied to Columbia University in the hope of obtaining a salaried post there as a tutor.

[9] Arturo Farinelli, Professor of German Literature at the University of Turin, was one of the three sponsors of Pavese's application to Columbia. The others were Ferdinando Neri and Augusto Monti.

To Giuseppe Prezzolini, New York

[Turin] 2nd September 1930

Honoured Professor,

I think one of my letters, dated 9th July and addressed to you, may have gone astray, since I have not yet received any reply. You will recall that, back in June, you passed to the Secretarial Department of Columbia University a letter from me, asking for information about the post in the University mentioned in your letter to His Excellency Farinelli.

Now the Administration department of Columbia has been in touch with me and has sent me a form of application to enrol as a student, advising me that I am expected to attend there on 25th September. Signor Farinelli has always spoken of a subsidy or a 'stipend' I might claim, just enough for my living expenses. At my request he has written you again, quite recently, to clarify this possible misunderstanding.

I find myself now in some uncertainty, not knowing what to decide about the journey. In any case I could not get to New York in time for the start of the scholastic year on 25th September. I also have certain personal commitments that will keep me in Italy until the New Year. Anyway, I cannot embark on such a journey without first making sure of what to expect when I get there.

So I beg you, Professor, to clarify the situation and if possible help me, if only for the sake of Arturo Farinelli, who encouraged me to study North American literature.

*To Antony Chiuminatto, Chicago**

[Turin] 22nd September 1930

My Tony,

. . . . Thanks to you for your happy intentions about slang. I'll be hanged if I am not owing to you my whole learning. Some day I'll try to reciprocate.

I called on Misses Franchi: they said me a lot of kind things about you and offered me a protector in America, whom I don't as yet want, as my dealings with Columbia are as yet unfinished and at least, for this winter, I think there will be nothing new. But patience is also a virtue.

Say, old socks, why are you so dissatisfied with your America? I know that one's country is always more captivating when abroad, but you must not forget that coming abroad is also intended to augment one's understanding of one's native country. You, who are in the tremendous situation of being both an Italian and an American, must try to comprehend the two nations and rise above petty difficulties. Moreover, you must not forget that we Italians are two distinct nations, the North and the South, and there is a deeper difference between us and them that nothing could repair. As for the money-making America, think that all great nations were in the beginning money-makers, also Italy, when in the twelfth century a bunch of republics. Look in Anderson and Lewis for an escape from that. The Americans of Lewis are good, very good people, in their somewhat childish psychology, and you've seen in *Arrowsmith* how this childishness can become a true human and brotherly suffering.

Anderson is somehow an Italian like you. His grandmother was Italian. Think of this: you are a son of two races and so you enjoy the odds of both.

I expect something by you about this. Now goodbye and a manly wallop by your Buddy.

To Arrigo Cajumi, Florence

[Turin] 27th September 1930

Dear Sir,

In reply to yours of the 17th, I am sending you herewith a note on the Whitman anthology issued this year. I did not write you about it at the time because I understood you had already heard of it from Ginzburg.

As for Anderson, I have not yet received all his works. Some of those I am short of are quite important, so I must postpone the article already promised, until my studies are completed.

Would you consider the possibility of publishing a translation of Cabell's masterpiece *Jurgen*? Unless I'm mistaken, that has not yet appeared even in France. It may be possible to do something with Hemingway and Dos Passos as well.

In one of his recent letters, Ginzburg indicated to me your intention of forming a publishing house to be called *La Cultura*. I take it that you will run it on extremely modern lines, and I would therefore suggest the great cultural value (and certain financial success) of including an Italian version of at least one work by H. Melville—*Typee* or *Moby Dick*—preferably the latter.

*To Antony Chiuminatto, Chicago**

[Turin] 28th October 1930

Dear Tony,

I'm shamefully late in replying to you. Anyhow, here I am. I got the Lewis short story and the two next Andersons, the *Testament* and the *Triumph*. You bought them, I think, and I'm now waiting for the bill. Buy some more, buy all you can.

Now rejoice, old-timer. Last week I rec'd the draught of *our* essay to correct! In another week it will appear and you'll get it in three more. They procrastinated the whole on account of its length. When they pay me I'll toast to your health till my own will be practically gone.

But let's come down to earth. I want you to explain to me: *usuer, stool-pigeon* and *pine-apple man*. Thank you for giving me the meaning of *put on the spot*.

A hundred millionaire-pupils to your fiddle-craft and only one she-pupil.

To the Bemporad Publishing House, Florence

[Turin] 14th November 1930

I write to confirm that I undertake to translate *Our Mr Wrenn*, by S. Lewis, as already agreed. I accept the conditions laid down in your esteemed letter of the 12th, and am counting on sending you the manuscript by the New Year, certainly not before.

Yours respectfully,
Cesare Pavese

To Giuseppe Prezzolini, New York

Turin, 25th November 1930

Illustrious Professor,

I have learned from a courteous note just received from your secretary that you have been in France all the summer and so have not yet been able to consider my letters of May and July, with reference to the appointment available in the University for an Italian student, mentioned in your letter to His Excellency Arturo Farinelli.

When I spoke to him yesterday, he urged me to add his name to mine in this request for a definite reply. With my letter in May I enclosed a few lines of recommendation from him, and I hope this has not been lost. As you may already know, I have been in constant communication with the University, but they seemed to know nothing about the subsidy which S. Farinelli told me of. Instead they simply and officiously told me to send them certain certificates which might enable me to be accepted as a student *on trial* for courses due to start on 25th September.

Naturally I advised the Secretary of their misunderstanding, and expected to receive a prompt reply, possibly an apology, too, but so far I've heard nothing. They already know I obtained my degree in July of this year, and that for some years I have devoted myself to the study of English and American literature.

It is therefore vital for me to know whether I can enter Columbia, as a lector[10] or in any other capacity. I beg you to do what you can to help me.[11]

Respectfully and gratefully yours,

*To Antony Chiuminatto, Chicago**

[Turin] 26th November 1930

Dear Tony,

I got your last letter of 11th November and make haste to reply. You'll receive separately the everlasting essay with the due dedication. I was greatly favoured by the Nobel Prize,[12] and many a guy, who should otherwise have ignored my work, has been obliged to sling his five lire on the counter. I am the only person in Italy today who knows all about Lewis, so I'm highly priced on the market.

But there is sad news, Buddy. My mother is dead.[13] I should be lonely as the devil, were it not for my good married sister with whom I am dwelling now. I only wanted you to know.

Do you know, my boy, I'm translating *Our Mr Wrenn*? The Nobel Prize awakened Italian publishers and I'm drudging now six hours a day about this book. New worries for you. Of course there is something here and there I'm afraid I don't quite understand, so I'll send you someday the very book with all difficult

[10] Lector = *lettore*, i.e. a post-graduate student.

[11] Prezzolini replied to this letter (on 18th December 1930) as follows: 'Dear Signor Pavese, I am indeed sorry that your letter, with an enclosure from S. E. Farinelli, did not at once reach me. However, it is too late now to apply for a scholarship for the current year, but I hope there will be a couple of them available next year. Please remind me about it towards the end of April. It would be helpful if you would send me a few copies of your articles on American literature. With good wishes, G.P.'

[12] Sinclair Lewis was awarded the Nobel Prize for literature on 5th November 1930. Previously he had been almost unknown in Italy.

[13] Pavese's mother died on 4th November.

words underlined. . . . Honestly, let me know before whether you have the time to send me some of your thorough explanations.

Surely, your bargains[14] are all genius strokes, and I can only compliment myself for having stumbled on such an agent. I'll pay you next time. I've now not the time to get the greenbacks and I want you to have this letter.

Thank you for your explanations on gangster life which truly is turning out every day more as the lovely Mafia. Take care of your health. You are lucky enough, gangsters did not put an eye on fiddling-teaching the way they did on beauty shops.

As yet you didn't know anything about my new English class. I keep in the same room, perhaps, where you had yours. What brazen-facedness! And say, among my she-pupils there are some exceedingly good-lookers, hot scorching mamas, we should say. My dear old-timer, I feel swoozie, while begetting English nonsenses in their youthful minds (ah!). I'm seriously thinking about love 'that way', love and death, all this stuff going wild, my boy.

Say, would it not be possible to let Sinclair Lewis, the actual Mr Lewis, have as a humble token of my admiration a copy of the everlastingly blooming essay? Try and find out his address.

To Arrigo Cajumi, Florence

[Turin] 28th December 1930

Dear Sir,

Herewith I enclose the manuscript of my Italian translation of *Our Mr Wrenn,* which I have managed to complete by the agreed date. It is somewhat of a problem to deal with slang words and phrases, but I have largely overcome the difficulty by communicating direct with an American authority. In some instances I have used terms borrowed from Italian dialects when these seemed appropriate. Throughout I have maintained a rather colloquial tone, bearing in mind the general atmosphere of the original work.

As you will see, I have added a few footnotes that I consider absolutely essential to an understanding of the text, particularly of the earlier, longer sections. With reference to page 309 of the

[14] Many of the books Pavese required were costly, and Chiuminatto had therefore been searching for second-hand copies.

MS., corresponding to page 283 in the Tauchnitz edition, I have reproduced the meaning of it as accurately as possible, but I must point out that it is in fact not connected with the main text and could be omitted without affecting the rest, should the editor so decide. I consider there is no need for an Introduction, but you will doubtless let me have your views on this.

I trust you will find my version satisfactory. Should there be any further opportunity of translating *North American* works into Italian, I would naturally hold myself at your disposal.

With my respectful and cordial regards,

1931

To Libero Novara,[1] *Parma*

[Turin] 13th January 1931

I am writing to ask you to do me a favour, perhaps two, both on the subject of languages.

The first is that I need several pages—as many as you like—of nautical terms in common use among sailors. You'll know the sort of thing: 'A point to port', 'Hoist your top-gallant' and so on. I know you have served at sea and still go sailing in the summer, so I feel sure you must be familiar with many words and phrases used aboard ship. I would stress that what I need is not slang but well-established traditional and generally accepted terms. This information is essential to me because I am just starting to translate an American novel that is full of such expressions.

My second request is for another list, such as you gave me last year, of terms used in music, especially any that apply to stringed instruments, in particular the guitar. This could be prepared at your leisure, but my first request is more urgent, since I am already working on the translation.

With warm appreciation for your help,
Cesare Pavese

[1] Libero Novara, son of a lawyer practising in Turin, was a year older than Pavese, but for a period they had been fellow-students and met again when they matriculated. Libero's father had sent him to sea in his early teens to serve as cabin-boy aboard a trading ship. Pavese was fascinated by his friend's tales of adventure and his experience of life.

To Federico Gentile,[2] *Milan*

[Turin] 19th January 1931

Dear Sir,

In reply to your letter of the 15th, I confirm that I am now beginning work on my translation of *Moby Dick* by Herman Melville. I accept all the conditions specified in your letter, requesting only that you will, if necessary, extend the date of completion beyond 30th April.

Yours faithfully,
Cesare Pavese

To Libero Novara, Parma

[Turin] 23rd January [1931]

First of all, please note that my name is Pavese, not Pavesi. I am singular, not plural.

I have received your postcard and letter, and send you my thanks for both, though you need not have replied to my queries quite so hurriedly. Your letter is most interesting. I already have the reference book you recommended, also another dealing with life aboard ship in 1850. Perhaps I did not express myself clearly in my last letter. What I wanted was information about the characteristic phraseology used by seafaring men when doing their normal jobs, the traditional terms in which officers give their orders, in short, the typical idiom of life at sea. This sort of thing constitutes a considerable proportion of the book I am translating. I'm working like mad at it and cursing over problems like this.

See what you can do to help me, and don't worry over the style of writing. No one but me will see anything you send me.

[2] Federico Gentile was a director of a bibliographical review, *Leonardo*, and editorial secretary of a periodical dealing with current affairs. This translation took a full year to complete and was eventually published by a different editor, Carlo Frassinelli.

To Libero Novara, Parma

[Turin] 2nd February [1931]

It has taken me a couple of days to get back to normal. You can discuss literary problems better than any of my colleagues and you know more about books than you do about taverns. Bravo!

You must know that I come about with you simply because, among your other virtues, you have the ability to talk like a god, describing things so smoothly, so fluently, that one cannot help stopping to listen. Your way of talking pleases me even more than wine. One evening, it was New Year's Eve, I went walking with a friend of mine and at one stage found myself in an office with anti-fascist posters on the walls. Close by were little statuettes of Garibaldi and Joshua.

My friend produced some wine, I brought out a corkscrew, and we started drinking. I can't drink much—I only drink to be sociable—but I stayed there listening to Berin strumming away on his *fruja*. Beside him stood a girl I did not know, while out in front, singing with the rest of the gang, was Emiliu. If only his voice had been trained he would have surpassed us all. Emiliu is my ideal of what a man should be—one of those sincere and straightforward people, but intelligent, and as quick-witted as any 'intellectual'.

By this time we had all had several drinks and I fancy my friend had already forgotten I was there. I was just one of his 'public'. Whenever I'm out with Berin I suffer from two handicaps. One is that I can't sing, so all I can do is listen, the other is that he has lived the sort of life I have only dreamed about, so in his company I'm merely a poor 'intellectual'. Berin spoke of many other things that evening, but what with the wine and my own wild fancies I was out of my depth.

So I went home, amusing myself on the way by smashing the bottle of wine. When I got there I was beset by another curse: the asthma that has plagued me for some years now. It almost suffocates me, and I breathe like a sack of sand or potatoes. Who knows what it will be like by the time I'm sixty?

To Arrigo Cajumi, Florence

[Turin] 2nd February 1931

Honoured Sir,

At last I am sending you my much-delayed article on Anderson.[3] You will see whether it is suitable for publication in your review. If it is, I beg you to issue it not later than April. Naturally I will correct the proofs myself.

Unfortunately my contacts in America, with whom I collaborated when working on this article, are now at an end. I should be grateful for any suggestion you may care to make about any other North American writer whose work merits review or translation.

C.P.

*To Antony Chiuminatto, Chicago**

[Turin] 11th February 1931

My Tony,

Hot letter I got, hot books, hot bill, too—I'm burning all over. (I'm only kicking sometimes out of jollity, in my humble endeavors to express my comradeship in a lingo which is not mine.) As for the books, they are O.K. and here's the dough. I'll say something about the contents when I've at least glanced them over: now I'm chocked with a flood of English books from a certain highbrow friend I got.

I'm sizing up *Hello Towns* and see it will cause me to change something in the essay I already wrote. I fancy this fellow Anderson exceedingly. You should read something by him. He's someone. If you someday stumble on the *Notebook* (1926), pick it up. I'll send you next time a hint of summer books, but I would not abuse of your kindness.

[3] Pavese's article on Sherwood Anderson appeared in the April 1931 issue of the magazine *La Cultura* and was later included in the collection published by Einaudi in 1951 (4th edn 1962), *La letteratura americana e altri saggi* (American Literature and Other Essays).

So you like my letters? Out of affection, I think, for, as for English I'm sure you're shrinking all over in reading them. Miss Franchi already pointed out some blunders of mine. Oh, well!

Hello old socks, *auf wiedersehen*

To Arrigo Cajumi, Florence

[Turin] 22nd February [1931]

Highly esteemed Doctor,

I am sending back to you my essay on Anderson, duly checked and corrected. Once again I beg you to publish it not later than April. It will mean a great deal to me if I can then show my work actually in print.[4]

I will think about the two authors you have suggested to me (Dreiser and Melville), but meanwhile I'd like to put forward an idea of my own. Would an article on *The American Village* be suitable for *Cultura*? It would deal with the literary revival that began in 1910 and is still continuing, showing the great advances made by men of genius in different parts of America—the central region, the provinces, the town, and dealing with works that could hardly be treated under any other title—as, for instance, *Main Street, Spoon River Anthology* (G. Lee Masters), *The Grandmothers* (Glenway Wescott), *My Antonia* (Willa Cather) and others of the same kind. To me the subject seems interesting and new. See what you think about it.

Meanwhile, I send you my respectful greetings,

C.P.

[4] At this time Pavese was making a further attempt to obtain a bursary that would enable him to become a student at Columbia University, and was anxious to send Giuseppe Prezzolini cuttings of his work that had already appeared in print.

*To Antony Chiuminatto, Chicago**

[Turin] 18th March 1931

Dear Tony,

Had I not already used up all possible expressions of wonder and 'speechlessness' I should now send you a whole dictionary of compliments about your new enterprise—the translation of a grammar—but things being as they are, I say only 'Buy you another typewriter'. What's worse, you're meaning business and your translations are getting home, one by one, all thorough and perfect.

I want also to thank you very much about the probable publication of my essay. It's grand to be read in America without having been there! But keep an eye. I don't know if Jesuits would like such stuff as mine. There's a page about *Elmer Gantry* I think would pickle their eyes. However, you're a knowing fellow. Do what you think best.[5]

Here is my summer list. You select from them:

Thornton Wilder, *The Woman of Andros* (I've read the other two of his)
Vachel Lindsay, anything
C. Sandbury, *The American Songbag*, *Smoke and Steel*, *Cornhuskers* (not *Chicago Poems*)
Countee Cullen, *Caroling Dusk*
Cabell, anything except *Jurgen* and *The Cords of Vanity*
J. Moncure March, *The Set-up*
Glenway Wescott, *Goodbye Wisconsin* (not *The Grandmothers*)
Langston Hughes, *Poems and Blues*
L. Lewisohn, *The Case of Mr Crump*
William Carlos Williams, *The Great American Novel* or anything else
Scott Fitzgerald, anything

As for Miss Franchi, you are a damned good psychologist. Pedantic, it's so! She knows however her rules and in this field

[5] Chiuminatto was hoping to have his translation of Pavese's essay on Sinclair Lewis accepted for the Catholic review *America*, through the good offices of a friend of his who was a Jesuit priest.

can yet teach me. I'm looking forward to the day when I'll speak American as no Englishman will ever be able.

I'm so crowded with work that I must steal from my sleeping the time to write you this letter and so you'll pardon me if I come so briefly to a conclusion. I'm teaching philosophy (! !) in a lyceum out of Turin and teaching Italian in Turin, so I must leap from a waggon to another and from table to bed.

I am your most devoted,

To Arrigo Cajumi, Florence

[Turin, 25th March 1931]

I am writing to thank you for your help in getting *Our Mr Wrenn* in print at last. Please convey my thanks to the publishers, the Casa Einaudi, for the five copies I have already received, and ask if they will send me one or two more. All that remains is for them to send me a cheque in settlement, since the contract stated 'payment on receipt of the manuscript'.

As for the critics who may review this book, the only one I know (and that only by name), is Alessandra Scalero,[6] the lady who translated *Babbitt,* but I doubt whether she will give a favourable opinion.

Awaiting your kind reply,
Yours very sincerely,
C.P.

[6] See p. 122 *n.* 3.

*To Antony Chiuminatto, Chicago**

[Turin] 26th March [1931]

Dear Old Tony,

I want to thank you infinitely for your swell results about my journalistic career.[7] You bet you are a Live Wire! I'm enormously glad to be given a chance in U.S.A., with the hope to enlarge subsequently my field. Moreover I think American review world is not like ours, so divided in quarreling groups, and it is possible to appear in a sheet without dyeing oneself with the color of this same sheet. I say so, with an eye to the tinge *Thought* certainly has got and my essay certainly hasn't.

So I'll begin to put down a new essay on Lewis. There's also another reason. Now I've got to speak to an American public, no more to Italians, and this changes a little, but you shall have the new article in April.

Now I want only to congratulate you and arrange businesses. If some mazooma will come out of our united literary strivings, we'll go fifty-fifty. Are you game? Say, Buddy, in a fortnight my *Anderson* will appear.

Take your time about summer books. Perhaps I'll already be over there by that time. I'll know in April.

To Enrico Bemporad, Florence

[Turin] 4th April 1931

Honoured Sir,

Thank you for sending on the balance due to me, for which I enclose my receipt, and for the extra copies of *Signor Wrenn,* as well as the two volumes by Anita Loos which reached me at the same time.

[7] Chiuminatto's Jesuit friend, the Reverend Wilfred Parsons, editor-in-chief of the Catholic review *Thought*, had accepted Chiuminatto's translation of Pavese's essay on Sinclair Lewis for early publication. Normally, *Thought* rejected any article that had already been published elsewhere, but in view of the special circumstances and the 'brilliance' of Pavese's work, as well as the excellence of Chiuminatto's translation, an exception was made in this instance.

I frankly confess that your comments on the quality of my translation came as a surprise. In all modesty, I believe my work is by no means below the standard required by your firm or, which is more important, unworthy of the original text. Allow me to state that my endeavours have always been to ensure that readers will understand the thoughts and behaviour of the characters in the novel. There is only one way to achieve this result. The original text must be studied until it is thoroughly understood, then precisely the same meaning must be expressed in the translation. Word-for-word equivalents are quite useless. In this work I took considerable pains to ensure that Italian readers would get the same impressions, colloquially rendered in their own language, as American readers did from the original text. When necessary, I may have used unfamiliar or even harsh terms so as to bring home to Italian readers the realisation that this is a *foreign* work, written from a point of view very different from their own. They would have found a literal translation quite incomprehensible. What I have given them is a re-creation of the original novel, a rendering that is in fact a literary achievement in its own right.

I must add that I cannot believe your statement that my translation of *Our Mr Wrenn* contains 'pages that are absolutely incomprehensible'. However, I would welcome an opportunity to discuss with you any points you may care to raise. Meanwhile I remain,

Yours sincerely,
Cesare Pavese

To Giuseppe Prezzolini, New York

[Turin] 19th April 1931

Distinguished Professor,

As you suggested in your letter dated 19th September, 1930, further to my letter of May 1930 (with which I enclosed a personal request from His Excellency Arturo Farinelli), I am writing to remind you of my application for a bursary that would enable me to study at Columbia University.

Unfortunately, to my great regret, I have now been called up for

National Service and shall not be free until the end of June 1932. (I fully expected to be exempted for reasons of health.)

Under separate cover I am sending you a copy of my essay on Sinclair Lewis, as requested, also my essay, only just published, on Sherwood Anderson. I am hoping that, with your help, I may be given a bursary for the following year, and shall look forward to hearing from you in due course.

To Arrigo Cajumi, Florence

[Turin] 28th May 1931

Dear Sir,

I have received the copies of *Anderson*, and thank you very much for your kindness and courtesy. I am thinking up something for *Cultura* that should turn out to be rather good.

I would beg you to do what you can to expedite payment for my *Lewis* (November 1930), Ginzburg tells me it should have reached me by now.

With my respectful greetings,

*To Antony Chiuminatto, Chicago**

[Turin, May 1931]

Dear Tony,

At last I succeeded in putting down another essay on that guy. Say, it's not so damn easy to rewrite on a topic! I had to plug along like a dog, believe me, but you'll soon get it. Now let Father Parsons decide.

And I'm not yet due to America. 'Tis sad, but 'tis so. On 1st November I'll enter under arms. That doggone doctor found me able-bodied to war and peace service. Eleven months! Till June 1932.

Adieu America! And I had already received an acceptance from Columbia! Surely, Daddy above is a funny guy, you bet.

So you can forward the library stuff I listed earlier, especially *Caroling Dusk*, which I want before all others. I'll mail Anderson's *Notebook* back to you, as you say. It's truly interesting and worthwhile. I'm only sorry I read it after my *Anderson* was already in proofs.

Say, you're really tough, my boy, when it comes down to brasstacks. You get along with the translation of that whole grammar. Methinks you'd spend less time and fatigue in writing a new one.

After my damned term in the army, I hope to find a new place somewhere in scholarly America and so embrace at last the only friend I have over there. Now I must hurry and get my everlasting essay typewritten. Toodle-oo. Come over sometime.

*To Antony Chiuminatto, Chicago**

[Turin] 14th June 1931

Dear Tony,

I got them eleven books, a wonderful cocktail of American life. You're so snappy in your doings! Would it be the straw on the camel's back if I asked you to help on my translation of Melville's *Moby Dick*? A little publicity would do me a lot of good. Which reminds me of Father Parsons and the hot stuff he will someday have to cry over. I don't really think my stuff will do for his magazines.

So you were made Prexy[8] this Spring and are even getting paid for it!

So you are feeling sentimental again, old chap! I began again to feel the same quite suddenly, some weeks ago—a trick of inhibition perhaps—and now I'm 'crushed' on four pink faces at once. There's even a fifth one looming on the horizon. Not so bad, eh?

PS. What do you Americans mean by 'You are perfection to a T'? I should like one of your page-long explanations.

[8] In May 1931 Chiuminatto was elected to the position of 'Presiding Judge of the State Examinations for College Musical Graduates'.

*To Antony Chiuminatto, Chicago**

[Turin, July 1931]

Dear Tony,

Your letter was an oasis in the wilderness, these hot days. 'Tis bracing in the maudlin dejection of Italy to get something of a handshake from over there.

So you're kicking about Melville, eh? Not you alone. Italian publishers also are kicking, but I got a crush on that fellow, and would it cost me my life-blood I'll push him along. I find *Moby Dick* an extraordinary piece of writing, but I won't worry you with an offhand lecture on his personality. Before long I'll scribble one of my famous essays about him and you'll hear.

Your lovely list of slang phrases touched my heart and I'm already studying them by ditto. Such things are sweeter than candy to me! In some days I'll mail back to you the eleven books on summer loan. If you can arrange a further loan for me, I'll be tickled.

So it's all hunky-dory with you and your Summer-school teaching? I must try to hustle in the world too. I'm now a totally lounging fellow, quite a philosopher, spending hours before the mirror to admire my perfect looks. (No doubt the army will spoil them.) Goodbye.

*To Antony Chiuminatto, Chicago**

[Turin] 28th August [1931]

Dear Tony,

I hope you have received the package of books I sent you on August 6th. Here's another set and so the whole is on its way home again.

Say, there's corking news for me and you to know. I'm not to go 'under arms'! I'll acquit myself with some pre-military courses on Sundays and remain a civilian all the time. America looms again in the skies.

Wishing you a happy father of many a spiritual child, here's my paw.

To Arrigo Cajumi, Florence

[Turin] 27th September [1931]

Dear Professor,

Herewith are the proofs of the *Anthology*, duly revised and corrected. I hope the additions I have made will not be long enough to cause any difficulty when the relevant pages are reprinted.

I have at last received from Milan an assurance that they will pay me early in October. Let's hope they do. I have in mind one or two new things for *Cultura*, and am up to my eyes in the history of the cinema. I've been trying to sort out its origins, but its records are so chaotic that there's no point in digging back into them. My proposed article becomes more and more hypothetical.

Cordially yours,
Pavese

To Ugo Ojetti, Florence

[Turin] 7th November [1931]

Your Excellency,

In response to your kind invitation I am sending you, under separate cover, an article for your *Pegaso*. I have taken care to follow the lines you indicated to me.

Spurred on by the recent translation of O'Henry's [*sic*] stories by G. Prampolini, I have touched on the difficulties encountered in any critical assessment of this writer's work. At the moment in America his reputation is going through the usual posthumous decline that always affects really distinguished men.

The argument seems to me to have considerable contemporary interest. In any case I felt bound to deal with it in the light of new discoveries and our own evaluation of North American literature. Will you be so good as to consider the matter and decide whether my article is in accordance with the policy of your review.

Yours respectfully

To Federico Gentile, Milan

[Turin, November 1931]

Highly Distinguished Doctor Gentile,

Taking advantage of your kind suggestion, conveyed to me by my friend Leone Ginzburg, I am sending you the manuscript of my translation of *Moby Dick*. I hope the book will please you and Dr Tumminelli. The Treves publishing firm agree to produce it when they think fit, but I maintain that the matter is urgent, in view of possible competition. There is the point, too, that they might decide against including a work of '*culture*' in a collection such as their popular New Library.

For this reason I must rely upon your judgment, hoping you will let me know your decision as soon as possible. I flatter myself that it will be favourable. As for my remuneration, we can doubtless agree on that. In any case I should be grateful for any help you may care to give me about the usual rate of pay.

Yours respectfully,
C. Pavese

To Federico Gentile, Milan

[Turin] 4th December [1931]

Dear Doctor,

About a month ago I sent you the manuscript of my version of *Moby Dick,* by H. Melville. Please excuse my haste, but I need to know at once what your decision is, and what would be the terms of the contract, especially in view of the competition caused by Emilio Cecchi's article in the *Corriere,* which has aroused considerable public interest. There is also the point that several other commitments require my attention.

Please be so good as to drop me a line.

With apologies and cordial greetings,
C. Pavese

To Luigi Russo, Florence

[Turin] 8th December 1931

Distinguished Professor,

On the advice of my friend, Leone Ginzburg, I venture to send you an article for your review *La nuova italia.* I hope you still remember me—one of the friends you made in Turin. Several of us used to climb together up to Barbara Allason's house and vineyard.

This article of mine is perhaps a trifle long, but it deals with a vast subject that, as yet, is hardly known or discussed here in Italy. A history of the United States, in Italian, remains to be written. See whether this article on *O'Henry* [*sic*] is suitable for your review, and be kind enough to write and tell me what you think of it.

*To Antony Chiuminatto, Chicago**

[Turin] 24th December 1931

Dear Tony,

Surely Americans are kinder than we. I got your card of good wishes and never thought to send you any myself. Here they are then, posthumous as always. I hear that your boosting in the world raised you to dizzy heights. When will you build an Institute all by yourself? Remember your Buddy when you're a big executive, and send me word to come over and bum some residence in U.S.A.

Now it's the winter season we'll have to let up books-sendings, so you'll enjoy some peace. Do you know I got a victrola? I've some of the cutest American trifles I ever heard—The Revellers, The Footwarmers, Ted Lewis, Whiteman and others. Should you hear about some hot American record send me title, composer and orchestra. Especially *blues* and *saxs*.

1932

To Federico Gentile, Milan

[Turin] 1st January 1932

Dear Doctor,

I am extremely sorry to trouble you again, but it so happens that I absolutely must have your reply—favourable, I hope—concerning the publication of *Moby Dick*.

Forgive me, please, for venturing to insist, but it is not without good reason. We can discuss terms and conditions later, but I must have a plain 'yes' or 'no' at once.

With my cordial thanks and good wishes,
Pavese

To Federico Gentile, Milan

[Turin, in reply to a letter dated 13th January 1932]

I have received yours of the 13th, and thank you for your promise. Like yourself, I hope for great success. Permit me, however, to remind you that my essential stipulations (more important than the question of remuneration), which must form part of any contract I may sign, are that my MS. will be printed without any alteration, and publication will be no later than April. I do not wish to press you further, but I beg you to write me something immediately, by the beginning of the coming week.

*To Antony Chiuminatto, Chicago**

[Turin, January 1932]

Thank you for the *Bookman,* a swell magazine. A friend of mine, a publisher in Turin (who is planning to translate *My Antonia*) will subscribe to it, so without any expense I'll look it over and keep informed.

Can you find for me some novel by Faulkner, the new famous writer of Southern stock mentioned in the *Bookman*? If it is not too costly, buy it and send it on. Otherwise send me word about.

As for records, I'll buy the *Saint Louis Blues,* on your advice. Send me the words of all these records, if you can, and your comments, I'll be tickled. Put down all novelties in this field—names and comments.

Say, you have an idea to treat me, over there in the States? You don't need to say it twice, old boy. In March, if all's well, I'll be free from the army, and after that. . . . Don't get too chummy with me. I'm just the sort of chap to take you up on an offer like that.

To Carlo Frassinelli,[1] *Turin*

[in reply to letters
dated 14th and 16th March, 1932]

Dear Frassinelli,

Here are the rough proofs, duly checked. I'm extremely dissatisfied with the haphazard layout, especially since the typescript itself was quite correct. I'll ring you tomorrow, about midday, to discuss it.

Antonicelli has already looked through these proofs. I shall be somewhat chary about accepting the alterations he has suggested.

[1] Carlo Frassinelli and Franco Antonicelli, Pavese's contemporaries at Turin University, were trying to establish a new publishing firm in Turin, Casa Frassinelli, which accepted several of Pavese's best translations. His first contract with them, for *Moby Dick,* was dated 10th February 1932, and his remuneration was fixed at one thousand lire.

Some of them, in fact, actually change the meaning. Then, too, he has a literary style of his own and strongly objects to such phrases as 'something of the sort' and the word 'No' used as an interrogation.

Bear in mind that next Wednesday I'm going to Bra,[2] and again on Thursday afternoon, but as long as you send me the proofs, fifteen pages or so at a time, I won't keep you waiting.

Greetings,
Pavese

*To Antony Chiuminatto, Chicago**

[Turin] 2nd April 1932

At last I'm here answering you. As for Faulkner, you're right! He's a tremendous bore, so far, at least. I haven't as yet got through the whole book. I buy it however as a curiosity and enclose here the dough. I cannot remember whether I'm still owing you something, so check your accounts-books and let me know.

This evening I'm swept along by the wanderlust. I swear I cannot any more stay here in Italy. My army duty is over at last. I've heard nothing more about the arrangements with Columbia. I dream, hope, long, die after Amercia. I *must* come.

Till now you've been so kind to me: try to make me the last and greatest favor. Call me to the U.S.A. You know we cannot come over without having a job already arranged there. So now your test of friendship is to find me an employment, however nominal, just something to get the passport. I'm ready to teach Italian or to marry the horridest heiress if only I could get there.

Apply to the University to find whether there's any possibility of a job as an assistant, an usher, or anything else. Only, help me through. Otherwise I'll try revolution in Mexico and bootlegging through the frontier. On any day, even tomorrow, I'm ready to pack. Only say the word, boy!

Pav.

[2] Pavese had taken a part-time teaching post there, during the Easter vacation.

To Alessandra Scalero,[3] *Settimo Vittone*

[Turin] 22nd May [1932]

Dear Madam,

I have received your letter, after a delay of thirty days or so, through the good offices of *Cultura.* Not that this delay mattered much, for even if it had reached me at once I could not have dealt with it then. I was busy with the final stages of my forthcoming book. It is now practically ready and will be out in a day or two.

I hope you are not already far advanced in your work on the same text. I should be extremely sorry, not because I imagine my translation could not be bettered, especially by yourself, but because of the quite unintentional rivalry that an alternative translation would occasion.

In any case, there is still a great deal of Melville's work awaiting translation—at least *Typee, Omoo* and *White Jacket.* The first of these was announced last year by the publisher Formica of Turin, but has not yet appeared. Just now, Italy has a real craze for tales of the sea, a craze fostered by the cinema, in my opinion, and Melville is so *up-to-date.*

I remember your excellent Italian version of *Back to Harlem.* In my opinion there is no one better qualified than yourself to translate *Typee* or *Omoo.* Please explain the position to the publishers who commissioned you to do *Moby Dick.* I should be delighted to hear from you now and then about the work you have in hand.

Yours,
C. Pavese

[3] Alessandra Scalero, a well-established translator from English and German, had written to Pavese, whom she knew only by name, asking if it was true that he was on the point of bringing out an Italian version of *Moby Dick.* She had been commissioned by an Italian publisher to translate that particular novel and had already started work on it, but would willingly give up the project if Pavese already had it in hand.

To Mario Sturani, Paris

[Turin] 1st July 1932

Hullo there! I expect you've heard from Ginzburg that I've managed to get his opera considered for publication. I could kick myself for not having composed such a fine, poetic flight of fancy myself. I expect that Ginzburg, as usual, won't have told you the important bit of information that I had nearly finished an opera of my own, on much the same lines, but it'll be no good now. Still, I'm very pleased with my (unsuccessful) effort and am enjoying myself eating, drinking and getting about. I shall write others and am growing more aware of my own individual personality.

I see from your letter you're having a fine time and getting a lot of satisfaction out of it—not merely financial success. I want to come to Paris if I can, but don't mention it to anyone yet. I've dreamed of spending this summer touring the Mediterranean coast in a sailing boat, if I can get hold of one. If not, I'll come to Paris. Can you tell me the absolutely minimum amount of cash I should need to get there and back?

While in Bra, I came across a girl from Santo Stefano, an old school friend of mine. We talked a lot about the old days there and went for long walks, eating picnics, being rude to each other and remaining the best of friends. Women! Ugly as a monkey, but thinks a lot of herself!

Pavese

PS. My uncle Olimpio[4] has died. A fine fellow, generally in a bad temper at having to pay for hospital treatment in Turin. After his death, his doctors discovered that for the previous three months he must have suffered atrocious pain in his head. He never mentioned it. Nothing was ever said to indicate he was really ill.

[4] Brother of Cesare's father, Eugenio Pavese.

To Alessandra Scalero, Settimo Vittone

[Turin] 15th July 1932

Dear Madam,

I am replying at once to your letter of the 13th, and was glad to have your comments. So much for what concerns your publisher and your own translations. The director is a friend of mine. Mention my name and ask him whether you may send him anything you have ready—such as O'Neill and the two Germans. Naturally without committing yourself, and solely in order to obtain their decision, which you should receive quite quickly, the normal policy of this particular publishing house. They have already announced a volume of O'Neill's dramatic sea stories and *Emperor Jones*.

Make sure of any rights due to you for your translations. The article by your sister[5] on O'Neill has been warmly approved by the Editor and by myself.

Thank you for all the nice things you have said about me, and for your interest in finding further work for me. At the moment I have nothing in mind that might suit your publishers, but should be happy to take advantage of anything that might crop up.

With cordial good wishes,

Your

Cesare Pavese

*To Antony Chiuminatto, Chicago**

[Turin] 24th July 1932

Dear Tony,

I haven't replied to you till now, because I was planning a short holiday at sea aboard a sailing boat, so it was impossible for me to send you my usual list of books for summer reading. Now my sea-trip has fallen through, so I'll go hiking round Italy instead. In

[5] Liliana Scalero, essayist and translator.

any case I shan't have a settled address and so would be unlikely to receive anything you might send me.

Thank you for your goodwill about getting me over there, but I see the difficulties. I had a few fits of hysterics, but now I can plainly see what a lot of salt water there is between us.

I'm philosophic enough to perceive that I might in time get tired of God's Country. I've already taught philosophy. Indeed, I don't know of any subject I haven't taught. Leaving on one side Italian and English, I can remember teaching Latin, Geography, History, French and Greek. Here's a brazen-faced bum, you can say! I've already had my fill of teaching. What I want now is experience of life!

Have a good holiday, old boy, on your Wisconsin lakes.

To Mario Sturani, Paris

[Turin] 26th July 1932

Sturani,

I'm not coming to Paris after all. My plans for a Mediterranean cruise have vanished into thin air. I've been invited by a family in Santo Stefano Belbo to spend August and September there with them, an opportunity I wouldn't like to miss. We'll talk about my coming to Paris in the autumn.

Now my book is out I realise it's no masterpiece and there's no point in discussing it. When I've written something else, we'll see. My latest poems please me very much—there are six or seven of them—but I doubt whether they'll be as popular as my 'dirty rhymes'.

Incidentally, Mila[6] is following your example. He took one of Foscolo's sonnets and altered it to convey certain indiscreet suggestions. It was a real hit the night we celebrated Giacchero's degree

[6] Massimo Mila and Mario Sturani were Pavese's closest friends during the period they spent together at Turin University. Their friendship lasted for some years after graduation, though Sturani left Turin to continue his studies in Paris.

award. (He's a 'doctor' now.) We were all terribly sorry you weren't there. As usual, I got so drunk at that party I had to have an injection of caffeine.

I realise my life is changing. I'm no longer interested in writing critical reviews of other men's work (I've never managed to take myself seriously in that particular role), nor do I want to become a teacher, still less a professional translator. I'm completely free to choose a job for myself. We'll see what turns up.

How we change! Even the prospect of spending my vacation on or in the River Po doesn't give me the same thrill as it used to do. At one time the mere thought of it would have made me sick with anticipation for at least a month beforehand. Now it doesn't mean a thing. I'd rather spend my time thinking out the books I want to write. So long. I'll send you my address in Santo Stefano as soon as I can.

Pavese

To A.E.[7]

[Turin] 15th September 1932

All day long I've felt ill with disappointment. You didn't meet as I hoped you would, and now Turin seems a dreadful place. What depresses me most is that we're starting to forget each other before we've really achieved any mutual understanding. I don't know what you see in me, but in you I see a miracle of tenderness and womanhood that has blossomed and taken shape before my very eyes all through this past summer.

I'm afraid those last days we spent together—will you ever forget them?—may well have marked a turning-point in our

[7] It is somewhat difficult to identify this lady with any certainty. In his letters Pavese sometimes addresses her as 'Elena', but gives no clue to her surname or her first Christian name, except for the initial 'A'. Some authorities suggest she may well have been a staff member at the school in Bra where Pavese had a part-time appointment. It seems unlikely that she was the 'old school friend' mentioned by Pavese in his letter to Sturani (1st July 1932), whom he describes as being 'Ugly as a monkey, but thinks a lot of herself'.

relationship. We could go no further along that road. Just at the moment I find that thought distressing, but what of the day when I no longer care? Grief and pain are not the most dreadful things in life. It is far worse to realise that the moment will come when we no longer mean anything at all to one another. We shall lose each other before we can attain any mutual understanding, with no memories to treasure, except the loving looks we exchanged, a kiss on your finger-tips, a caress or two.

There are so many things about you I shall never know. Why do you tremble so, when I am with you? What do I see in your eyes when they smile at me and then grow cold, even hostile, before their smile returns?

I cannot weep for love. My tears are for the unfairness, the cruelty of it all, the fact that our love has been spoiled. All I can do is to let it die, not even lifting a finger to save it. What else can we do? It's pointless to lie. What really matters in love is body and blood, exhilaration, the breath of life itself, but we must be parted, use our powers of judgment and be reasonable, though reason counts for nothing, compared with life.

Unless I'm close beside you, I'm not really sure I love you. Certainly I don't love you as much as you'd like me to, though I know I shall never forget those afternoons we've spent locked in each other's arms, gazing deep into each other's eyes. Must it all end like this? Won't you give me a chance to love you more, be more faithful to you in my thoughts, prove myself more worthy of you?

But at what stage can we end it, Elena? Is there something inherently absurd about love? If we enjoy it to the full it soon becomes boring, even distasteful. If we keep it on a strictly moral plane, so that we can remember it without regret, one day we may bewail our stupidity, our cowardice, in not daring to take the plunge. All too readily, love can become a habit, and when two are made one flesh, sharing life in common, love soon dies. Love is life itself, and life does not follow any hard-and-fast rules. Must we then let it degenerate into hopelessness? I cannot find words to give you any real consolation, except to remind you of the utter bliss we both found in each other's arms.

So I'll send you a kiss, the special kind of kiss you like so much, even though you were naughty enough to keep me waiting in vain for you, on the road to Crevacuore.

To A.E., Bra

Turin, 14th October 1932

So we have lost our lovely friendship! Now you're no longer with me, I realise I've been in love with you all this year. I'm just a great fool who gets about a good deal and likes most people, but tries not to show it and pretends to be morose, unsociable. I've always felt I could depend on you, and we understand each other more than most people do. Sometimes you led me a fine dance, sometimes my mind was occupied with other things. Sometimes you seemed a helpless woman, sometimes a kind sister. Now you are all that and something more—an enigma.

As we were sitting close together yesterday, with our knees touching, I was reflecting how strange it is that we ever met, though we share such similar ways of acting and thinking. It seems incredible that there was a time when I could have been alone with you without wanting to hold you close and kiss you.

I got used to having you with me at Bra. Now I've lost your company, I feel I've lost more than that, the pleasure of seeing you with other people, moving about in their homes, busily occupied with all the usual activities. Still, it must be even worse for you, to go on living in places that keep reminding you of this last summer. Keep in touch with Alda Manfredi, the girl who was at school with you. You'll laugh together and be constantly reminding each other of me.

It will be very different for me, here, studying and striving to make the best I can of my life. My future seems a bit uncertain just now, but I'm not afraid. I've known a few terrible moments in my life, but I'm still here. Even if you don't write to me, never see me again, or forget me altogether, I shall never forget teaching you to kiss me on the lips. As my arms held you close, I could feel a new vitality surging within you, a thrill you may never have felt before, but which you now remember with surprise and delight. That means a great deal, Elena. If you do come to me again, I'll hold you tight and we'll be happy together again, as we were in those secret moments when I would steal a glance from you, a caress or a thought.

To Alda Manfredi [8]

Turin, 23rd October 1932

I will be at Porta Nuove on Friday at about 6.20. I'm so glad we are comrades in distress, all the more so because I'm not in the least methodical in any other way. I run into crisis after crisis, with such modest powers as I have at my command.

To A.E.

Turin, 23rd October 1932

I've written to Manfredi to say I'll be at the station on Friday. I'm sorry you've lost your job. But cheer up. Now you'll have a refreshing period doing nothing.

Do you still feel the same about me? I earnestly hope we'll manage to spend a little time alone together, especially if you mean to give back to me all the kisses I've given you. Unless you tell me otherwise on Friday evening, I'll take it that you'll come and find me on Saturday morning.

What do you want to know about me, Elena? That I'm proud, an utter fool, a coward, a mere child, a potential criminal, a would-be seducer without the courage to carry it through, a persistent delinquent? I mean it all quite seriously, but console myself with the thought that all men are much the same. Once I hoped to become something different from the rest, but now I know I'm just an ordinary biped. I write poetry, sure, but have you ever seen anything more inept, useless, trite or blasé? I spout politics, but what do they matter to me anyway? I have no convictions, no aptitude and no capacity. I might at least have become a good commercial traveller or a factory hand, but by now I'm completely spoiled for a job like that. For two pins a man becomes a cynic

[8] Alda Manfredi, whom Pavese mentions in his letter to 'A.E.' (14th October 1932), had written to him on the 22nd to say that both she and 'A.E.' had lost their jobs as 'supply teachers' and would come to Turin on Friday, 28th October, arriving at 6.30. She suggested they might all spend the evening together.

in Turin. Let's hope you may change me a little, for otherwise I don't know how it will all end.

To Ugo Ojetti, Florence

[Turin] 15th November [1932]

Your Excellency,

I fear that the typescript I sent you a month ago, 'Dos Passos and the American Novel', may not have reached you. Would you be so kind as to relieve me of this uncertainty and, if you have received it, to give it your consideration with a view to publication in *Pegaso*.[9]

To Arrigo Cajumi, Milan

[Turin] 21st November [1932]

Dear Cajumi,

All's well with *Typee*, which reached me yesterday.

With reference to translations, for some months now I've been worn to a frazzle by an urge to translate *Spoon River Anthology*. Naturally, Frassinelli won't hear of it because he's got to build up his business and poetry doesn't sell. However, Ginzburg has suggested I should turn to you again, in case the firm of Treves might feel like taking a chance.

It is a particularly fine book, presenting personalities rather than lyrics. Americans themselves have said it gives a complete portrayal of America as it is today. In short, this book is no more likely to land you in bankruptcy than many other volumes Treves have

[9] This essay was in fact published in a different periodical, *La Cultura,* between January and March 1933. It was later included in the volume of essays by Pavese on American literature (see p. 106 *n.* 3).

already published with considerable success. See what you can do about it.

I enclose (feeling somewhat embarrassed about doing so) an article I offered to Ojetti in Florence. He doesn't want it because, he says, he's expecting an article by Praz on the same subject. No doubt something in my article has put him off and his decision has nothing to do with Praz, but his judgments are sometimes very odd—on Dos Passos, for instance. Would you please give me your considered opinion on whether this article is 'cultural' or not?

*To Antony Chiuminatto, Chicago**

[Turin] 1st December 1932

My dear Tony,

At last I got something from you! I thought you were dead! It seems that Roosevelt's hit knocked you on the head and made you remember old friends. If that's politics, all the better.[10]

Speaking seriously, I'm glad you're not forgetting me. As for books, slang and so on, you are but too kind. It's your old need to be of service to someone and I can only thank you for it. For now, I want nothing in that line. I'm getting crammed with English literature to hold some professional exams, and by those gentlemen American literature is ignored. But it will not be long before I need some service. (For instance, ferret out for me some cheap edition of *In Our Time* by Hemingway. I am told it is marvellous.)

By the way, I've got a very stingy fellow as a publisher and I've already used up the copies of my translation due to me. Now I know you are still kicking, I cannot immediately beg another copy from him to send you, but I'll remember it the first chance I have.

So be merry,

[10] Pavese is referring to Franklin D. Roosevelt's staggering success in the American presidential election of November 1932. Standing as a Democrat, in competition with Hoover, Roosevelt secured an unprecedented majority of over twelve million popular votes.

1933

To Enrico Piceni, Milan

[Turin] 22nd January [1933]

I have received your welcome note. Please observe that my name is Cesare Pavese.

As for the Aldington, are you sure it could be published in Italy?[1] In general, English writers interest me less than Americans. I'll make you a proposition: I would translate one of the following American works: *Jurgen* by Cabell or *Arrowsmith* by Lewis, the MS. to reach you by the end of May. (Just at the moment I am deeply involved in another short work.) My fee to be 2,000 lire. If this suggestion is acceptable, send me the contract without more ado.

*To Antony Chiuminatto, Chicago**

[Turin] 24th January [1933]

Dear Tony,

Now that I'm out of danger with Xmas and New Year turkey-stuffings, I can write you off a good old letter. As for politics, here's to you, hoping to encounter you at my machine-gun's end and have you cry mercy. We'll yet see that, someday, old boy. Perhaps only in the next world-war we'll find our true calling.

Honestly, I don't care a damn about the whole lot of it. I would soften a little, however, thinking about your 11 million unemployed, if I hadn't learned from my old school text-books that world history is only a great shambles. Never did our ancestors bring about anything like fairness and humanity. I can't help grinning at the

[1] On 20th January Enrico Piceni, chief director of Mondadori, the publishers, had written to Pavese (mis-spelling his name 'Pavesi'), inviting him to translate Richard Aldington's novel, *Death of a Hero*.

thought that your 11 millions are the result of ten years of boasted 'prosperity'. Your unemployment figures are being quoted merrily here in Europe. Do you know what people are saying? They consider you are damned lucky to have had this calamity, and that your national pluck and boldness will be perfected by suffering. To make a long story short, they say you'll profit immensely by the unheard-of depression. How do you like that?

So you also are looking out for books? My opportunity has at last arrived. You want something to translate into *American*. That will be rather hard to find, for our writers have been asleep for two hundred years. The most obvious name, S. E. Pirandello, is no use here, for your playwrights have already rifled it. But perhaps one of his novels remains unknown over there and you could reveal it to an eager public. *Il fu Mattia Pascal*, for instance. Naturally it's out of print, but I'll find out at once whether it is already translated and will try to find a copy of it to mail you.

Meanwhile, giving you no chance to change your mind, I'm mailing you another novel, a masterpiece by our Sicilian novelist Giovanni Verga, who wrote the plot of *Cavalleria rusticana*. He and Alessandro Manzoni are perhaps our greatest nineteenth century novelists. I have made enquiries and don't think it has already been translated into English. Think about it.

Of course, I'm here ready to help you on any points I can, from the meaning of some of Verga's idioms to copyright matters.

To Enrico Piceni, Milan

[Turin, 30th January 1933]

Dear Sir,

Why the devil d'you want to get more of Anderson's work translated? *Winesburg, Ohio* and *Dark Laughter* are already out and haven't been too successful anyway. At a push one could do *Poor White*, a novelette that came out in 1921, or *A Storyteller's Story*, an autobiography of 1924. This last is possibly Anderson's masterpiece, but it has already appeared in French translation and there's not much chance that it would be well-received in Italy.

Re Dos Passos, I'm told that *Manhattan Transfer* (*New York*) is not selling well. In general, any translator of *The 42nd Parallel* would have to do the sequel to it, *1929*, though I don't suppose it would have much popular appeal.

You offer me a choice between an Anderson and a Dos Passos. I would much prefer a Dos Passos, but in that case I could not undertake to send you the completed MS. by the end of May. One very seldom comes across such a slangy, colloquial writer. Consequently this long volume demands the greatest care and a close study of his style if the translation is to be in any way adequate.

Keep in mind that I'm translating to earn a living and could accept a contract only on these terms: on delivery of the final forty pages of the MS. I am to receive full payment of the amount already agreed between us. (As you see, I'm giving you a few little problems.)

Your
Pavese

To Enrico Piceni, Milan

[Turin] 9th February 1933

All right. I agree to do Dos Passos by the end of June. Send me the contract.

I don't need a copy of *The 42nd Parallel*, but I should be glad to receive *Manhattan Transfer* (*New York*) translated by A. Scalero, so that I can glance at the Italian style of her work.

To Enrico Piceni, Milan

[Turin, 14th June 1933]

Dear Sir,

I received your letter of the 10th, asking me to send you an extract from *The 42nd Parallel* by Dos Passos, which I am at present translating for the *Medusa*. I shall be pleased to do as you suggest, but since I am just starting the final check of the typescript of my translation I must ask you to give me a few days' grace so that while reading it through I can give due thought to the selection of a suitable passage to send you.

I will take advantage of this opportunity to ask you whether you would be seriously inconvenienced if I were a few days late in submitting the MS. of *The 42nd Parallel*? Say the first or second week of July. This is simply to allow me time to check it through again at greater leisure. I will add an introductory note that will, I hope, satisfy your requirements.

Will you be so good as to let me have a reply from you about the points I have raised? Meanwhile I add my distinguished greetings.

To Luigi Rusca [?],[2] *Milan*

[Turin, in reply to a letter dated 26th June 1933]

Dear Sir,

I have received your letter of 26th June, asking me to submit, for your periodical *Almanacco*, an article on Dos Passos, 'not excessively critical but acceptable from a literary point of view'. After considerable thought, I see no way to satisfy you. As it happens, I have already said what little I know or could find out about Dos Passos in an article published in *Cultura* in the issue of March '33. Anything further would be simply a repetition. Furthermore, I should be totally incapable of writing a single page that would not be 'excessively critical' and, I fear, extremely boring.

If, after what I've said, you feel you simply must have a few words from me about this writer, I will do what I can, if you will get hold of the following works for me: *Nouvelle découverte de l'amérique*, Waldo Franck; *A Pushcart at the Curb* by J. Dos Passos, and *Orient Express,* also by Dos Passos.

[2] Luigi Rusca was director of the Medusa series published by Mondadori.

If you still think this a practicable suggestion, write and tell me how long the article should be, and when you would want it, not too soon, I hope.

To Luigi Rusca, Milan

[Turin] 12th July 1933

My dear Sir,

I am sending you herewith the final proofs of Dos Passos, typed and corrected. Since I could do no more than read it through once, I'm afraid there may still be a few misprints or spelling mistakes. While checking these proofs I have had time to make one or two corrections.

Do please let me know the date of publication.

As my contract mentions payment on receipt of the typed MS., I beg you to make sure it reaches me, since my plans for the summer depend on it.

I have thought over your suggestion about *Ulysses*, and feel sure there are Italian writers better fitted than I am to undertake this work. Before I could commit myself I should need more time to consider it, and examine my conscience a little. In general, each work you suggest would take me at least a year to complete, and the remuneration must be commensurate with the time involved.

For now,
I remain yours sincerely

To Luigi Rusca, Milan

[Turin] 25th July 1933

Dear Signor Rusca,

Referring again to yours of the 20th July, has nothing new cropped up about the proofs of *The 42nd Parallel* by Dos Passos? I had to be away for a few days then, and I should not want them to lie overlong on your desk or mine.

Meanwhile, I would beg you to take an interest in ensuring that I am given adequate compensation for my translation. My contract specifies 'full payment on receipt of the MS.'. The figure it mentions is 3,000 lire on completion of the MS., but so far all I've had is 1,000 lire. See if there's anything you can do to help.

1934

To Alberto Carocci, Florence

[Turin] 30th March 1934

Dear Carocci,

Since you have so kindly suggested it, I will leave the matter to your discretion. I should warn you that the poems of mine you already hold have not yet been revised or checked, and may need a few corrections to prepare them for publication. In addition, I have some more fragmentary poems you have not yet seen. These, together with the earlier ones, total about thirty. If you do decide to publish, would you please return the copies I sent you earlier, in case they need some correction or amendment.

As for my friend,[1] we are still as much in the dark as you are. He is not alone—he has a dozen or so of his followers with him—but apparently things aren't going too well for him and for one of the others. I shouldn't be surprised if the case ended up in Rome. Perhaps we can take comfort from the fact that he's quite prepared for it all. If it is merely a question of his personal importance and integrity, he'll soon be released, but one of the others, it seems, is not in the same position.

I've heard, however, that the movement is not confined to Turin, and this may be a favourable sign. I often see his mother and will certainly mention your name to her. She is an admirable woman, capable of appreciating the importance of sticking together. However, we can't bring ourselves to talk about him. Nobody can, not even his wife.

[1] This friend was Leone Ginzburg, who had been working to organise a secret resistance movement, 'the League of Justice and Liberty'. Pavese himself took no interest whatever in politics, but out of respect for an old friend he attended some of his meetings. Ginzburg and several members of this group were arrested, but most of them were soon set free. Ginzburg and a friend of his, Sion Segre, were sentenced to four and three years respectively, but Ginzburg was released from the penitentiary of Civitavecchia on 13th March 1936 (see also my note p. 140).

To Guido M. Gatti [?], *Turin*

[Turin] 12th September 1934

I'm here with Debenedetti, who is working desperately hard to revise my dialogue. Tonight he's only half-way through the film. His greater experience in synchronising dramatic dialogue has involved him in rewriting a good part of the work.

If only there were no great urgency (and one must remember that Debenedetti has other work to do), the revision could have been completed without prejudice to the rest of the text, but, things being as they are, all I can do is to send on the MS. only partly revised. You must therefore decide whether the revision should be done by someone in Rome, or whether it should be completed here by Debenedetti. We shall await your reply.

Pavese

To an unnamed gentleman, Vercelli

[Turin, during autumn 1934 (?)]

Highly distinguished Professor,

Some time ago I wrote to inform you that I would be available to resume supplementary teaching on a part-time basis, provided I could have two clear days off per week and could still live in Turin.

I gather my letter did not reach you, and on the whole it's just as well, for we have made no binding decisions. My idea now is to spend the coming winter working on my translations, devoting myself entirely to this work, in which I have already gained considerable experience. (Teaching and translating are quite incompatible activities.)

I did not forget to take into account that there are plenty of Latin teachers better qualified than I am, so by giving up the class I shall not penalise it too much. You still have time to appoint a suitable part-time tutor.

My English class has gone fairly well. Writing and reading are good, but the exam went badly. I'd appreciate a line or so from you, and an appointment to see you at Vercelli early next month. I should like to drop in to say good-bye and to return a few books.

Yours,
Pavese

1935

To Giulio Einaudi, Turin

[Turin] 13th January 1935

Dear Einaudi,

I wish to inform you that as from next month, February '35, I will no longer allow my name to appear as the director responsible for the review *La Cultura*.[1] I am giving you plenty of notice so that you can take your time over selecting my successor.

Of course, should you find yourself in difficulty, I would willingly collaborate with you again in the production of your review.

With cordial greetings,
Cesare Pavese

Translator's Note: Italy's war with Abyssinia had caused a good deal of unrest among the Italian people, and the Italian police were actively searching out any groups which might be guilty of spreading subversive ideas. Suspicion fell upon the literary review *La Cultura*, and its director, Leone Ginzburg, was arrested in May 1934, with several associates. He was accused of using that review as a cover for the activities of a group of young intellectuals working to forward 'Social Reform', 'Justice and Liberty', Ginzburg himself being their leader.

To help his friend Ginzburg, Pavese agreed to serve as director of *La Cultura* as a temporary measure, and continued until January 1935, when he resigned. Early on the morning of 13th May, police raided the house where Pavese was then living with his sister Maria, her husband and their

[1] Pavese had accepted this position in May 1934, in succession to Sergio Solmi, when the publishing house of Einaudi found itself in difficulty because several members of the staff had been arrested, charged with spreading political dissension. In a letter to his sister (26th July 1935), Pavese said he had resigned because an issue of *La Cultura* had been suppressed, but his real reason was that he was tired of being nominally in charge of a periodical that, in actual fact, was directed by Arrigo Cajumi.

family. A detailed search of Pavese's room brought to light a letter addressed to him from a former colleague who was then serving a prison sentence in the Regina Coeli, Rome. On the strength of this evidence, on 15th May Pavese was arrested and thrown into prison in Turin, at the Carceri Nuove, where he remained until 6th or 7th June, when he was transferred to the Regina Coeli and then, on 5th August, to Brancaleone (Calabria). He was sentenced to three years' imprisonment, but was actually released from Brancaleone on 15th March 1936.

Pavese's letters from prison were addressed for the most part to his sister Maria in Turin, and these are given in the pages following.

To Maria, Turin

[Carceri Nuove, Turin] 16th May 1935

They're treating me magnificently here. Let's hope it will last. Since I have money in my pocket I can get plenty to eat. For instance, I've had four meals already today and it's only three o'clock in the afternoon. All I'm short of is something to smoke, so I collect the butts of Tuscan cigars and smoke them in my pipe. I even have plenty to read and, taking one thing with another, I'd rather be here than teaching. If anyone had come to see me, or if any school had made a protest on my behalf, I should have been told. Here we are careful not to mention any names, so as not to involve people who really know nothing about it. We even have central-heating of a kind, when the sun shines through the window-panes. If the weather turns cold we shut the windows, though actually I have plenty of bedclothes.

As for what will happen to me, you know more than I do about that. I can't tell you anything. If Carocci writes from Florence asking for my poetry, let me know at once.

One result of living in a prison cell is that every now and again I give a tremendous belch, a companionable sound. I doubt whether I'll ever be able to control this habit when I'm released, no matter what company I'm in.

Now I think of it, please go and tell the Headmaster what has happened, so that he can appoint someone else.[2] Don't disturb anything in my room, and leave all my books and papers just where they are. Otherwise I'll have no idea where to start on them when I'm released.

Don't make a fuss, don't ask anyone for advice, and don't write any letters. Once I'm set free I'll soon sort things out, and I'd better do it myself. In the last few months I've been working hard, with no time to keep everything neat and tidy, even if I'd had any inclination to do so.

Give my regards and best wishes to all the family.

So long,

Cesare

18th May 1935

Dear Maria,

Nothing new to tell you, but I'm still keeping well. I received the parcel of clothes and am wearing them all at this moment. I still believe I shall be out very soon, and meanwhile I'm becoming even more aware of my own personality. Since I've never served as a soldier, I'm reckoning this as my military service. The limitations on personal freedom are much the same in each case.

I'm still worrying about my school work, particularly the evening classes, because the students need to complete their courses. Without me they'll be wasting time, and will all fail their exams. Dainotti is not on the phone, so you must contact him yourself (his address is Via Mercanti 3). If this letter reaches you in time, see him before Monday evening, or even on that evening, when my usual class starts at 8.15. Tell Sturani I'm expecting something to drink and plenty of it, in view of the half-million lire his wife has just won.[3]

I hope you won't come to see me every day. I don't want a

[2] At the time of his arrest, Pavese had already signed on as a part-time teacher at the Liceo D'Azeglio.

[3] Sturani's wife, Luisa Monti, had just won a prize in a state lottery.

queue at the door. If you feel you must discuss something with me, you must start arranging it well ahead, otherwise I'm quite capable of refusing to see any visitors at all. Living here is like being in a monastery. Everyone is most kind and helpful, except that they keep the doors locked. When I leave here I shall have a good idea of what a religious life is like and whether I might become a monk myself. (Probably not, though.)

Every now and then we enjoy smoking long cigars, specially selected by the man who sends them in. Anyone who hasn't smoked in prison can have no idea how good a smoke can be. When I'm released I really must lay in a stock of these cigars. Unless, of course, I decide to come and live here permanently.

We don't go short of anything in this prison. There's even a spider I'm trying to tame. If God means me to remain here, I shall spend this summer catching flies for my new pet. I may even try to grow a few flowers on the window-sill.

If anyone enquires for me, say I'm enjoying a long holiday. Otherwise, don't even mention me.

Warm good wishes,
Cesare

18th May 1935

Dear Maria,

Your second letter has come, the one in which you complain about the cold.

As for the food we get here, every now and then I take a little extra. I don't know why, but I'm growing miserly, and am concentrating all my ambition on getting out of here and claiming interest on the money I deposited when I came in. I'm all right for clothes. I'm allowed to write a letter on Wednesdays and Saturdays. If my stay here is to be prolonged, I should very much like to have a new pipe, if possible one of those marked G.B.D. They cost forty lire and are quite big. The family might like to give me a present of one.

At the moment I have plenty of books here. I'm still anxious about my schools. We shall see how things go. I hope you've given a plausible excuse to my English student. I hope, too, that my friends will rally round and keep him company. If any girls try to reach me by phone I'd like to know.

Here I'm behaving most discreetly. Living in a cell has the advantage that I never have to shout 'Shut that door', as I did at home. You know what that means to me in terms of serenity.

I can't be sure, from your letter, whether any proofs have arrived for me to check. If so, just put them aside and keep them carefully. Don't let any busybodies catch sight of them. I want to be away from here when those poems are published.

The chief officer here has told me you called on him and asked how I was. He really is most courteous, and as soon as my poems are published I will certainly send him a copy to show my appreciation.

Give my regards to that pig of a millionaire, if he's still around. I see from my bank-book that you've deposited another hundred lire. I hope I shan't need it. I suggest you go to a gaming house in Turin and play roulette, backing the numbers 15-5-35, the date of my arrest. Or buy a government lottery ticket with that number. It's too good a chance to miss.

All the best,
Cesare

29th May 1935

My laundry still arrives regularly, I eat with discretion and smoke my pipe whenever I like. I still don't know why I'm here, but hope it will be explained some day. With this note I'm sending you a poem I've written, just to keep my hand in. It's not very good, but it's the first I've written from memory, so I think it's quite commendable.

I'm still waiting news of my friends. You might ask them to send me a postcard, or, better still, a letter. It's not good to neglect friends who are in trouble. Tell Pinelli, a good Catholic, to get busy obeying the injunction to visit prisoners. If he can't visit me, he can at least write to me.

I hope you are all well, and that when Cesarina[4] is studying Pellico's *Le mie prigioni* she bears in mind that her uncle is in

[4] Maria's daughter, the elder of Pavese's two nieces.

the same unhappy state. However, I fancy that, of the two of us, she is more bored with life than I am. I'm rather afraid that, under present circumstances, the Headmaster will hold the exams in my absence. Try to tell her this, so that she'll be forewarned.

With affectionate greetings to you,
Cesare

1st June 1935

Dear Maria,

In reply to yours of the 10th, we are allowed to write letters only to a near relative and a few close friends, but anyone can write to us. Tell Bertola and Dainotti that I can't take classes for them any more this year, for their school closes early in June. As for what they owe me, use your discretion and take what they offer.

I don't need winter clothes yet, don't even wear pyjamas, but I'd gladly exchange the smart suit I'm wearing for a rough tweed one. I certainly don't want to cut a dash here. I've had a touch of asthma when it rained in the night, but it was nothing much. I've bought myself a pipe, here in the gaol, for we're not allowed to go outside.

Keep carefully the poems of mine you have. Don't lose them. I'm glad you gave Sturani a copy. I already knew that *La Cultura* had been suppressed. Probably that was how all this trouble started. But I cannot understand why the editor of an authorised review, particularly a literary review, can be sent to prison for doing his job. All I had to do was to read the articles submitted and decide whether to accept or return them.

Greetings,
Cesare

5th June 1935

Dear Maria,

As you see, I'm still here, and starting to find it boring. On the other hand I have books to read and am allowed to come and go as I please. Contrary to popular opinion, I find the days in prison pass very quickly. To me it seems only yesterday I was brought here, but it's a month now. Some little while ago I requested an interview with the Chief of Police, to ask him, among other things, why I'm here and how long I'm likely to stay, but so far I've had no reply.

Could you possibly see him yourself and ask the same questions? Alternatively, will he give me an appointment to meet him and discuss the matter? It seems little enough to ask.

You've sent me a whole lot of clothes. The little Chinese pyjamas are no use to me and I've returned them to you. Instead, I'd like a plain, hard-wearing suit. There's no point in spoiling the better quality suit I'm wearing now. I'm eating well, though the food is a bit monotonous, and I smoke as much as I can. I've nothing else to tell you. Give my regards to everyone and take things quietly.

Cesare

PS. I see you have deposited another two hundred lire. You should know I'm still living on the 175 lire I had in my pocket when I was brought here. I've told you before, I don't like you giving me money, though I know you mean well.

Rome, at the Carceri di Regina Coeli,
8th June 1935

Dear Maria,

As I expect you already know, I've been brought here to be at the disposal of the Public Security Police. I still don't know what I'm accused of, but I hope I'll soon find out. Anyway I've nothing to fear, for my conscience is perfectly clear. In the end, all it will probably amount to is a serious interference with my school work and the publication of my poetry.

I have a good supply of clean things, and I've found out that I can get washing done here. I have more than 400 lire in cash. If I find I need more, I'll write and ask you to send me a money-order, but I don't think it will be necessary.

The weather here in Rome is perfectly lovely. On the whole it is generally better here than in Turin. I can't tell you what my food costs per day, because it varies so much. My cell is a treasure of convenience and good taste. It has everything—wall-brackets, clothes-hangers, a bed that's not fixed to the floor, all I could possibly need. Through the windows comes a blue and orange reflected light, typical of Rome. There is even a pathway of archaeological interest, but I had only a glimpse of it from the car that brought me here. I hope I shall soon visit it again, on foot. What was my dearest wish this year? To come to Rome for my final exams. And here I am, without having to take any exams at all (which is a pleasure).

I can buy as many books as I like, and if I have to stay here long I shall study another foreign language, the only effective way to pass the time.

Give my greetings to all my friends who enquire after me, and try to cheer up. This stupid fuss and bother can't last long.

Cesare

14th June 1935

Dear Maria,

Yesterday I received your letter of the 7th and am replying in the same strain. I have all the equipment I need for the moment. It's infernally hot, and I'm taking advantage of the fine weather to sunbathe during our periods of exercise. Since I am not allowed to take off my singlet, I thought out a little trick. I wear my singlet and nothing else. It is cut away like a waistcoat, so I unbutton it and soak up as much sunshine as I want.

Everything is kept very clean here. Just imagine! Any bugs are hunted with a blow-lamp! It gives us a few minutes of healthy and amusing sport!

The most serious thing is that I keep on buying books to help pass the time and I'm spending fabulous sums of money.

Every now and then I get a touch of asthma, due, I think, to sweating so much and then feeling chilled. Oh well, I must put up with it.

This is important: send a reply by express to Alberto Carocci (Via Maggio 13, Florence), telling him to proceed with the publication and sales promotion of my book.[5] There's just one thing I'd like to alter, if it's not too late, and that is to cut out the last poem, 'Una Generazione'. The more I think about it, the less it pleases me. It is really one of a different series I was working on when I was arrested, and so could not complete. I would prefer to take it out.

The more I think about my present situation, the more sure I feel that the world is a vale of tears. Where is the greatest living poet in Italy, perhaps in Europe? Here, in the prison of Regina Coeli.

Greetings to you all,
Cesare

17th June 1935

Dear Maria,

I'm down in the dumps today. Let's hope it will pass. The days go by smoothly enough, but it's difficult to get hold of new books. I have ordered several, leaving a credit balance in my account of only 380 lire. It takes at least a week for me to receive your reply to my letters, so it will be best for you to send in something to increase my funds.

Everyone here is kind and helpful, except that they have a craze for keeping the doors shut. I hope they'll open them one fine day. They were asking me if I'd brought in a pair of shoes. I'm afraid I left them in Turin, and have asked if you could be allowed to go there and collect them for me. Will you please do so?

I still know nothing definite about what's going to happen to

[5] This was a collection of Pavese's poems, published in 1936 under the title *Lavorare Stanca*. The particular poem he mentions, 'Una Generazione' had a strong political bias, and Pavese may well have feared it might be prejudicial to him when the authorities came to consider his 'case'.

me. You could consult Tullio's father, the lawyer Ferdinando Pinelli, and ask his advice.

I'm doing a lot of physical exercises in our gymnasium here, and my asthma has disappeared. Now and then I put on my hat and stroll round my cell, imagining I'm in Piazza Castello, Via Roma or Corso Vittorio.

Just then I had to break off to eat pasta and peas. It was a good meal. One thing (among others) that I find annoying is that I cannot revise my poems in a serene state of mind. Let's hope they'll come out in a decent edition. I'll hope, too, that all my friends are still alive, though none of them have written to me. Have I got the plague?

It's infernally hot here. If only it were allowed, it would be much more comfortable to go around naked. They've just fired a cannon, so I'll break off this letter.

So long,
Cesare

21st June 1935

Dear Maria,

The worst thing about being in prison is that there's never anything to say when writing home. Never anything new to talk about. I'm sick and tired of life, wondering if it's worth the trouble of being born if it all ends up like this. The other day I had a bath, but it's so hot here that I stank like a goat again as soon as I got out. Being isolated in a cell turns a man into a beast, in every sense of the word. I should be glad to be given my sentence. Then I could at least mix with other men, even behind prison walls. But it never seems to get to that stage, and the devil of it is that it should.

I hope you are all well and have no other worries. Within the limits of the regulations they treat me very well here. You are not to waste time and money in coming to Rome. See if you can help me in some other way, that's all.

I feel a bit more cheerful now. My depression comes and goes in waves. I hope you got my letter asking you to send me some cash. Do send some if you can. I have enough clothes for now and can get them washed.

It's terribly sultry here today, ideal for going swimming in the Po. Let's hope we'll be able to, another year. Write and tell me if anyone has enquired for me. I realise your difficulty,[6] but I get the impression that all my friends must be in gaol.

Greetings,
Cesare

PS. Someone who might give you advice would be my friend Avv. Vaudagna—Ces.

24th June 1935

Dear Maria,

I've had my interrogation, but have heard nothing since. It appears that some acquaintances of mine banded together between themselves to carry out heaven knows what silly enterprise. Naturally the authorities assumed I was involved. Everybody knows I've never been concerned with politics, but now it seems that politics are getting concerned about me.

Since I fully expect to be set free any day now, I'll add that my stay here has been little short of delightful; tranquillity, rapid service, plenty of leisure and every attention. Still, I think you had better consult Pinelli's father or Vaudagna, to see if either of them can lend a hand to get me out.

I note the good wishes expressed by Tullio, Mario, Chabod and Norberto. I can't tell you how much I envy them. Though they live in the same atmosphere as I do, they are lucky enough to be free to go wherever they like. I don't wish them to be placed as I am, but I'd gladly change places with any one of them.

Good wishes to you all,
So long,
Cesare

[6] Maria's difficulty was that only very few of Pavese's friends knew he was in prison. Others had either been told or had assumed he was away on holiday or had taken a job at some distance from Turin.

28th June 1935

Dear Maria,

It's some time now since I've had any news from you. The last was your letter-card of the 16th. Haven't you had anything from me since then?

On the other hand, what point is there in writing? I'm fed up to the teeth with it. All I can do is go to sleep, just to forget it all. Nothing else to do but wait. It's up to you, now, to tackle the job of getting me away from this place, out into the fresh air. It's easy to get into prison, but knowing when one will get out is a different matter.

I expect you've received my letter asking you to send me some money, if you possibly could. I spend, on an average, 4 lire per day, plus the cost of books and papers. It's a sobering, instructive thought that I cannot spend anything whatever in any other way—no smoking, nothing.

Apart from all that, I can't say I'm treated badly. What wears a man down is not what he is, but what he can't be. That's enough of my grumbles for now.

I'm still waiting for press reviews of my poems, and letters from my friends and yours. I asked you a little while ago to make arrangements about Serralunga, as if nothing was wrong, so just keep me informed. I don't know whether you've told Luigi of my misfortune, but if not, do so now. Tell Mario I hope he'll go to prison one of these days. It just isn't fair. He gets married, wins half a million in the Tripoli lottery, and travels about, whereas I, as much like him as one drop of water is like another, have to stay inside. I only hope his riches won't prove to be a golden cage.

I dream I'm bathing in the sea, and wake up sweating, which starts me coughing. It's not exactly asthma, just enough to keep me awake all night, conscious of the hours as they pass. It's most unfair to rob a prisoner of his sleep. With us, things are either done or not done.

So long,
Cesare

1st July 1935

Dear Maria,

I'm beginning to appreciate the importance of family affection. Yesterday I felt like shooting myself (though we have no firearms here), but then your letter of the 23rd arrived and gave me some respite. Today I had a postcard signed by several friends of mine. Thank the senders for me, if you can.

You seem surprised that I had written you on the 14th and 17th of last month. I wrote on the 11th,[7] too. Aren't you getting my letters? I told you I had my interrogation 15 days ago, but have heard nothing since. I expect you had my letters suggesting you should seek advice from those highly qualified men of law, Pinelli and Vaudagna. All I can do here is to wait, leaving you to take action, if you will.

I'm starting to wake up every morning in a bath of sweat. Already my face is chapped and sore from being washed so much. Every now and then a prisoner cries: 'If it's like this in July, however shall we get through August?', and we tear our hair in desperation. That's why I already have large bald patches all over my head. All because some acquaintance of mine chose to play the fool and ruin an honest man. If I get out I'll break every bone in his body.

I still have just over 300 lire. Quite apart from my special expenses (books, papers and medicine), I'll be getting 150 lire per month. Not too bad as a pension, is it? I may even manage to smoke!

I enjoy a glimpse of the country when they open the little shutter in the door of my cell to give or tell me something, and through a window I can see a green hill, the Gianicolo I think.

The best moments of my life are when I'm not troubled by asthma, i.e. when I'm asleep. I dream a lot, and all my dreams convince me that I'm back in Turin taking a walk or out in a boat, visiting a friend's house or enjoying the company of a lovely girl. But a moment or two before waking I become conscious of the walls and bars around me. Once I open my eyes I'm only too aware that I'm still in prison, as I was yesterday.

It's a strange thing that there are no flies here. I haven't seen any bed-bugs, either, but those are hunted with a flame-thrower.

[7] Pavese's letter of 11th June is not included in this collection.

I'm still in solitary confinement. It's enough to drive a man mad. I must break off now, to go and enjoy the fresh air in the prison yard, formerly called 'the lion's den'. When I come back inside I'll be dripping with sweat, and to cool off I'll strip myself here in my cell.

So long,
Greetings to you all,
Cesare

Friday, 5th July 1935

Dear Maria,

You'll have noticed, I expect, that letters written on a Friday are more cheerful than those I write on Mondays. The reason is quite simple. On a Monday I still have to get through the week, but on a Friday the week is nearly over. It's amazing how keen a prisoner is on noting how the weeks go by, even though he's getting older all the time.

My health remains good and I think I'm putting on weight. Chickens are shut up in a coop to fatten, and men in prison. Your 300 lire reached me safely, so did Guglielmo's little note you told me he'd be sending. I appreciate your sympathy for my misfortunes, but naturally that's not enough. As long as you're the only one who believes I'm innocent, I'll remain in gaol. It's not even enough that people like Pinelli and Chabod,[8] whose reputations are beyond question, know I've never had the slightest interest in politics and can vouch for my good faith from their personal knowledge. What we have to do is to convince Rome.

As for Vaudagna,[9] he's been moved to Asti, not Alessandria, and you can get in touch with him through Sturani. A man who knows me as Vaudagna does, who has lived with me for weeks at a time and knows I'm a serious, right-minded poet, should have no difficulty in finding a way to help me. Provided, of course, that he felt disposed to concern himself with the matter.

[8] Renato Chabod was one of the politically minded students in the group led by Giulio Einaudi.

[9] Giuseppe Vaudagna, a school friend of Pavese, had been recently appointed to the post of Secretary of the Fascist Workers in Asti.

The heat? Don't mention it. Tell me instead about the girls who ring up to enquire for me. I wish I knew who they are. I'm naturally flattered by their interest in a bit of human jetsam like me.

Don't remind me about boating on the Po. The mere thought of it makes me foam at the mouth. So much water waiting there for me, and so much sweat here. To console myself for the loss of those delights, I'm reading Manzoni's *Observations on Catholic Morality*. I've asked for a Bible, too. It's a great book and an extremely long one, with enough material to keep me occupied for ages.

'Bye for now,
Cesare

8th July 1935

Dear Maria,

I've just found out that my case no longer concerns the Director General of Public Security, but has been transferred to the Chief of Police in Rome. I'm not clear as to what this means. I'm glad to know that a man who was arrested with me is now free. It gives me hope for myself.

You did well to write to Luigi, but it would be wrong for you to come to Rome. There's no need for you to spend money on useless travel. A visit would do no good at all at this stage. Wait at least until we know definitely what is to become of me.

I asked permission to buy a few books, but so far only one has arrived. We have a circulating library that allows me two volumes a week, and also a Special Library from which I can borrow six books every fortnight. I also buy newspapers and reviews, so the time passes pleasantly enough.

I've become aware of my own cleverness. I had never been in prison, never even dreamed of being sent to one, yet I wrote a poem describing with absolute fidelity the feelings of a man who finds himself in prison. I also wrote a poem expressing his happiness when he's set free, but so far I don't know if I was right. Let's hope I shall soon find out from my own experience.

Cesare

12th July 1935

Dear Maria,

On the 10th I learned that someone denounced me to the authorities as being a danger to the established order of national security. I've been allowed to prepare a statement in my own defence and will send it in today.

I'm delighted to know that some of my friends have been freed, but I withdraw the good wishes I sent to Sturani. Let him enjoy his good luck while he can, dropping any friends of his who are in trouble.

You did well to write to Luigi in Rome. Even now, if he knows in time, he might manage to help me. I have your long letter of the 3rd and must tell you again it would be useless for you to come to Rome. By the time you arrive I might well have been moved somewhere else. Tell Carocci he's played me a dirty trick by postponing publication of my poems just because I've had a bit of bad luck.

I've at last received some of the books I asked permission to buy. Among them is a Bible, and I'm studying the highly complicated genealogical details of the patriarchs. When I've finished that I shall study the Psalms of David. After that I may ask to enter a monastery, if they'll have me.

Here's good news. Our fruit allowance no longer consists of cherries, but peaches that smell of vineyards and honey, filling the cell with their perfume and making my eyes shine. If only I could get married, I'd ask for nothing better than the way I'm living now. It's a job like any other and I'm sheltered from wind and rain (but, alas, not from the heat). Still, in one way or another it will soon be over.

My head aches from smoking my pipe too much. Once my skin smelt like some exotic fruit, but now it stinks of tobacco, sweat and animalism [*sic*]. (The last is a pleasure.)

Give my regards to everyone,
and wait to see how I'll end up,
Your brother in disgrace,
Cesare

15th July [1935]

Dear Maria,

It's two months now since I came here and everything is going quite pleasantly. I'm still waiting to hear what decision the authorities have reached.

I've received Guglielmo's note of the 4th, his letter of the 5th, and three postcards dated the 6th, 7th and 8th, apparently written from various railway stations. If you think it gives me any great pleasure to hear about trains coming in or going out, you are mistaken.

I see you've been talking to Vaudagna and others, but it doesn't seem to have had much effect so far. If, as they told you, my position is not really serious, why am I being kept here so long? Prison seems to me like a cupboard. Apples left there too long go soft or turn bad. I suppose when the authorities consider you've been softened up enough, they'll decide what sentence to give you. But I haven't turned soft, inside or out. It's like having some dreadful maggot gnawing my life away, but I fumigate it with my pipe and manage to keep it quiet.

I'm annoyed that you wrote to Luigi suggesting he should come and see me. He's an intelligent fellow and hasn't come so far, but if he were to come, what on earth should we find to talk about? We should just stand there like a couple of fools with no notion of what to say. Don't do anything like that again. I'd much rather hear about the girls who have rung up to enquire for me. That's the only thing likely to cheer me up.

I have a great longing to be sent somewhere near the sea, and I fancy that wish may soon come true. A lot depends on what the weather's like when I get there. I hope I shan't be expected to live on fish.

Our paradise of peaches didn't last long. Now they give us baked apples that look and taste like ashes, but they have their uses as a remedy for constipation, which troubles me nearly as much as my asthma. Every day I dream up all sorts of long-term illnesses in the hope of being transferred to hospital, where I should at least have a little company. Actually, I don't think I've ever felt as fit as I do now. No doubt, if I were set free, I should instantly fall ill with some long and painful disease.

Finally, I beg you not to write me a lot of tittle-tattle about those friends of mine who have been freed, or assure me that my innocence must triumph in the end. Just get me out of here. That's all I want. Now I'll get back to Kant's *Critique of Practical Reason*, so good-bye for the present.

With my cheerful good wishes,
Cesare

Telegram to Maria

17th July 1935

SENTENCED TO THREE YEARS IMPRISONMENT. DESTINATION UNKNOWN. CESARE.

19th July 1935

Dear Maria,

Further to my telegram, I still don't know where I shall be sent to serve my sentence, but I shall be there within a week and will let you know. As for the statement I was told to make, I'd hardly sent it in before my sentence was announced. I've been told I could appeal against it and I'm doing so, but meanwhile I'm to be sent away somewhere. If my appeal succeeds, I shall be released there, wherever it is. It will, in any case, take months before my appeal is heard.

I'm now sharing my cell with another fellow, a fine little chap with a beard like a prophet's. We lend each other books. Later on we'll see if it seems suitable to invite Sturani and a few others to visit me.

All good wishes,
Cesare Pavese

22nd July [1935]

Dear Maria,

This will probably be the last letter I shall write you from Rome, but I still don't know where I am to serve my sentence. It doesn't much matter to me, since I have plenty to read and write, but the idea of having to spend three years in prison is a nuisance, because I had things to do in Turin that I shall hate to put off. I would rather have had 100 strokes of a bastinado on the soles of my feet, or have had my left hand and right foot amputated, than having to spend three years far from Turin, not that I mind being away from my family.

If you still insist on seeing me again, one way of salvation is still open. My appeal was sent in on 20th July and sooner or later it will be discussed by the Central Commission in charge of prisons (Ministry of the Interior). Take an interest in this procedure, through Luigi, for I can certainly do nothing more from here. Tell those true friends of mine, who 'won't be bothered', that if they've got no more influence than that they can go to the devil and take their good wishes with them.

Cesare

26th July 1935

Dear Maria,

I received your letter of the 13th, two postcards and two telegrams. Thank Irma for her card. My appeal, dated 20th July, was rejected, mainly because I spent two or three hours of my life (in 1932) talking to the editor of Treves. Now that you know it all, sleep on it. My further appeal may be considered at once, or may take months. Meanwhile I may be transferred, or may be kept here.

Your letters and cards mean precious little. If it wasn't for the messages you send from my friends I'd ask you not to write me any more. It's not worth the trouble. It's all very comforting to me to have you grumbling because I couldn't take my exams, telling me there's nothing more you can do and that innocence will prevail. It's shameful for you to add that your days seem endless. What do you think mine are to me?

I can say all this because at the moment I have no need of money. When I do, I shall again become your affectionate brother,

Cesare

26th July 1935

Dear Maria,

I've already written you today, but I've just had permission to write another letter, so I'll reply to your telegram asking for details of my appeal. If I was denounced because of my position as a director of *La Cultura,* I must protest that this is a literary review, in no way concerned with politics. I was personally invited to undertake this purely managerial post by friends of mine, who would certainly not have asked me if they had considered there was anything wrong with this publication. It may be that certain contributors to this review in the past have since attracted the attention of the authorities, but the general intention of the publishers and directors was to promote discussion among young students in a perfectly legitimate manner. When a recent article seemed open to question, the whole issue was suppressed. What better proof of good faith could there be?

If the cause of my arrest was the fact that I had received certain letters from a friend in Milan, I protest that they contained nothing whatever about politics, and I agreed to receive them simply as a favour to an acquaintance. I reaffirm that I know nothing about politics and that my whole time is fully occupied by my literary activities.

Cesare

Telegram to Maria

Brancaleone, 5th August 1935

HAVE ARRIVED HERE BRANCALEONE IN CALABRIA AT THE ALBERGO ROMA. PLEASE FORWARD WHAT YOU CAN SPARE FOR MY EXPENSES AS QUICKLY AS POSSIBLE. CESARE.

To Alberto Carocci, Florence

Brancaleone, 7th August 1935

Dear Carocci,

I expect you've already heard of the trouble I'm in. I'm at Brancaleone, sentenced to three years. My sister has told me that my book has been approved and given the Official Stamp, but you wish to postpone publication until October. In my view the reasons you expressed for this delay no longer apply, and I should be grateful if you would reconsider the matter and let me know your views. I think the volume (i.e. cutting out 'Una Generazione') could well be issued now, but the proofs should be passed to the Minister of the Interior for his authorisation. All I can do at present is to leave everything in your hands.

Pavese

Brancaleone, 9th August 1935

Dear Maria,

I reached Brancaleone at 4 o'clock on Sunday afternoon, to find the whole population strolling round outside the station as if they expected to see a criminal in handcuffs, escorted by two *carabinieri*, emerge from the train and march firmly towards the municipal offices.

My two days' journey, with my handcuffs and suitcase, was an undertaking of tourism in the highest degree. Henceforth our family name is compromised beyond all hope of recovery. We passed through the stations at Naples and Rome at the height of the rush-hour, and unless you had seen it for yourselves you'd never believe how the crowds stood back to allow ample room for the sinister trio—a handcuffed prisoner escorted by two *carabinieri*. At Rome a little girl asked her father: 'Papa, why don't they send an electric current through those handcuffs?' At Naples, handicapped as I was by my handcuffs and suitcase, I had a bad fall on the steps. After that, someone carried my suitcase for me.

At Salerno we had to change trains, so providing an educational spectacle for all the small boys of the neighbourhood. It was dark when we got to Paestum, so we didn't even have the pleasure of seeing the Greek temples. Changing trains again at Sant'Eufemia and Catanzari gave us a welcome break in the journey. On arriving at Brancaleone I was given a great welcome by kind people who did everything possible to make me feel cheerful and in good heart. I'm the only prisoner confined here at present. Conditions are so dirty it's a positive scandal. Everything is baked hard by the sun. The women comb their hair in the street, but at least all the inhabitants go to the baths. They carry huge pitchers on their heads. I must learn how to do that myself, then perhaps I'll be able to earn my living at it on the variety stage at Turin.

People here have no idea what grapes are for. If you were to send me a score or two of bottles I'd have to drink them myself. I've received the money you sent me, and I very much fear that unless the Minister changes his mind about my needs I shall be allowed only two books a month. I'm still waiting for the box of books you sent off to me some time ago.

I have arranged to rent a bedroom for 45 lire. Every day there's some new expense or other, for light, a wash-bowl, sugar, drinks, etc. I manage to eat—cold stuff, of course. The beach is at Mar Jonio, just like any other beach, and for bathing it's almost as good as the Po.

I've received a quantity of cards that have been held up, but all I ask for is books, money, and greetings from my friends.

So long,
Cesare

PS. Send me the following books of mine: Two volumes of Molière's *Comedies* (with yellow covers and written in French); Kipling's *Jungle Book* and *The Second Jungle Book*; two volumes of Ben Jonson's plays (rebound in dark green and gold), written in English; two volumes of Rocci's *Greek Grammar* and *Greek Exercises*; and finally my *Italian-Greek Dictionary* (rebound in green).

[Brancaleone] 19th August [1935]

Dear Maria,

I have received your letters of the 10th and 12th, and have already sent off, duly signed, my petition to the Minister for National Education.

I've had enough of Brancaleone already. I get up early in the morning, when the milkman comes, and boil my quarter litre on my little spirit stove, otherwise it would turn sour by midday. Then I go out to have coffee in the little town and sit over it till 10 o'clock, trying to read or compose a poem, but the heat is so intense and my surroundings so uninspiring that I don't have much success.

I go down to the sea. I used to swim a great deal, but one day the salt water affected one of my ears, so now I have to keep my head above water and cannot dive—another pleasure now lost. I stroll back to the prison, buying myself some bread and fruit on the way. At noon I drink my boiled milk and eat my bread and fruit, or sometimes an egg that I cook for myself in a little pan.

Then I try to take a nap. If, as often happens, I can't sleep, I idly turn the pages of a book until 4 o'clock, when I go out again to report at the Municipal Offices. On my way back, through the town centre, I sit trying to compose a poem or join in the local chit-chat, though I soon feel bored. If I haven't spent much that day, I go and enjoy a beer, returning to my cell about 7 o'clock to have supper and wash the plates. Then I take a stroll round the house until 8, still dreaming of poetry, then go indoors and tuck myself into bed, having first taken a quinine pastille—a good precaution against illness, according to the prison governor. From 7 o'clock onwards, cockroaches swarm all over my poky, tiny kitchen cell, and I simply can't get rid of them. Flit merely fattens them up and other alleged repellents they treat with scorn. They're as big as my thumb, and enjoy licking my milk-bowl and egg-pan. They disappear at the first light of dawn. My cell is at ground level, so one evening I enticed a hen inside and shut her up there, hoping she would kill them. Actually she not only blasted all my hopes, but also ate a bunch of grapes I was keeping in reserve.

Once or twice a week I go out for a good lunch, to keep up my strength. It's almost incredible, living as I do, how much I have to spend. When I first came it cost me between twenty and thirty lire a day (covering things like my bed and bedclothes, tips, postage stamps and so on). Even now, just for food and odds and ends I need to buy, I can never get away with less than five lire. I keep a careful note of what I spend every day, but even so my cash just vanishes. In the evenings I can economise a little, for the smell of this place and of the cockroaches, the rustling noise they make and the dreadful heat, all combine to destroy my appetite.

I'm told that in the winter here the weather is very humid, and any form of heating is quite unknown, yet I certainly don't want to be sent anywhere else. The country round here is very good, and the translations I'm doing give me a feeling of travel. I'm looking forward to having the 'grappa' wine you are sending me, which will certainly help me through the winter. I've applied for a subsidy, but without much hope of getting it.

In front of my room is a little yard, then the railway line, then the sea. Five or six times every day (and night), passing trains rouse my nostalgia as I follow them in spirit. On the other hand I am completely indifferent to the ships on the horizon and moonlight on the sea. (All that glimmering brightness makes me think only of fried fish.) The sea is merely one great void.

Re my translations, I would like to do *A Storyteller's Story*, by Sherwood Anderson. Mondadori told me he was doing it, but so far nothing has been seen of it. If you can manage to get hold of Signor Rusca, at the publishing house of Mondadori in Milan, put the position to him. Tell him I would, for 800 or even 600 lire, produce a translation finer than the original text. For 1,000 I'd make it a really first-class job. If they accept, all we'd have to do is to ask the Minister of Internal Affairs to give his authorisation.

Greetings to everyone. Show this letter to any friends of mine who are interested.

Cesare

[Brancaleone] 24th August [1935]

Dear Maria,

I've received a flood of mail—an old postcard dated 31st July, in which you tell me I'm a fool, another dated the 14th and a letter of the 18th.

My journey here cost me nothing, but I had to ask you for money as soon as I arrived because I still hadn't received the cash taken from me when I was arrested. That has now reached me, and with your two consignments I now have 700 lire, so I'll see a bit of life for a change.

My room is as good as it's possible to make it. I was lucky to find one with a bed already installed. Generally one takes just the room and has to buy a bed for oneself. For 45 lire I was even supplied with blankets—washed. I pay 8 lire per month for lighting, 12 for laundry (mending included). Those are all my fixed expenses. Other details of my life I told you about in my letter of the 19th.

I've received the little box quite safely, but you're no good at choosing pipes. I've tried them all, but have had to put them aside because they do not draw properly. The three new ones I've discarded. They were cheap and may perhaps last a month, or even less. One has already split.

As for new books, you did the right thing in not buying *Psyche*. It was too expensive and I don't need it now, nor do I want the *Aeneid*. Here is a list of those I do want, if you or a friend of mine will look them out from my bookshelves: Montaigne's *Essays*; the works of J. de Maistre; Pascal's *Les Provinciales*; John Milton's *Areopagitica* (Dent's Everyman edition); D. Defoe's *Robinson Crusoe* and *Moll Flanders* (both in the Everyman series); Nathanial Hawthorne's *The Marble Faun*; the Earl of Chesterfield's *Letters to His Son* and David Garnett's *Lady into Fox*.

Ask Rossi to send back the Anderson books I lent him; get Galeazzo to return my copy of Defoe's *Captain Singleton,* A. Huxley's *Point Counter Point*; and Brantome's *Les Dames Galantes*.

Don't write so many letters. Postcards are quite enough—and a help to the censor. I've reckoned up that since I came here you have already spent in postage alone, 14.50, without counting telegrams or money orders. It's all money wasted. My system of giving you a choice of books to send me every now and then, has the advantage that if you send two or three at a time the cost is small; but sending a lot together makes a parcel and costs the earth.

Cesare

To Alberto Carocci, Florence

[Brancaleone] 16th [or 24th] September [1935]

Dear Carocci,

Herewith, God willing, are the final proofs of *Lavorare stanca.* I have taken into account the advice of the Minister in charge of Printed Matter, and have, as you see, cut out 'Il Dio Caprone' (most reluctantly), 'Pensieri di Dina', 'Balletto' and 'Paternità'. Henceforth the volume could be used as a prayer book, even by a virgin.

With my usual obstinacy, I could not resist the temptation to include eight other poems after 'Una Generazione', written during the period of tranquillity I've recently enjoyed.

If you think this would be possible, they can appear in the order I have numbered them. If, however, this would hold up publication for too long, use your discretion. As you will see, they are all perfectly innocent poems and in no way at variance with the ascetic tone of the book itself. They would also serve to add a few pages to replace those poems cut out by the Prefecture and the Minister.

If you agree, you will need to correct the proofs yourself, for it would be such a pity to delay publication for another couple of months or more by exchanging our views by post. I beg you most earnestly to grant me this favour without any lengthy argument. These poems really date from the summer of '34. The municipal authority here has told me that, provided I send this folder to the censor's office, it will be passed automatically.

Pavese

To Mario Sturani, Turin

[Brancaleone] 20th September [1935]

Dear old friend,

It's useless to send me letters headed with the name and address of some luxury hotel on the shore of some famous lake. We all know only too well how humbly born you are and how much money your father left you. You put on too many airs. If I felt so inclined, I could (with more justification), style myself as 'The

Con.(-vict) of Brancaleone', to impose upon the good faith of honest men.

In a word, old chap, you are common. Still, remembering our former fellowship, I'll be your friend again and tell you how thrilled I was to get your letter. I'm only sorry you took so long to let me know you're still alive. I lost my temper when you spoke to me about Monferini. God knows why, but I've taken a strong dislike to him.

I'm not living in a hotel, but in a small furnished room full of cockroaches. When it rains (as it does all winter), my room is flooded. I'm only mildly interested to learn that in Turin you're having a heat-wave, but I was moved to tears to hear about the motor-cruiser *Vittoria* and your period of national service.

The last time you came to see me, I didn't mention how shocked a certain police-officer looked when he read my poems. He decided they were pornographic. Faced with some of them he forgot everything else—his country, his duties and his family—took off his cap and bellowed like a cow.

In view of your present financial position and the way you boast about it, I think you might send me some of the books I need. Second-hand copies would do, if you can find any:

(1) A modern German novel—I haven't yet read one.
(2) Any book about the interpretation of the Bible—Old and New Testaments—in Italian, French or English.
(3) Any work about pilgrimages or travels in general, fanciful or erudite, during the fourteenth, fifteenth or sixteenth centuries.
(4) Frassinelli's new book, *Kafka*. (He might even give you a free copy.)
(5) Any other book you consider worth reading or re-reading (but not your own novel).

Also, if you can find one, a copy of the *Thousand and One Nights*. A translation would be acceptable, but *not* the French translation by Antoine Galland.

Won't you tell me something about your wife, my friend? Isn't she even a little bit pregnant yet? She would be even lovelier if she were. I kiss your hand, Madame. In me you see a wretched victim of fickle Lady Luck. What of tomorrow? Who knows where either of us may be tomorrow?

Affectionate greetings,
Pavese

Brancaleone, 2nd October 1935

Dear Maria,

I am to be given a subsidy of 5 lire per day, plus 50 lire per month for lodgings, with arrears as from 5th August. No one understands why it was refused in the first place.

The English book you sent me I enjoyed very much, in spite of its rather melancholy title. Possibly that was meant as a challenge. You *must* get after Alberto Rossi more fiercely and *make* him return my books. He's still in Turin, since he's writing stupid commentaries on films for the *Gazette*.

My neuralgia is gone now, but I expect it will come back any day, since winter has already begun. Sturani has written and sent me two pipes, better than the ones you sent. Please send me as quickly as you can my long-sleeved shirts, together with my little copies of the *Iliad* and the *Odyssey,* in Greek.

Make a note of the following books I'd like to have :

Jonathan Swift's *Tale of a Tub* and *Journal to Stella* (both published by Dent)

Edmund Spenser, *The Faerie Queene*, 2 vols (also in Dent's edition)

William Congreve, *The Complete Plays,* 2 vols (Oxford edition)

William Faulkner (an American writer) *Light in August* (?) and *Pylon* (?) (recent publications)

I'm amazed that you ask me whether I want to come back to Turin. It's no use grumbling—there's always someone worse off than oneself—but I'm not yet so philosophic as to put up with toothache calmly. It gives me some comfort to take things easily on Sundays, and smoke my amber pipe, pleasures that not all men would appreciate, but then, not all men are at Brancaleone.

Cesare

Brancaleone, 11th October 1935

Dear Maria,

Sturani has sent me all the books on my list of 24th August. I've written to thank him, but would you please thank him personally, too? I haven't yet received the money you've sent, but it will come all right. Amen.

Cesare

To Alberto Carocci, Florence

Brancaleone, 24th October 1935

Dear Carocci,

I drew a breath of relief on hearing that the proofs have finally reached you (via the Prefecture of Florence). Even the eight new poems now have the approval of the appropriate official department, and I shouldn't be surprised if various civil servants in Florence and Rome already know them by heart. When I was transferred to the Regina Coeli in Rome, one of the staff complimented me upon them, half seriously and half jokingly. Once the book is published and is available to general readers, my fortune will be made!

If ever you come across a book that you consider quite objectionable, I'd be grateful if you'd send it on to me. I'm in the mood to read anything at all, if only to pass the time. My curiosity extends from commentaries on the Bible to yellow-back novelettes, a range that includes Japanese lyrics, occultism, literary criticism and love-letters. Indeed, I assure you with my hand on my heart, the only subject that doesn't (and never has) interested me in the slightest, is anything to do with politics.

Pavese

To Augusto Monti, Turin

Brancaleone, 29th October 1935

Dear Monti,

I've received your letter of 10th October and given it a good deal of thought.

You meant to cheer me up, I'm sure, but it's no good. Only last night I was foaming at the mouth, doing my best to kill off cockroaches and smashing a chair in the process. Then I sank back into bed, a prey to asthma. When I get these attacks I sleep the best part of a week and then blossom forth on the Lord's Day, full of accumulated energy.

Sturani has flooded me with books and pipes, and I have overwhelmed him with thanks. If you want to do something worthwhile, send me something in Greek. I found several Greek texts here, including Sophocles's *Oedipus Rex*, and I've already translated them, apart from the last, which I'm just finishing. I need hardly add that I loathe Greek and the man who invented it. It's a dead language, illogical and artificial. *Oedipus* is enough to fell an ox, but that's the way it is. It's up to us to tackle it with a gay and resolute mind.

Be good,
Pavese

[Brancaleone] 29th October [1935]

Dear Maria,

So you dream every night that I'm coming home, and you're living in hope? That's a good beginning, especially since I've often had the same dream myself.

The clothes I have here are all in fairly good order. All the summer I've worn only the lightest clothing, but now the evenings are growing chilly I've started using the thicker things you sent me a little while ago. When I catch cold it leads to an attack of asthma, and vice versa. The heavier suit you sent me I haven't yet started to use. I need handkerchiefs, socks, shirts, underwear to change into. Very soon, short-sleeved shirts will not be enough. If you haven't any with long sleeves I shall have to wear what I have, underneath a jacket. I have three pairs of shoes in good order, for all through the summer I have worn tennis-shoes that I bought here for 6 lire, though generally I should prefer some not quite so flat.

Go and see Rossi and tell him that his book on the *Works of Daniel Defoe* was passed on a year or two ago to Franco Antonicelli, who wanted to read it in case he decided to translate *Moll Flanders*.

If everyone is amazed at my imprisonment and very sorry for me, I might be relieved to hear it, but the opposite simply bores me. Such tales are pointless. If my friends have something to tell me, let them write to me, as many others have done, others for whom I still retain considerable respect.

I've racked my brains to discover what the little things are you want to know about, but all in vain. Do you mean the cockroaches? I've told you about them. Money? I've told you. How I eat, what I do all day, whether I sleep well or not? I've told you. What I spend? What do I need? What poems have I written? I've told you. There is a popular saying that when something isn't mentioned, it means that all is well. Just remember that!

I can't fathom your mysterious hints about the salame, but thank you for sending it. The only thing wrong with salame is that, before you know it, there's only a half left.

Thank you for the copy of Byron, which has been my greatest pleasure ever since I first came to know it, on this very coast. With this letter I enclose two photographs, the only ones that came out well. The other four are no good. Altogether they cost me 12 lire. How expensive little things can be!

I have at last received my subsidy from 5th August to the end of September. I've brought myself an umbrella with a handle like the head of a bulldog. I call it Beethoven.

Cesare

[Brancaleone] 5th November [1935]

Dear Maria,

Here is a summary you may like to read, of the American book *Autobiography of a Suicide*. It's nothing out of the ordinary, just the sort of thing America turns out every year, dealing with sex and nervous tensions. Here I'm living the same sort of life as the author of that book, but I don't suppose it will end in the same way.

Cesare

To Mario Sturani, Turin

Brancaleone, 27th November 1935

Dear Sturani,

So you press me to send you a further list of the books I want. Actually, my family has already sent me several, and I am reluctant to trespass further upon your kindness, and your purse. It does not do to be too generous, for there comes a point when the recipient begins to hate the donor.

Winter has now set in, with rain, gale-force winds and humidity at night, all of which affect my asthma worse than pepper. This is hard to bear, since sleeping is the only way I can pass the time without irritability, and these afflictions drastically curtail the hours when I *can* sleep.

What poetry I manage to write is insipid and tame. It doesn't even help to kill time, for only very rarely do I feel any real interest in the work. I spend countless hours gloomily concentrating on an idea that as yet hardly exists.

Even in summer I don't much care for the sea, and in winter it is dreary beyond words. The shore is a yellow strip of rough sand.

On the horizon the water has an edge of green, so tender, so evocative, that it drives a man mad with longing.

The main attraction of this part of the country is the fish that are caught here—but I do not care for fish, so I eat meat no more than once or twice a week, when someone has slaughtered a calf.

I bought a strong rope and made a running noose in it. Every morning I rub it well with soap to keep it supple and swift to use. With it I can sometimes earn a joint of meat. When the local people have a sow, fattened by being forced to lead a life of stern chastity, they invite me to help them string it up.

Even you must be aware that Pinelli has written and produced a thoroughly bawdy comedy with the title *La pulce d'oro* [The Golden Flea]. I've read it and found it very much in his usual style, but amusing this time. It's filthy, even worse than *Tutto Banda*, but that's the way of the world. He cannot bring out his *Dio-Caprone* as yet. It is absolutely full of the most chaste resolutions, but what it really presents is sensuality. He would do better to use his present popularity to get me out of here so that I could go home. All he thinks of is begetting sons and writing comedies, two functions involving the exercise of the same physical organs.

Pav.

To Mario Sturani, Turin

Brancaleone, 15th December 1935

Dear Mario,

In your last letter you reproach me for being so harsh with everybody. Can it be that, in spite of knowing me for twelve years or so, you still do not understand a fundamental element of my character? When Pavese is displeased or bored, suffering from indigestion or a flea-bite, he can't let anyone else be happy and contented, and does his best to spoil their peace of mind. It's just the way he's made. That's why he says he's feeling fine, even though he may be far from well.

I don't understand where you read that I was feeling discouraged. What does the word mean anyway? Being in torment is something else, as you very well know. Would you advise me to go on working? Actually I need no advice. In four months I've written fourteen poems, seven of them being beyond praise.

In strict confidence I will add that I'm well and am treated with every courtesy. I'm being paid for doing nothing, and, in short, am enjoying my ideal way of living. If I have periods of boredom, they add to my importance. There's only one thing I lack, and it's because of this that I'm sometimes irritable. I can hardly explain to a married man just what it is I miss. If you haven't understood my problems in twelve years, you never will.

I have heard from you, your father-in-law and my sister that you have all been sent advice notes, confirming the publication of my *Lavorare stanca*. I still can't convince myself that the book is coming out at all. When a man writes the finest poetry of the century, his agony is necessarily long drawn out.

P.

Brancaleone, 23rd December 1935

Dear Maria,

Yesterday a new prisoner arrived here, a gipsy girl, far advanced in pregnancy, who offered to tell my fortune. There are two women in my life, she said, one a long way off who is dying for love of me, the other close at hand, but so far unknown to me. 'Cross my hand with silver,' she went on, 'and I will foretell your whole future.' I replied that I already knew enough about that. So this pretty little mother-to-be spoiled my day.

Several evenings lately a group of herdsmen or boys in filthy rags have congregated outside our main gate and raised a terrible din with horns, bagpipes, flutes and triangles, to honour the *novena.* Yesterday they were due to be paid. Some pious women give them a meal of meat and macaroni, or a bag of dried figs, oranges or some other treat. As for me, I had to wipe a tear away with the back of my hand. This for me was my Christmas festivity.

I have received the package you sent me, with a list of the contents. Nothing was missing. With my asthma I cannot drink spirits, so I make do with sucking sweets. I note that the salami are from Irma. Thank her from me and tell her those salami were the best of the lot. All the rest was from you, I suppose, or are there any other donors I ought to thank?

I'm not expressing my thanks to you because you would be forever nagging me about the cost of it all and the transport charges. I've become quite resigned and have been considering castrating myself. Then I should no longer feel I was missing anything.

Cesare

Brancaleone, 26th December 1935

Dear Maria,

It's a year since I felt as happy as I do today. I'm not surprised that you and certain dull-witted friends of mine imagine me thinking out ways of getting my own back. I know human nature well enough to feel sure that when some poor devil with nothing else to do starts grumbling or giving vent to his feelings, his relatives and dear friends will seize the opportunity of saying in chorus: 'What a silly fellow he is, so weak, so bad all through. He can't even put up with the consequences of his own actions.' What they should really say is: 'At last we've found an excuse to free ourselves from our natural embarrassment at the trouble he's in. Now we can regard him as a rogue and thus become his judges.'

I'm not complaining about it. I'm an ordinary kind of fellow. It's highly unlikely that some miracle should bring me into contact with people of more than average intelligence. If in my letters I mention certain things when you expect me to say something different, I'm sorry, but I cannot change. I tell you things I consider important and the rest can go hang. Any man in the whole solar system would do the same. You give me all the local gossip—Franco's wedding, for instance—and it makes me foam with rage. If you would only stop to think for a moment what that sort of thing means to me, placed as I am! It nearly drives me mad! So why should I stop to consider what I should or should not write to you?

However, I won't write you any more exasperating letters. It would be pointless, anyway, as so many other things are. I won't even write to Serralunga. I'll just include in my next letter a card addressed to our grandparents for you to send on to them as from Turin, to bolster up their blissful illusion as to my present whereabouts.

Cesare

1936

To Luigi Sini, Turin

[Brancaleone] 5th January [1936]

Dear Luigi,

I have read your letter with much the same blend of curiosity and awareness of something unusual that one feels when the parish priest comes to arrange details of a funeral, a wedding or a baptism. I would never have believed you were such a stickler for traditional ecclesiastical observances!

You tell me how you have transformed your little room into an attractive studio where you can please yourself what you do. You are full of Christian humility, peace of mind and hope—precisely the qualities that the parish priest would recommend to a parishioner suffering, for instance, from venereal disease.

Naturally I appreciate fully your intention to cheer me up, but it's no good. I have two sorts of trouble, one physical, such as my asthma (and it would certainly take more than a compliment to relieve me of that), the other physical-moral—the lack of company—which nothing can alleviate except the presence of other people. An insoluble problem. Let's leave it. From now on I shall say I'm well, then there will be no need to say more.

I note that you're slaving away like a dog at the office. Do you really think it's worth-while making all that effort to become such a highly respected citizen, when it absorbs your whole life? I don't envy you in the least, nor do my fellow prisoners. My troubles are mere trifles compared with what you have to suffer. You're precisely the sort of man for whom *Lavorare stanca* was written. Go and buy a copy, read it and find out how many ways there are (all legitimate) of enjoying a good time and cocking a snook at your department head. But how stupid of me! I was forgetting you are a department head yourself.

Wishing you every advancement in your career, I thank you for your letter and send greetings to you and your suffering family.

Your
Cesare

To Maria, Turin

[Brancaleone] 16th January [1936]

Dear Maria,

I received your card of the 1st, also the two American books *Tragedy of Lynching* and *Treatment of Delinquency*. Both of them are now wet with tears, as is the bread I eat. If I may be allowed to make a gentle reproof, sending me such books about American delinquency, with vivid details of prison treatment and electric-chairs, is not the best way of keeping me happy. Overcoming my instinctive repugnance I will, however, read and summarise them.

You hope my asthma will soon be better. So do I. It's a month and a half now since I've been able to write any poetry. A great disappointment to me.

I find much to console me here. For example, I'm collecting pretty coloured stones on the beach, studying the flight of birds, waiting for the cuttlefish season to begin and choosing a name for each of my sons, whom I shall bring up in strict chastity, for chastity is the first virtue of all. Unquestionably my sons will be chaste and very handsome.

Cesare

[Brancaleone] 4th February [1936]

Dear Maria,

Take pity on a man who has not slept all night, because of :

(1) Dreadful pain in the penis, due to an oedema
(2) A bad attack of asthma
(3) The need to prepare a statement declaring my relationship to any member of my family to whom I write letters. If I also wish to write to anyone who is not a blood relation, I must

first obtain permission from the Honourable Minister, stating the purpose of my letter.

(4) Some time ago I sent in an appeal, as you advised me to do, but so far have had no reply.

(5) Now, on 3rd February, I have received a communication stating that the Appeals Commission has rejected my petition of 20th July.

Try to remember me.

Cesare

To the Minister for Home Affairs, Rome

[Brancaleone] 7th February 1936

Sir,

On 3rd February I was informed that a regulation now exists requiring a political prisoner to obtain permission from your department before writing to anyone other than a member of his family, giving names and addresses of any such correspondents and his reasons for doing so. I therefore request permission to correspond with my lawyer, Alberto Carocci, Via Maggio 13, Florence, a director of the publishing firm Edizioni Solaria.

This firm is publishing a volume of my poetry and I need to keep in touch with Signor Carocci to maintain the necessary contact and be able to deal with any emergency that may arise.

In addition I request permission to correspond with Mario Sturani, Via Cassinis 55, Turin, a close friend of mine since boyhood; also with Professor Augusto Monti, Via Napione 5, Turin, with whom I have maintained a cordial friendship ever since my school-days when he was my teacher.

Trusting that my requests will be given sympathetic consideration,

Your obedient servant,

Cesare Pavese

[Brancaleone] 15th February [1936]

Dear Maria,

I have received your cards of 20th January, 29th January and 2nd February, a letter from Sturani and one from Monti, with nothing much in any of them. By the same post, however, someone sent me a present, a copy of that novel by Stendhal I wanted so much, a gift that moved me deeply.

For some time now I've been rather afraid my poems might give rise to a certain amount of discussion, and I'm extremely sorry about it. Can a book be much good if students from here and there, journalists and all the ragtag and bob-tail of the literary world describe it as 'an exquisite, romantic expression of what life means to an artist and observer'?

I could not check the final proofs myself, and rather fear there may be several errors. I don't yet know whether I shall be allowed to write to Sturani and Monti, so would you please thank them both for their letters? I know Sturani feels somewhat overshadowed by my success, so tell him I'd far rather be able to spend my nights in bed with my wife, as he can, than win fame as the author of this book. Most young fellows of my own generation seem to have no idea how dreadful life can be, so tell him he's the only one who understands what I'm trying to convey. Monti has a lot to say about my 'good intentions', but he has fallen into an error I should never have expected a teacher like himself to entertain for a moment. He has confused biography with aestheticism, praising certain poems for their documentary value, not for their merit as poetry. It is true that they record my personal reactions to the excruciatingly painful crisis I was living through at the time. Now I am recovering, but any relapse could be fatal.

Cesare

[Brancaleone] 25-28th February [1936]

Dear Maria,

I have your note of the 17th. The book, Richard Hughes's *The Spider's Palace*, is in the bookcase, rebound in green.

I feel very depressed and will try to describe my condition as well as I can. I'm like a man with a thick crust partly torn away but attached to his flesh by wires. It is terribly painful, for every movement—even breathing—jolts the wires connecting the crust to his body and makes him cry out in pain. One solution would be to tear away the crust firmly, and this I do *every* day. But the crust renews itself, pulling on the wires and causing great pain. This little game has been going on for nine months already, and the sores make me writhe in agony. If I seek consolation by thinking of the past, the same crust obliterates my memories. I cannot cut short my sufferings by the old method of suicide, because of the theory that even after death that crust persists. If I keep still it hurts me, and if I move the pain gets worse. For the last two months I haven't had a moment's peace. Even washing and dressing myself is an ordeal. Think kindly of me,

Cesare

Note: We have a beggar here, Ciccio by name, who at one time was a head-waiter in Reggio. His eyes are bright and very quick. His face is covered with curly hair. Six years ago he was driven mad and has been sleeping on the ground. When anyone gives him alms, he spends it on smoking and drinking. We have long conversations that have shown me how boring a cuckold can be. He cannot understand why a man like him, good-looking and young (he's thirty-eight now), should have been deserted by his faithless wife. After it happened he wandered about for days without eating or sleeping, and it drove him mad. The curious thing to me is that he still mourns for his wife and holds long, imaginary conversations with her, his beard bobbing up and down all the time. I almost forgot to tell you that on 21st I sent in another request for clemency. You have to keep on at them.—Ces.

[Brancaleone] 2nd March [1936]

Dear Maria,

When a man who should be writing poetry writes letters instead, he's finished. Memories can be cruel. I put my nose outside of an evening and look up at the constellation of Orion, so clear and limpid I remember a book I read a long time ago. I breathe the scented air at the window, and remember the period, two years ago, when I taught in the school at Corradino.

A train rushes by, reminding me that tomorrow morning one of the four that pass daily will go through the pinewoods of Viareggio. I gaze at the distant mountains and shiver with cold, remembering the three days I spent there—it seems three years now. I undress to go to bed and feel pity for my naked body, so young and beautiful and so much alone.

I go out as early as possible in the morning and remember how I used to go to the café at dawn, smoking my pipe and waiting for something to happen, reading in the *People's Gazette* about the films being shown in Turin, gazing for a quarter of an hour at a time at a view of the Gran Paradiso in a geography textbook. I finger a mole on my cheek to reassure myself of my own identity. I think back to the period when I was translating *The White Whale* and all my troubles were still to come. Once I stayed awake all night to brood over what I now know was a mild attack of jealousy, quite unaware of the pangs of hunger and pain the future might have in store for me.

I remember how furious I was with three fellows who wanted to come boating with me on the Po, and I mourn for my past unhappiness. What an utter fool I was to believe, as I did then, that personal isolation, even for a moment, would be bliss. These are the thoughts I turn over in my mind all day long.

To Giuseppe Cassano, Turin

[in reply to a letter
dated 8th June 1936]

Dear Sir,

I am delighted to have your letter, particularly because you must be taking my *Lavorare stanca* seriously, otherwise you would hardly have written me twenty pages about it, full of home truths you felt obliged to put before me. Naturally I have something to say in rebuttal when your view differs from mine. Even when you agree with me, I should like to add a word or two of explanation to certain passages you mention.

The most comprehensive attack you make against myself, as the writer of these lyrics, and against the characters introduced in them, seems to me a clear indication of your moral instability, especially of your sexual complacency. One critic may describe the book as a pleasant commentary, another may be convinced that what matters most in the world is intelligence and sound common sense. But you regard the book almost as a 'period piece', saying to yourself as you open it, 'Let's see what young people are doing nowadays, what they believe in.' But when you consider just one of those young people and see what he is doing, what his beliefs are, you shake your head in disapproval.

It may perhaps surprise you that one at least of the critics who reviewed my book is convinced it revealed to him his own moral taint, his weakness and lack of human kindness. If that is the general reaction it is not surprising that I should become highly unpopular.

In a way, books are like children. Once they are conceived and brought into the world, it is too late to change them. If you want better, you must start all over again.

As for your opinion of 'Deola' and 'Ritratto d'autore', the former expresses poetically an act of human kindness towards that unhappy woman. The second should record everything of interest about the author, not only his beard and his reputation, but also his ability to relax completely and spend the summer doing nothing at all. In all probability this is what moved you, as soon as you read it, to seize your pen and give vent to your moral indignation. So what is in question is not whether the poetry is good or bad, but whether one conception of life is better than another. I compliment you on having assessed so accurately the moral viewpoint of a man who loves luxury, and also for having brought home to me the fact that, to a cultured and intelligent reader such as yourself, the impression of ethical standards I meant to convey is not adequately stressed. In fact, though, my poems are not much concerned with ethics anyway.

If I were skilled in debate, or thought it worth my while to become so, I could readily counter many of your objections to some of my subjects—a woman treated as a machine, a mother despised by her swinish son, and so on. But this collection of poems should be considered as a whole. There can be no question that its moral *timbre* either rings true or sounds false. Obviously I have failed to convey to you a fair impression of a world that I once believed in, so I can only conclude that my work sounded false.

The idea behind my poems, expressed in abstract now and then for reasons of brevity, was to present a world of young men living happily enough, interested in the wonders of reality, moving around with an air of early morning freshness. They are not averse to giving a burst of laughter when they feel inclined, going swimming, enjoying a drinking-bout or (and why not?) having a good time with the girls. They like simple things, clear-cut situations, rest after work and work after rest. These young fellows are no longer adolescent, they know better than to regard young girls as angels, but they are not yet men, not ready to accept responsibility or undertake any constructive or complicated work.

The women in my book consider themselves as *'companions'*, meaning they are not merely instruments for occasional use. They are all unmarried and are friendly comrades. Sometimes their comradeship leads to marriage and maternity; often they find themselves betrayed, left to manage as best they can.

Later in my book I may have stated that women are of no account in family life. This does not mean that I regard my mother in that light. It simply means that at one particular period in life my gay young fellow clings desperately to his awareness of his strength and virility, a typical peasant tradition firmly established in the heart of every man in Piedmont.

This, then, was my ethical purpose in composing *Lavorare stanca*, presenting a 'landscape with figures', showing with simplicity and power, perhaps a touch of humour too, their virtues of sturdy optimism, their love of life and of all living things, their ready smile. I felt that my style should be in keeping with the purpose I had in mind, so I made it frank and straightforward, swift and masculine, shorn of every scrap of excess verbiage.

Why did I introduce certain low-down, common types? In the first place because they were all around me, and secondly because I found them congenial. There was a bond of sympathy between us. They moved and inspired me, as other types did not. To fire off one final broadside, I'll assure you you are quite mistaken in assuming that my poems are being praised in social drawing-rooms or literary clubs. Their atmosphere is too redolent of filth, wine and sweat, their sympathies are too involved, their situations too clear-cut for them to appeal to people of that sort. I only wish they did, but in fact these readers simply murmur 'How clever' and never read the same verse twice.

Having sorted out all that, let us return to your criticism: the moral tone of my work savours of perversion, rather than of sane thinking. I will be frank enough to confess that is what I've always been afraid of. I've always felt concerned about how frequently, how complacently, I touch upon erotic themes. I kept saying to myself: 'My words are as fresh and pure as water. There is no vice in them, no decadence.' But I could not free myself from the fear that these fantasies of mine served as an outlet for physical impulses. How could this question be answered? By waiting for the verdict of a sane and normal person, I told myself.

The verdict has now been given, and I accept it. Perversion it is. You, unbiased and with no axe to grind, are the oracle I was waiting for. Ethically, and therefore aesthetically, the book is not a success. It is ambiguous and far from clear. It must all be done again.

Since I have told you about the (shall we say) moral intentions of my book, it is obvious I did not write it to show off my own abilities, but out of my love of justice. That was my purpose, and I have succeeded in doing it. I hope that my explanation has thrown a certain amount of light on the text. I've been brooding over the pages of *Lavorare stanca* for too long (four years now), and have poured into it too much of my own youth to cast it aside like some bastard production. My somewhat vague apprehensions have found dreadful confirmation in your comments, and for this I thank you. If you were to ask me why my book was published, I could only beg you not to be so cruel.

I am hardly likely to visit the Vigna Allason in the immediate future, but with the whole summer before us, who can say?

Your
Pavese

1937

To the Minister in charge of Telephone Services, Turin

[Turin] 19th February [1937?]

Dear Sir,

In reply to your letter of February 13th I write to confirm what I have already stated verbally, viz. I cannot accept the statement made in your letter that my home should be classed as a professional studio, nor will I agree to change my subscription rate from the fifth category to the second.

Since I am a Doctor of Literature and an ex-political prisoner, I need hardly add that I am not a member of the National Fascist Party, nor am I listed in any professional register. I cannot discuss with you, even confidentially, what my activities may be in the future. Broadly speaking, I do a certain amount of literary work and am more or less dependent upon my sister, whose home I am sharing. She has been paying the telephone bill for this number, which includes my calls as well. I should perhaps add that while studying for my present academic status I have done a certain amount of translating, and have had a few literary articles accepted for publication, but I cannot see how this could be considered as a professional occupation or be connected with my use of the telephone.

A year ago your department treated me most courteously, allowing me a few months' grace while I was doing my best to find a co-subscriber for this party line, when I was called away unexpectedly for several months. It would distress me considerably should you reject my appeal and so force me to cancel my subscription, not as a reprisal but for the simple reason that my use of the telephone is hardly sufficient to warrant increasing the subscription rate from 380 lire to 1,070, as your letter suggests.

I am quite prepared to discuss the matter with you personally if you wish. Meanwhile I look forward to receiving your reply.

To Valentino Bompiani, Milan

Turin, 29th April [1937]

Dear Sir,

I am interested in *The Way of All Flesh*, by Samuel Butler, which as far as I know is not yet being translated into Italian, though possibly Enso Giachino may be considering doing it for Einaudi. If you care to enquire about this point, Einaudi would probably reply personally, as he generally does.

With kind regards,
Pavese

To Luigi Rusca, Milan

[Turin] 2nd June [1937]

Dear Signor Rusca,

Herewith the MS. of *Quattrini a palate* you asked me to send you early in June.

I have scrupulously followed the Ministry's instructions, anglicising Italian names, cutting out any references to Lenin or Soviet affairs and substituting fascist views, omitting or finding dignified equivalents for such terms as 'wog' or 'dago'. When I considered it necessary to make these changes I have indicated as much by enclosing in red brackets the corresponding words or phrases in the original English text I am sending you herewith. In my Italian version I have been careful to retain the democratic atmosphere of Mary French, Don Steven's travels in Russia and one or two other matters I considered should not be sacrificed.

From a literary point of view, this work has been sheer murder, but I flatter myself I have more or less succeeded in reproducing the tone of the original. My own work on *The 42nd Parallel* has been most helpful in this connection, enabling me to interpret the idiomatic phrases of North American English. However, some such terms have several different meanings, so I must reserve the right to amend them, if necessary, when checking the proofs. Please, therefore, make sure nothing is sent to the printers until I have approved it.

Cordially yours

To Valentino Bompiani, Milan

Turin, 9th October 1937

Dear Sir,

I have received *Mice and Men*, by Steinbeck, which seems good to me. Send me the contract on the terms already agreed. Re the delivery date, will the end of November suit you?

I must, however, make it quite clear that when dealing with such a book as this, full of colloquial expressions and conversations in dialect, I must be allowed complete freedom to employ comparable terms currently used in conversational Italian.

Cordially yours,
Cesare Pavese

To Valentino Bompiani, Milan

Turin, 13th November [1937]

Dear Signor Bompiani,

I have done my best to conform to your wish for an early completion date, bearing in mind that my previous commitments were already occupying most of my spare time. I usually send in my completed MS. well ahead of the agreed date—a strong point in my favour.

I am sending herewith the original English text for your perusal, but must ask you to return it to me together with the proof-sheets, in case I may need to reconsider the meaning of certain dialectal terms.

This volume, in my opinion, is beautifully written. I shall be happy if my Italian version manages to convey the same light-hearted atmosphere.

With my best respects and awaiting your acceptance,

Yours,
Cesare Pavese

To Valentino Bompiani, Milan

Turin, 30th December [1937]

Dear Sir,

I should be very glad to have information about my translation of *Mice and Men*, since the question of the payment due to me seems to be a secondary matter, less important than my correction of the proof-sheets.

Seizing this opportunity of expressing my good wishes for you in the New Year, I am sincerely yours,

Cesare Pavese

1938

To Enso Monferini, Ancona

Turin [January 1938]

Dear Enso,

I have often meant to answer your letter of last summer, but, as you know, pressure of work leaves me hardly time to breathe.

You gave me excellent advice, as far as it went. I should be sincere in everything I do and learn to accept responsibility. But you took no account of the influence of women or, rather, of one particular woman, on a man's life. The very thought of it drove me to make a half-hearted attempt to gas myself.

How are you? And your new 'friend'? Those happy days I spent at Ancona now seem incredibly remote. At that period I still had a shred of illusion and was deeply moved by the serenity of life in your home. I thought I could follow your example, but today I know I cannot. I still think enviously about your way of living. If a man's misfortunes stem from his own ignorance and weakness, if he is by nature incapable and lacks any vestige of common sense, how can he escape his own destiny?

This isn't a matter of moral sensibility. (As you know, I do not believe in any mystic divinity with supernatural powers). It's a question of understanding, of coming to terms with life and managing to get along, the very art of living, and I'm convinced that unless a man has acquired these aptitudes by the time he is eighteen, he will never get them at all.

I beg you to believe that as I write this I am not blinded by passion. Day by day I reach a better understanding of myself, and I have come to the conclusion that, but for the education I absorbed involuntarily, which taught me to be afraid, I should have become a common cutthroat.

To think I was dreaming only of marrying her, working and being faithful to her! Good sense tells me: if it hadn't been this girl, it would have been another. But I'm ready to swear that isn't true, if only because of the knife-thrust she gave me when she said that sexually I could not satisfy a woman. It would be pointless and indecent to explain it to you, but I know it is true.

Please, please, do not spread this story when writing to friends, not even with the well-meaning intention of having me examined by a psychiatrist or someone of that sort. I have already done everything possible and have nothing to add.

In November I found a little peace by working like a dog on three translations at once, feeling like a starving man chewing paper. To you, happy in your own home with your little son, all this will seem like an ugly film-script, but to me it's as real as a cancer.

When you reply to this letter, I should be grateful if you would refrain from making any reference to the matter. I'm writing to you as one would write an epilogue to a story, so as not to leave you in suspense, but I want no condolences, no sermons. I know how pointless they are.

Charity is useless, too, unless one has faith in God. 'If there is no God, nothing is forbidden.' Power is the only law. One can either live apart from the world (and how can that be possible, if it means remaining in the world?) or accept the rule of power. I'm a pessimist, too, this time seriously. If you can forget your home and children for a moment remember the conflagration of the '14-'18 war, which destroyed not only humble people like me but a whole generation of intellectuals who opposed the rule of force. My dearest wish would have been to join them. In short, I live with the idea of suicide always in mind. That is far worse than having actually committed suicide, which, after all, is simply a sanitary operation.

How I wish I could live a little while with you, as I did last summer, chatting with Ernesto and roaming around with you. Though I'm convinced that all human intercourse falls short of one's desire, I have a terrible thirst for friendship and communal living, a longing shared by all elderly spinsters. You might well be my ideal friend, but I'm not threatening to visit you, if only because I have work to do.

1939

To Luigi Berti,[1] *Florence*

Turin, 3rd April 1939

Dear Berti,

We haven't quite finished yet. The biographical write-up is excellent, but I think we should add, in brackets, the dates when the various books mentioned were first published, so as to give the reader a clearer historical perspective. The concluding sentences could be amplified a little. At present they seem unnecessarily brusque and consist mainly of a list of errata.

The Introduction seems to me rather obscure, with too many abstract terms. Fresh lines of thought follow one another in quick succession, leaving the average reader somewhat bewildered and by no means convinced. (I am referring, of course, to a reader who has not yet read *Esmond.*) Furthermore, though you explain to him certain anachronisms and other apparent anomalies, attributing them to artistic licence, you do so too briefly, too hurriedly.

What amazes me most is your unexpected desire for a hermit's way of life. From your letters and the articles you contributed to the *Nazione*, I was expecting something very different from you. I believe I told you so at the time. The function of a preface is to eliminate any misunderstandings, historical or aesthetic, as I did in the prefaces to my *Translations from Foreign Novelists*. You, dear Berti, could do much better and express your meaning with Tuscan clarity. Is it too much to hope that you will?

I've been discussing the possibility of translating one of Meredith's books and may start on it almost at once, since the translation I've been working on is just finished. I have carefully noted your own proposition, but cannot give you an immediate reply, as I would have wished.

Coming to the question of punctuation, I see from your letter, and from the many commas and full stops scattered all over your preface, that you are trying to introduce English punctuation

[1] Luigi Berti, a professional translator commissioned by the publishing firm of Einaudi, had just completed an Italian version of Thackeray's novel *Henry Esmond*.

into Italian. But I know from experience that punctuation can never be transposed as it stands. Even if the translation is literally correct, word by word, incorrect punctuation would make the book incomprehensible. There is a whole world of difference between English punctuation and our own.

With all good wishes

To Valentino Bompiani, Milan

[Turin] 7th May [1939]

Dear Sir,

I have received your book, *The Importance of Living,* which I already knew. Several times last year I thought of suggesting it to a publisher, but various things cropped up to prevent publication just then. I believe you have obtained permission to translate and I congratulate you, for it is a most interesting book, sure to be a hit.

Unfortunately I cannot undertake to do it now. When I first had your proposition in general terms I imagined it would be something like *Of Mice and Men*, which I would have been happy to do. This volume is so massive, and presents so many difficulties, it would drive me mad. I am already translating certain history books that keep me busy all day.

If you are really at a loss for a translator, may I give you the name of Mme Lidia Rho (Via A. da Bassano, 16, Padua). She has already given proof of her quality in a selection of stories by Poe, published by Utet in a series *Grandi scrittori stranieri* [Great Foreign Story-writers].

I shall always be happy to consider a proposition from you, when I have a moment to breathe.

Cesare Pavese

To Valentino Bompiani, Milan

[Turin] 14th May 1939

Dear Sir,

I have returned Brett Young's book to you at once, to save time. There must be some misunderstanding between us, I would be prepared to translate another book like *Of Mice and Men* (200 pp.), but not one of 750. I just haven't the time. It would need four months' intensive work, and actually I am already up to my eyes in translating history books.

I'm sorry this difficulty has arisen. If I may give you a hint (and if the translation rights are still available), you might well consider doing Faulkner's *The Unvanquished*, an excellent book from all points of view.

[*To Valentino Bompiani, Milan*]

[Turin] 17th June 1939

Dear Bompiani,

I must confess I know nothing about *In Dubious Battle.*[2] By Steinbeck, I imagine? If so, and if it is not very long, I should be happy to translate it this summer. Forgive me if I seem unco-operative, but I am extremely busy and I therefore hesitate to take on any fresh translations. When one is already producing fifteen pages a day, one is apt to regard a new proposition somewhat coldly.

However, if this book has the same terse style as Steinbeck's *Of Mice and Men* I will accept it. Can I see a copy?

Many thanks and cordial greetings,
Pavese

2 This novel by John Steinbeck was translated by Elio Vittorini and published by Bompiani in 1940, under the title *La Battaglia*.

To Tullio Pinelli, Bordighera

[Turin] 6th November [1939]

Dear Tullio,

Having made sure of your address, I am sending you the MS. of my latest work[3] and will enclose this personal note. I advise you not to leave it about where virgins and other innocents could read it. It calls for kindly broad-mindedness. This is the only copy, so take care of it.

Naturally I have already started writing another one and am reckoning on finishing it before the war makes martyrs of us all. Every morning when I wake up I say: 'So God is pleased to grant me another day.' It's a good thing for Him as well as me, since if we, His creatures, were no longer alive, who would there be to praise Him, bear witness to His greatness and glorify His name?

I am living through long, very mild days, misty yet bracing, the air suffused with golden or rosy light and the scent of vine-shoots. Such days make Turin a city peculiarly our own. We were born for her. Which does not rule out the possibility of my getting away from her, one fine day. I must be careful with the money I have coming in, or, better still, keep it in a safe.

So you're reading *Strange Interlude*. I'm glad you like it, and that you tell me so with such youthful enthusiasm. In my opinion, you would be wise to model your own style upon it, cutting out all excess verbiage and so developing a more trenchant method of expression. I myself find the need to do the same thing, otherwise my prose would be about as sharp as a bit of polenta.

I will take advantage of this opportunity to send my very kind regards to you, your wife and your children.

Pavese

[3] This was a translation of Eugene O'Neill's play, *Strange Interlude* (1928).

To Tullio Pinelli, Bordighera

[Turin] 4th December 1939

Dear Tullio,

I have very much enjoyed your critical essay, admiring yet again the versatility that allows you to pass so smoothly from one subject to another. You have stated supremely well, in a few sentences, matters that one of our long-haired professional critics would have rambled on about for half an hour. It seems you have acted on my recent advice to good effect!

Re *Paesi tuoi,*[4] I assure you it was not my main purpose to portray scenes of rural life, but rather to show the reaction of a town-dweller when faced with such crass stupidity that neither subtlety nor humanity nor legitimate self-defence can affect it in the least. This confrontation must be expressed at the obvious and crudest level, contrasting city and country. No matter if the cityfied atmosphere does not quite come over, it's enough that the shrewd city-dweller, convinced of his own cleverness, sees himself continually fooled by a stupid yokel.

Your own appraisement of this peasant world stems simply from the fact that you regard it as a place where corn grows thickly and the people are earthy and blind, yet they always get the better of an 'outsider', no matter what his resources may be. Which means: 'My countryside is beautiful, not because that statement is more or less true, but because it gives me the sort of backing I need for my real function in life, a battle of wits.'

In short, reverting to certain ideas I had, the work is symbolic. The characters and the atmosphere surrounding them are setting forth a little parable—the basic root of its interest and inspiration: the 'path of the soul' of my personal *Divina Commedia.* As for the way the characters speak, except for one or two instances of dialect that just slipped in, I presented their thoughts, their sneers and bewilderment as they themselves would have done, had they been able to speak Italian.

You had better send my notes back to me. I don't think I can come to you, it's a long way and expensive, and I don't know whether you'd be free. I'm slaving away at the office, because the firm is moving to fresh premises almost immediately in the Piazza

[4] Published 1941, and in English under the title *The Harvesters,* trans A. E. Murch (Peter Owen, 1961).

San Carlo. God has lifted a finger, and kingdoms and empires have crumbled into dust. Every day may be our last. That's totalitarianism. Anyone thirsting for that kind of justice will soon have more than enough of it. At the cinema I saw a film about Tiso, the President of Slovakia. He's very much like Don Brizio, only fatter.

Greetings to your wife and children.
To you I send my love.
Pavese

To Messrs Valentino Bompiani, Milan

Turin, 25th December [1939]

Dear Sir,

I acknowledge receipt of your courteous proposition of collaboration, but must first point out that I could not begin working on the book you suggest before March. In any case I could not send you the typescript of my translation until the autumn, particularly since I do not already know the book you have in mind.

I should, however, be delighted to collaborate with your firm, provided I find the volumes you suggest are congenial to me. If *In Dubious Battle* is that kind of work, and you are not dismayed by the difficulties stated in my first paragraph, then consider the matter settled.

Please give Dr Bompiani my cordial greetings when you have occasion to write to him.

Yours,
Cesare Pavese

1940

*To Gertrude Stein, Paris**

[Turin, 1940?]

Dear Miss Stein,

Your letter pleased me very much. Thank you for it and also for sending me *The World Is Round,* which I found delightful, an ideal adventure story, especially in its second half. It set me dreaming of the mountain and the chair. Of course, like all children's books, it is meant for grown-up people. What you call your 'commonplace style' (which is not commonplace at all) is admirably suited to a subject like this.

My foreword to *Three Lives* was simply intended to bring you to the notice of Italian readers, and I hope I have succeeded. Mr Einaudi is satisfied with it and, since you are also, so am I. Should you reply to this note, please include instructions as to where my bookseller should apply when seeking any available book of yours.

To Messrs Valentino Bompiani, Milan

Turin, 31st July 1940

First of all, let me thank you for *Piccolo campo*[1] which strikes me as a fine translation.

I have received *The Trojan Horse,*[2] a work I already know, and

[1] Elio Vittorini's translation of Erskine Caldwell's *God's Little Acre*. Government censorship compelled Vittorini to make several modifications to the original American text. Griselda became a servant; a reference to her breasts had to be altered to her legs; Vittorini's title, *Il piccolo campo del signore*, was considered unacceptable by the Ministry, who cut out *'del signore'*.

[2] By Christopher Morley, published 1937. Pavese's translation into Italian was published in 1941, after some delay because the Ministry of Popular Culture withheld authorisation for several months, and Pavese was forbidden to start work on it until official permission had been given.

I gladly agree to translate it. There are, however, quite a few problems to settle, for instance the chapter-headings in verse. Can you give me a ruling on this, or shall I do as I think best? Another difficulty, purely editorial this time, is the underlying note of parody, somewhat reminiscent of Shakespeare's *Troilus and Cressida.* How can we deal with this without upsetting the Italian reader?

I hope you have already made sure you will be allowed to publish this book? It deals with war, and has little to say in favour of nationalisation. I mention it in case the point has not yet occurred to you.

All being well, just send me the contract, allowing at least three months for completion. There's always the risk of my being recalled to the army.

With my thanks and cordial regards,
Cesare Pavese

To Fernanda Pivano, Turin

Turin, 22nd August [1940]

Holiday Task: Describe how you spent your holidays and state your plans for the future.[3]

What delightful bicycle-rides we enjoyed in the countryside around Turin! Every morning, as soon as I woke, I would telephone my friend Nando and arrange to meet him at half past ten, the time he usually gets up. I love to see him come rushing from his front door, almost always wearing something different from the last time. The colours that suit him best, I think, are white and bright red.

[3] Writing to his friend, Pavese jokingly presents his letter in the form of a typical schoolboy's essay, even to the extent of using foolscap paper with lines and a wide margin. His reference to 'Nando' really apply to 'Nanda', the nickname by which Fernanda was known to her friends.

We mount our cycles and Nando, who is much tidier than I am, always tucks in his trouser turn-ups very neatly. Then we make our way towards open country, pedalling away with all the breath we have and talking about our school-work, for during vacations we generally take a book with us. I often go about with Nando because I know I could learn a thousand things from him. He never talks nonsense or filth as so many young people do nowadays. When I'm with Nando we discuss our teachers and school affairs. Though we know one shouldn't poke fun at other people's misfortunes, we sometimes have a good laugh about some of our friends who have done no real work all the year, and now have to work all through the vacation frenziedly trying to catch up.

Sometimes Nando confides in me, especially when we've been pedalling along for some considerable time and stop for a rest, sitting on a low wall at the edge of a wood. (We call it our own little wall.) There we stay, close to the road and in full view of any passers-by. What would people say if they saw us disappearing among the trees? One must avoid even the appearance of evil, and some people are only too ready to spread malicious gossip. Nando and I decided, once and for all, never to hide away. Anything we do is done in broad daylight and bright sunshine.

As I was saying, at such times Nando talks to me confidentially, as I do to him. Some of the things he tells me are quite staggering! For instance, he'd like to stop his parents worrying about him, and come to terms with life and its perils for himself. He wants to marry, and feels he's wasted too much time already. I advise him to wait at least another year and finish his studies, but Nando gets all worked up and insists he will do as he says. I'm well aware that young lads like us get stupid ideas during adolescence, a period full of dangers and temptations. Nando and I are lucky to have got through it unscathed.

This idea of marrying has never occurred to me. I ask him with a smile whether he knows anyone he would like to marry. He lowers his eyes and looks thoughtful. 'That's a difficult choice,' he says, 'and all the rest of your life depends upon it.' One of his ideas struck me very forcibly. He thinks every school should run a course on betrothal and marriage, side by side with the usual curriculum. The professor in charge should be someone like our old Italian teacher, kind and paternal. A student who does well and completes this course satisfactorily would be declared fit to marry. There would be no women teachers. (I agree with this, because women of any age and status can do nothing but harm to an adolescent lad.) How I wish I could change my sex and become

Nando's girl-friend! I love him so much and would gladly marry him. But all I say in reply is that he must finish his studies so as to compensate his family and his teachers for all the sacrifices they are making for him. One fine day his parents will choose a wife for him. Nando pulls an ugly face, but actually he is well content.

I've just realised that you do not know Nando, so I will describe him. He's a sensitive, intelligent fellow. Seen in profile, he looks a man already, but face to face he looks very young. His great brown eyes reflect his laughter and bewilderment alternately. He is always very clean and tidy, unlike me, for sometimes I even forget to comb my hair. The mere look of him makes me feel good, eager to show myself worthy of him by studying very hard, so that next year I shall pass my exams with honours. Then we can spend our holidays together again and be happy.

Cesare Pavese

To Fernanda Pivano, Turin

[Turin] 20th October 1940

An analysis of F. and her attitude to love:

A girl who as yet knows nothing of love and sex, but has a secret, abstract idea of it that she doesn't really understand. She's like a man who has never known danger, and so has no knowledge of how he would react to fear. Can it be really true that she knows nothing about love? Certainly she has no experience of its ultimate expression.

Listening to her conversation, one becomes aware that she has built up for herself a sober way of life in which sex does not exist. If she were an ordinary girl, this might be simply a shiver of reluctance before taking the plunge, but F. is not at all ordinary. She has, for a long time, been aware of the social side of love and (even more to the point) has built up for herself a way of life based on her own sense of responsibility. She can take a stand, make her own decisions and work out an active part to play. I'm not referring to the gay, 'worldly' social life that attracts all young girls in her position, to a greater or lesser degree, but to the life she has evolved for herself, expressing her own taste and spirituality in sport, music and study.

She sometimes says she is too 'mannish', firmly believes that real friendship is possible between a man and a woman, discusses other people's love-affairs with unbiased frankness and is always talking about 'femininity'. She is not being 'bold', as pert young girls so often are nowadays. She 'confesses' personal things, too, such as 'I don't like cats, because I should suffer so much if I lost them'; 'Three men have said they loved me dearly'; 'I feel soft and damp. I know someone is making a plaster cast of me. It must be that man we saw.'

Her confession about cats is quite significant. She is terrified of becoming attached to any living creature, and this is important. It shows that her 'shrinking' is not an affectation, derived from her virginity, but a painful confession of weakness, a fear that, for her, love will mean loss of control, taking a plunge, not into the unknown but into a vortex of passion. This is not the voice of inexperience, but rather of a realisation that she is capable of complete dedication. She recognises that love is of the highest importance, totalitarian, and trembles at the thought of falling short of that standard.

F. is not a 'good-time girl'. Or is she? This is the problem that only a great step forward can solve. There are the clearest possible reasons against it: first, her education, her inner sincerity, her sense of a person's overall value. But other considerations are in favour of it: her intellectual brilliance, her enjoyment of sport, and particularly her awareness of her own great worth, side by side with her doubts as to whether her value will ever be realised.

How will F. end up? For her, more than for another girl, that will depend on whom she meets. An ordinary girl living with her family knows perfectly well what her own future will be. She may be more or less happy or unhappy in her marriage, but that in no way affects the importance she attaches to herself and her social status.

Fernanda is different. She will always be the outstanding personality in any group she joins—a serene mistress of her household, a lonely matriarch, the central figure in a scandal. Her view that 'sex does not exist' (though she's always talking about it), is primarily a confession of failure and resentment. Evidently F. needs a masterful man and has not yet found him. Her home life adds to her disillusion, for her father is a typical poor-spirited little man. The most enigmatic member of the family is her mother. Perhaps

F. sees in her a forecast of what her own fate may be if she marries the wrong man. Her mother never complains of her own condition yet, all unawares, she has convinced F. that this is the normal position of married women.

Hence F.'s determination never to give herself to any man. It's as though she says: 'If Mama, who is so good, so understanding, so amenable, has made such a poor success of marriage, how could I do any better?' Something F. said to me one evening struck me very forcibly: 'Mother tells me that *all* men are faithless to their wives.' Her tone was so resigned, so subdued, so free from resentment, that it instantly reminded me of how my own mother used to speak. Much of F.'s restlessness and petulance stems from the placid, melancholy way her mother talks. F. tests all her plans for the future by comparing them with what she thinks her mother (whom she loves) would approve. The reaction is always discouraging.

Hence the characteristic pose F. adopts of being foolhardy and always 'on the go', an instinctive defence against the strangeness of the world, especially the world of men. Fundamentally, she is trying to create an imaginary picture of the man she might fall in love with tomorrow. She would like him to be open-minded, happy-go-lucky, smartly dressed and sufficiently 'virile' to satisfy her own longing for tenderness and understanding. She is trying to allay her own instinctive dread of a 'grand passion'.

F. believes that men are born for action. They are useful and practical, capable of organising themselves and their social life. In all this she tries to imitate them. The error implicit in this course of action is that she sacrifices her delightful (and in her case irresistible) feminine charm. Actually, real men are not active, but contemplative; dreaming of action, but not putting it into practice; not 'sociably inclined', but (the best of them at least) preferring to be alone.

In view of all this, she will probably marry (as late as possible) some puppet or other who has no idea of what solitude is, and who will never realise what a treasure he has won.

If I'm wrong, forgive me.

C.P.

To Fernanda Pivano, Turin

[Turin] 5th November 1940

Dear Fernanda,

Don't worry over your troubles. We all have them. I'd like you to read this analysis of myself that I wrote during the worst days of October. You will see how one can find peace and comfort simply by trying to *understand* what is happening.

If sometimes it seemed I was giving you the cold-shoulder, you will see I was really cold-shouldering myself. That's how one can make progress. The pages I enclose will tell you such shameful things that you will quite understand I had no ulterior purpose when I wrote them. I give them to you out of friendship, for I am still very much your friend.

Pavese

[Enclosure, dated 25th October 1940]

Analysis of P.:

Without any doubt, P. is an unusual man, which does not mean a man of any importance. He has traits that clearly show his unconventional ways, his lack of any social routine, the facility with which he can up-anchor and be off, but at the same time he has a capacity for concentrating on one particular thing—work or passion—that allows him, if only occasionally, to achieve results and acquire some self-assurance.

His fundamental tendency is to give his actions a significance far beyond their actual importance; to regard his days as a sequence of individual moments, each with its own value. Hence, in anything he does or says, P. reveals his dual personality, one sharing in a human drama, the other, more intimate, seeking to discover some symbolic significance in his actions. This 'duality' is in fact a reflection of his capacity for writing poetry.

Though P. is convinced that Art and Life are two quite different things, and writing as much a job of work as selling buttons or digging a garden, he still regards his existence as some huge spectacle arranged for his benefit. When a man does that, it generally means he is not taking it seriously, but P. plays his part in deadly earnest, with the air of a tragic poet mingling in person among his characters, to kill or be killed.

A spectacle is a public display. Herein lies P.'s worst fault. After spending an evening drinking with friends and feeling he is being overlooked rather than admired, he decides to let himself collapse in the street, simply to make himself the centre of attention. I remember once that, when set on his feet again and held up by his friends, he wept with rage because he had not seemed 'pitiful' enough.

P. is undoubtedly a solitary man. As he grew up he learned that nothing worth-while can be done except at a distance from the world of commerce. He wants to be alone, and is, but wants to be so inside a circle of people he knows. He wants to feel, and does, a deep attachment for certain persons, so deep that he cannot find words to express it. Then he torments himself day and night in search of those words and complains that he cannot 'communicate' and has lost his powers of 'self-expression'.

What can a man like that do when he encounters love? Obviously, nothing. (Or rather, a number of extravagant things that amount to nothing.) Once in love, P. will do just what his innate laziness suggests, i.e. nothing. He will let it be understood that he is no longer master of himself, that nothing in his day matters as much to him as the moment of meeting the one he loves. He pours out all his innermost thoughts to her and never remembers to put her in such a position that any attempt to leave him would compromise her, the first elementary precaution of a libertine. So he ignores the tactics of love and ruins himself completely. He forgets to love the girl for herself and instead reveals all his inner life to her. When he is in love he is physically incapable of approaching any other woman—a weakness that no woman, not even the one he loves, can forgive. Why such naïveté? Obviously he is mounting the stage like an actor of the old school and playing out the drama with intense seriousness. He hopes this proves he is noble, so, symbolically, are his actions. In short, he makes an idol of her, worth the sacrifice of his life and his powers, great though he thinks they are.

But who asks him to make such a sacrifice? The kind of woman who expects a man to cast aside all restraint, every scruple, and make love to her with the pointless cosmic intensity of a thunderstorm in August. In other words, a 'vamp'.

What P. really needs is the love of a wife to whom he can give his whole heart. This frenzied longing for a home and a life he will never have, found its expression in an arrogant phrase that P.

used one day, when a certain love-affair (by now too well known) was at its peak: 'The only women worth the trouble of marrying are those a man cannot trust enough to marry.'[4] It's all there, a vamp and frenzy, a wife and an unshakable dream. P. is, as it were, crucified on this dream, and nothing could be more pitiful than the struggles he makes to free his hands from the nails. Since he knows he is a captive, unable to move or free himself, any prospect of a new passion makes him tremble.

P. has a vivid imagination, and merely to envisage such suffering is to feel physical torture. When over-sensitive men feel the same pain it is generally only for a short while, but P. is not an ordinary man. Some years ago he endured this agony for three months on end, feeling as if breast and heart were being torn away.

That's what happens to a passion as it dies, but that is natural. With P., passion becomes merged into his poetry. It becomes the very flesh of poetry and so identifies itself as a breath of fantasy.

P. regained his stoic philosophy by renouncing every link with humanity except the abstract one of writing. He felt stunned, bent his head, tried to write, but month after month, year after year, he wrote less and less. His life was being drained away, yet he held firm to his purpose, knowing that for him to mingle again with his fellow men and women, or even with one, would be a relapse not a rebirth.

Nevertheless, he let himself be swept away once more, and though he tried to stop half-way, he could not. With him it was all or nothing. Now he has to suffer for every moment of the fictitious loneliness he created for himself. In revenge, Life has brought him real loneliness.

To Messrs Valentino Bompiani, Milan

Turin, 5th November 1940

Dear Sirs,

Here is my translation of *The Trojan Horse,* which I have managed to finish before the due date. I have not had it typed, thinking that would save time. I know you want to get it out quickly. (I have written it as legibly as I could.)

[4] Cf. entry for 30th September 1937 in Pavese's diary, *This Business of Living* (p. 42).

As you will see, I have made two or three changes in the text, because a literal translation, especially of the introductory verses and the references to Chaucer and Shakespeare, could not convey the delicate subtlety of the original. The Italian reader might even find it meaningless, or a stupid parody. However, we can discuss it if you wish.

For now, I'll take the opportunity of sending my cordial regards,

Pavese

1941

To Mario Alicata, Rome

Turin, 28th April 1941

Dear Alicata,

Messrs Einaudi have shown me their correspondence with you, and I quite realise your time must be very fully occupied with organising the forthcoming series—the Struzzo Library.[1] Since the first volume to be issued will be one of my own stories, I can hardly presume to praise the project too highly, but I feel sure that you and I, working together with a certain amount of skill and intelligence, should manage to make a good thing of it. After all, we can still call ourselves 'young fellows' for a year or two longer. However it goes, I'm happy to have this opportunity of corresponding with you.

Here in Turin we live completely out of touch with the world. A literary man, born anywhere else in Italy, would have ample time to make a name for himself, become an editor with a public of his own or even change his job before we so much as heard of him. The advice and help you can give us from Rome will be invaluable in this connection.

Keep your eye open for clever new writers. (I'm told the city is swarming with them!) Preach the art of telling a good story well, particularly the kind of narrative that uplifts and inspires the reader, such as you 'wheelers'[2] regard as your special province.

Einaudi's idea of limiting us to 'short romances' seems good to me, since it excludes any tendency towards a flood of 'omnibus' volumes, I take it to mean that literary style is of the first importance. Also, on reflection, that writers of 'short stories' and whimsical essays are excluded. I don't at the moment quite see why Einaudi proposes to republish rare or forgotten books that are not strictly narratives, but doubtless you'll give me your views.

[1] The 'Struzzo Library', a project just promoted by Einaudi, was to comprise a series of contemporary novels by Italian writers. The first volume, due out in May 1941, was Pavese's *Paesi tuoi*.

[2] A group of anti-fascist intellectuals, led by Alicata, had begun to express their political views in the Roman literary review, *La Ruota* ('The Wheel').

By the way, Einaudi intends offering a prize of 500 lire for every Italian author whose 'romance' is accepted by our consultative body in Rome for this series. You agree, I imagine?

With cordial greetings,
Pavese

To Giambattista Vicari, Rome

Turin, 22nd June 1941

Dear Sir,

I thank you for your very kind review, and your cordial note.

Your suggestion of publishing my work in volume form is most flattering, but there is a difficulty: the two long novels I could let you have now are, first a presentation of my life in prison (in '36), and second a story of lesbianism which is not precisely 'up to date'.[3] The first has something good about it, but it says too much of prison life.

Re translations, the only foreign language I know is English, and even that is none too pure. At the moment I've had to lay aside all translation and devote myself to creative work of my own.

Yours,
Cesare Pasese

[3] These were, respectively, *Il carcere* (The Prisoner) and *La bella estate* (The Beautiful Summer), published in one volume in English under the title *The Political Prisoner,* trans W. J. Strachan (Peter Owen, 1955; repr. 1969).

To Mario Alicata, Rome

[Turin, July 1941]

Dear Alicata,

I'm pleased with your review, especially the historical part. It's the most comprehensive one that has appeared, so far. American critics are somewhat cautious and link it with *Lavorare stanca*, which actually is a better book. They seem amazed that my 'tramps' are not all 'scroungers', nor are all my women characters 'blonde'. They also want precise information about my 'personality'.

Thank you very much for studying my work so closely, and for expressing your warm approval of it.

Yours very sincerely,
Pavese

To Alberto Carocci, Florence

Turin, 12th July 1941

Dear Carocci,

After discussing my work with Einaudi, I find I rather like the idea of republishing my *Lavorare stanca* in a revised and augmented edition. It would then serve as a kind of final summary of my poetic years, for I have given up all hope of writing more.

Would it, do you think, be possible to persuade Parenti to relinquish whatever rights he has in the first edition, naturally provided I indemnify him for any copies still on hand? I'm rather afraid this may amount to a good deal, so I haven't ventured to suggest it to Parenti myself, for he may well consider there is no justification for a new edition. Now I'm with Einaudi, the book could be presented as my farewell to youth before passing on to more serious things.

If this would not offend anyone's sensibilities, I should be most grateful for your opinion. If you consider I have 'room to manoeuvre', I would write to Einaudi and Parenti, making it official.

All good wishes,
Cesare Pavese

To Giambattista Vicari, Rome

Turin, 12th July 1941

Dear Vicari,

Forgive the delay. I've been thinking over, at some length, your courteous suggestion that it might be worth-while for me to glance at the possibilities of writing crime fiction, but I think it would not be practicable.

Instead, I am sending you the first ten pages of a short novel to be called *La spiaggia* [The Beach],[4] just a couple of chapters, but in my view they have 'body' and would hang together. See what you think.

Cordial good wishes,
Cesare Pavese

To Fernanda Pivano, Ancona

[Turin] Monday [August 1941]

Your letter about the gipsy has a different air about it—or am I wrong? A suggestion of ploughed fields and lands beyond the sea. It seems only yesterday we were on the hills together and you said to me: 'There's something about those pine trees, something formidable.' But all I could see was your head against the background of palms or the meadows of paradise. Nothing can be lovelier than to be alive against a background of antiquity. How well I remember watching your head, so full of life against the background of those marvellous subdued colours! You told me the sea was worth watching too, particularly in the midday heat, when it looks as cool and fresh as a lagoon.

You remember the letter I showed you, the one from a girl who said she admired me? She had the nerve to telephone me! A fat

[4] Published in English in one volume with *Fuoco grande* (A Great Fire) under the title *The Beach,* trans W. J. Strachan (Peter Owen, 1963). *La spiaggia* was first published in 1941; *Fuoco grande,* written in collaboration with Bianca Garufi, posthumously in 1959. See p. 238 *n.* 1.

lot of good it did her! I realised instantly what a terribly bad Piedmontese accent she had. Her very sighs seemed in dialect. She told me she had a whole gallery of modern paintings and often entertained well-known writers in her home. She added that she owned various cinemas in country places around Turin and could arrange a free pass for me! So much for my gipsy!

Fernanda, my dear, I'd gladly exchange a whole gipsy camp for a chance to be with you again on the beach of San Marino, spending another afternoon like the one I remember so well. Do you think of it sometimes? Really?

To Giambattista Vicari, Rome

[Turin] 15th August [1941]

Dear Vicari,

It's now settled that *La spiaggia* will appear in instalments. Actually it's too short to fill a volume—only about sixty pages in typescript. Instead, would you consider accepting another romance for your *Lettere d'oggi* [Today's Letters]? I enclose the opening pages for your consideration, but please take good care of them. I have no other copy. It deals with lesbianism and other filthy practices. The title will be *La tenda* [The Pavilion].[5]

If you think it a practical proposition, I'd be grateful to have your views. Please send this MS. back to me at once.

Yours sincerely,
Cesare Pavese

[5] Pavese changed the title to *La bella estate*. Cf. *n.* 3 above.

To Giambattista Vicari, Rome

[Turin] 25th August [1941]

Dear Vicari,

I find that *La spiaggia* is in fact shorter than I told you, speaking from memory. It is not about 60 pages, but only just over 40. This rules out any idea of making it into a book. I have absolutely no other stories that could be put with it. They have already appeared in various journals, and reviews of them are still coming in. It would be ridiculous to reprint any of them so soon. Send back to me the MS. of *La tenda*. I have changed my mind about it.

Now I have a proposition to put to you. A young woman writer,[6] who at one time wrote for *Solaria,* has entrusted to me certain novels she would like to have published under a pseudonym. (They deal with racial problems, you understand.) Could you find time to glance at them? Perhaps even publish them? They seem very good to me. If you are interested, I'll send you one or two.

With warm thanks for all your kindness,
Cesare Pavese

To Giambattista Vicari, Rome

[Turin] 13th December [1941]

Dear Vicari,

I have received the MS. of *Mio marito* and will send it on to the author. Now I've put you in touch with one another I seem to have lost interest even in my *Casa al mare*! [House by the Sea].

[6] This was Natalia Ginzburg, wife of Pavese's friend Leone Ginzburg, who became leader of the resistance movement in Turin. He was arrested and interned when war broke out, and died under torture in the Regina Coeli prison on 5th February 1944. For her novels Natalia chose the pseudonym Alessandra Tornimparte, and the first of her tales (published by Vicari), was *Mio marito* (My Husband).

As for the contract, will you draw it up for me? I should be glad if you would. Here are a few points that occur to me and details you asked me to send. You are to publish *La spiaggia*, by Cesare Pavese, who retains the translation rights and those of any other adaptation. As from two years after publication, any literary rights in the work will revert to the author. On publication, the author will receive the sum of 50 L. as an advance against his rights, fixed (as before) at 7% of the price of copies sold. A statement of accounts to be made in December 1942 and 1943. I think that's about all, except that I can claim the first ten copies printed.

You ask for details of work I have done to date, and certain personal information. I was born in 1908 at Santo Stefano Belbo and now live in Turin. I am a bachelor and have translated English and American works—seventeen in all—among them *Moby Dick*, by H. Melville; *Daedalus*, by James Joyce; *Moll Flanders*, by Defoe; *The Hamlet*, by W. Faulkner; and *Three Lives* by Gertrude Stein. In 1936 I published *Lavorare stanca*, a volume of poems that no one has yet noticed. I'm thinking of republishing it, revised and augmented, in a month or two. I collaborate with a few periodicals, notably *Messaggero* and *Lettura*. There's no point in my telling you my political views—you know them already.

Congratulations on having acquired the services of Giovanni Macchia as a contributor. I know some of his work that came out in *La ruota*, and he seems to me a fine man.

Cordially,
Pavese

1942

To Fernanda Pivano, Turin

[Rome, 6th February 1942]

Dear Fernanda,

It's cold here in Rome. No one came to meet me at the station last night and I had to wander round in the dark, up and down all those highways and byways, trying to find a bed for the night. In the end a charitable janitor telephoned all the other janitors he knew and found me a boarding house in the Via delle Quattro Fontane (doesn't that sound lovely?), where I was offered a more than matrimonial room with three beds. Take it or leave it! I took it. Since I was wearing new shoes for my visit to Rome, my feet were rubbed raw. I wandered up and down, trying to find the fourth fountain, and felt I was treading on my own bleeding heart.

I slept in the middle bed. I'm afraid I'll have to stay here till heaven knows when. My boss can be seen only on a Sunday or Monday. So far I've heard nothing of the 1,000 lire prize. The lady who keeps him fighting fit is in bed with an attack of bile. I haven't yet spoken to her, or indeed even seen her. Keep working at your translating.

I'll see you again, the first chance I get,

Pavese

To Fernanda Pivano, Turin

Rome, Sunday, 8th February 1942

Dear Fernanda,

I can't resist the temptation to write to you from this luxurious boarding-house. Not that I've anything new to say, except that I've got a touch of fever. So has everyone else in the place. The man I came to see went down with it today. His wife remains invisible, so do the 1,000 lire she is supposed to hand over to me. Anyway, with or without them, I shall leave here this afternoon.

Pavese

To Mario Alicata, Rome

Turin, 3rd March 1942

Dear Alicata,
The list of Japanese films you sent me is certainly unusual, with their dignified elders like those in Hirth's book.[1] The Chinese verses are simply pastiches borrowed from Paris, from *The Book of Jade*. Hearn has already been improved upon by Laterza, and I hardly think it's worth doing again. Three items, however, are interesting: Tsen Tsong Ming, Lin Yutang and *Popular Japanese Poems*. I should like to examine them, and can probably get the volumes on Thursday or Friday, when the principal will be here.

Cordially yours

To Mario Alicata, Rome

Turin, 14th March 1942

They'll probably slaughter Maupassant.[2] It's a splendid idea, though. If you do get permission you'll be doing very well. Naturally, the Ministry won't allow you to include his stories of the

[1] The German-born Friedrich Hirth (1845-1927) spent many years in the East, as an official in the Diplomatic Service. He wrote several books on oriental culture, notably *China and the Roman Orient,* to which Pavese is referring.

[2] An application to translate Maupassant's novels was already being considered by the Ministry of Popular Culture.

1870 war. Personally, I would advise cutting out *Bel Ami* as well. Keep on pestering them and stressing the great tradition of neo-Latin novelists.

Good wishes

To Mario Alicata, Rome

Turin, 2nd April 1942

Dear Alicata,

This doesn't seem to me a good time to translate *Father and Son*, by Edmund Gosse, or to adapt it for the screen.[3] From what I've read, I think it would bore Italian readers. Remember, too, that a great many pages are full of controversial subjects, as in *The Way of All Flesh*. Besides, why annoy Gaeta[4] unnecessarily?

Cordially yours

To Giulio Einaudi,[5] *Turin*

Turin, 14th April 1942

Respected Editor,

I have received six cigars, for which I thank you. I found them of such poor quality that I feel compelled to say I cannot continue to honour a contract initiated under such unpleasant auspices.

[3] Alicata had passed on to Pavese a suggestion made by Vittorio Gabrieli that this novel should be translated into Italian and used as a basis for a scenario.

[4] Gaeta was the official of the Ministry of Popular Culture responsible at that time for authorising the publication of any book and the preparation of translations of works by foreign writers.

[5] This letter, written as a joke, was a retort to a letter in similar vein, (dated 4th February 1942) from Giulio Einaudi to Pavese.

Furthermore, your never-ending demands for revision and all the other jobs you fob off on me, leave me no time to attend to more important matters. So, worthy Sir, the moment has come for me to tell you, with all due respect, that as long as you persist in exploiting the people who work for you, you cannot hope to get out of them better results than they are capable of producing.

We have a life to live, bicycles to ride, footpaths to explore, sunsets to enjoy. In short, Nature calls, and we must follow. Get somebody else to do the job on Bini.[6]

Cordially,
C. Pavese

To Elio Vittorini, Milan

Turin, 27th May 1942

Dear Vittorini,

I'm writing because I think you'll be pleased to hear we are all solidly behind you.[7] The whole value and meaning of the *Americana* lie in your notes. I've been studying American literature for ten years now, and have never before come across such a well-balanced and enlightening appraisal of it as you give in your *Piccola storia della cultura poetica americana* [Short History of Poetic Culture in America]. It is precisely because their poems generally tell a story, a romance if you prefer, that they are so informative.

Leaving on one side the soundness of individual opinions, based on so many intimate and well-informed monographs, I want to

[6] Pavese had been asked to edit, for a forthcoming issue of the Struzzo Library, a book by Carlo Bini—*Manoscritto di un prigioniero* (Manuscript of a Prisoner). Pavese was required to write an introduction to the book and also to provide all necessary footnotes.

[7] Vittorini had run into difficulty with his anthology of American poetry. It was published by Bompiani in March 1942, but since the work had not yet been approved by the censor (the Ministry of Popular Culture), it could not be offered for sale. A few copies come into Vittorini's possession and he sent one to Pavese.

applaud your delicate treatment of dramatic contrasts, corruption and purity, ferocity and innocence. It is not by chance, nor by an arbitrary decision, that you begin with abstract emotions and end with something very reminiscent (though unacknowledged) of *Conversazione in Sicilia* [Conversation in Sicily].

In this sense it is something grand. You have brought into it the intensity, the exclamations of delight, so typical of your own views on poetry, and providing controversial comparisons with literature in other parts of the world.

Naturally there are details I cannot agree with (e.g. that *The Scarlet Letter* is finer than *The Brothers Karamazov*, and some of your general comments on Whitman and Anderson), but the fact remains that in 30 pages you have written a fine book. I've no wish to flatter you, but for you this work has the same value that *De vulgari* had for Dante.

Till we meet again, dear Vittorini,
Cesare Pavese

To Fernanda Pivano, Turin

[Santo Stefano Belbo, 27th June 1942]

Dear Fernanda,

I'll send you greetings and all good wishes at once, in case I forget later. I want to talk to you about myself.

Always, but more than ever this time, I am deeply moved to find myself back among my native hills. Primordial fancies come to me, inspired by a certain tree, the house, the vines, the path, the evening light, the bread, the fruit. At a certain fork in the road there stands a large house with a red gate that creaks, and a terrace, green with the verdigris forever dropping from the pergola. My knees were always filthy from it when I was a boy. To gaze at those trees again, those houses, vineyards and footpaths, gives me the feeling of being caught up in a fantasy of extraordinary power, as though a complete understanding of them was quickening to life within me. I feel I am an infant again, but an infant rich in memories of sights and sounds from those early days. Not for nothing have I lived another twenty years since then.

I know my true purpose in life was to express all that in poetry. Not an easy thing to do. My first efforts were feeble, composed on stereotyped patterns, completely failing to reveal the individuality of those trees and this landscape as I knew them.

Having gone farther along the road that ends with a leap into the void, I know now that very different words are needed, different echoes from the past, different conceptions of their character. In short, they need to be expressed as myths. I thought it was enough to describe country people (psychoanalysed or transfigured, perhaps), but that is not enough. To describe landscapes is stupid. Such places, such crags and ravines, trees and vines are as much alive as people are, each with its own personality. They are mythical. That great hill, shaped like a woman's breast, is the very body of the goddess to whom, on St John's night, the traditional bonfires of stubble will rise. Now at last I understand the *Georgics.* I burn with love for them.

They are lovely, not because of their sensitive presentation of country life, but because they imbue a landscape with its own mythical reality, going deeper than its outward appearance and expressing, even in such actions as studying the weather or sharpening a scythe, an awareness of the presence of the deity who made it.

So long,
Pavese

PS. A pretty little mouse has been running up and down the balcony where I'm writing this. It is afraid to enter the beam of light from my lamp, but will get inside the house tonight.

To Mario Alicata, Rome

Turin, 12th October 1942

Dear Alicata,

I'm returning to you the MS. of Bacon's *Essays,* translated by one of your women contributors. The proposed selection seems to me unsatisfactory. The essays she has omitted, on 'Gardens', 'Plantations' and 'Fortune', are among the clearest, most vivid examples of Elizabethan English prose.

Her command of Italian is commonplace, lacking the style and resonance essential to any adequate rendering of Bacon's work. Still worse, the original text has been wrongly translated in at least ten places. (I have indicated them on the relevant pages of the MS.) From a Cambridge graduate, this is a bit too much. Personally, I would turn it down.

Cordially,
Pavese

PS. Have you heard any more about the *Spoon River Anthology*? We sent it (in manuscript) two months ago to the Minister, requesting permission to proceed.

To Fernanda Pivano, Mondovi Breo[8]

[Turin] 22nd December 1942

Dear Fernanda,

I'm glad to see, comparing your second letter with the one you wrote earlier, that you are recovering your normal spirits and clarifying your outlook on life. I don't know whether this is due simply to your physiological recovery, or to the fact that you are getting more accustomed to wartime conditions, or, frankly, to my own good advice. In any case, you are better, and I'm sure that if you will settle down to a working routine, you will be better still in the future.

I was particularly moved by your confession of submission. If that is true, if after all the war is to continue and will leave its traces on us all, I could almost feel thankful for the bombing and your own precipitous flight, because of the valuable experience you should derive from it.

Here, things are in the very devil of a mess. Even travelling to Rome is a chancy business, and who knows what will happen to the firm.

[8] After the bombing of Turin, Fernanda Pivano had taken refuge in the country district of Mondovi.

I remember with tenderness and regret my last trip to Mondovi. Regret because, if I'd only had the luck to walk arm in arm with you then, two years ago, I should have felt I could touch heaven with the tip of my finger. Now I'm older and far away from you. We are all evacuees now, clinging to one another for company, not for love.

After Christmas, say from the 28th to the 31st, I'm thinking of coming over to see you again. Remember me to your mother and the rest of the family.

See you soon,
Pavese

To Fernanda Pivano, Mondovi Breo

[Turin] Tuesday 29th [December 1942]

Dear Fernanda,

I meant to come to Mondovi this morning, but, instead, fever has come to me. I would have come all the same, for nothing can hold me back from my pursuit of beauty, but at the end of last week I had a most exhausting visit to Rome. For the present, at any rate, I must stay in bed.

Perhaps I shall see you if ever you come to Turin, and we can spend a Saturday or Sunday together. I must tell you that Einaudi will be all right. We have notices about not spreading rumours and taking care not to cause any panic. Hence the need for visiting our office in Rome, sending on material, organising the services we offer and all the rest of the commercial side. I'm working like a dog, and so are all the others.

Kind regards to your mother and the family,
Pavese

1943-1944

To Fernanda Pivano, Mondovi Breo

Rome, 7th January 1943

Dear Fernanda,

It seemed unlikely, but it has happened. The Minister of Popular Culture has given us permission to go ahead with the *Spoon River Anthology*. I haven't yet heard from the typing service, so I beg you to get hold of your own copy, in Turin, and send it on to me by registered express post. I believe the limitations on sending MSS. and printed matter through the post have been cancelled as from today, but find out and send it on as best you can. I must have it quickly, because—taking the rough with the smooth—I'm afraid of being called up for military service early in February and I'd like to have the book ready by then.

Excuse haste. Take care how you go, and read Kierkegaard's *Diary of a Seducer*, just republished by Bocca. You'll find it very useful.

Your
Pavese

To Fernanda Pivano, Mondovi Breo

Rome, Saturday 13th February [1943]

Dear Fernanda,

I've been thinking a good deal about my own affairs, and realise I'm no longer a little boy. If I were, I should have enjoyed or suffered many things, thought beautiful thoughts and spouted poetry. Instead, I was stolid, reserved, rational and polite. That's how grown-up men seemed to me and I envied them a lot. What a fool I was! Now I'm growing old, Fern. If I'm thinking of writing a novel, I turn it over and over in my mind, getting no pleasure from the story or from myself. If I think about love, it is in terms of a house, money, the future, my responsibilities. I'm an old man.

I feel like a father (though I don't know whose), responsible, boring, haughty. I was more intelligent, more adventuresome, when I was twenty-five. Then I wrote a book nobody would give tuppence for, though it was better than anything I've written since.

I've drawn up the contract for *Farewell to Arms.* Einaudi will sign it on Tuesday, I hope. Then we can get on.

The truth is, Fernanda, that I'm turning egotistical. I suffer dreadful pain and shall end up by calling a doctor in, to check up my liver, lungs, ribs and bladder. I no longer enjoy anything but the pleasure of eating and drinking, and am convinced that all one's spiritual life is conditioned by physical causes. They are a determining factor, like any other. To hell with them all. It means that one cannot write something beautiful simply by wanting to, nor can one find any pleasure in company.

I'm very unhappy, Fernanda. Still, I can send you a discreet embrace.

Pavese

To Fernanda Pivano, Mondovi Breo

Rome, 26th February [1943]

Dear Fernanda,

This is it! I'm called up and am to report at Rivoli on 4th March. I'll keep you informed. I shall be in Turin on the 2nd and 3rd. *Spoon River* is already in print.

Cesare Pavese

To Fernanda Pivano, Mondovi Breo

Rivoli, 9th March 1943

Dear Fernanda,

I'm still here, waiting to get through my medical at the hospital. I'm very pleased to know you at last have a house and a roof over your head, and shall hope to visit it soon. It's so long since I wrote to your mother that I daren't do so now. Give her my apologies and tell her how much I've had to do.

It's fine to stroll about, free as air. The other day I bought two mandarin oranges, annoyed a couple of girls and ended with a grand booze-up. I've been solemnly promised my uniform very soon. Then I shall be a magnificent little soldier. Is there any way to become an officer at once? That would be fine. Would you dare to refuse me again? I hope not.

Remember me. I think of you all the time, so very much.

Your own little Cesarino Cesare

To Fernanda Pivano, Mondovi Breo

[Rome] Sunday, 9th May 1943

Dear Fernanda,

It's hardly likely, I imagine, that you have handy the three poems I wrote in your honour in the days when I used to write poetry?[1] I'm preparing a second edition of *Lavorare stanca* and would like to add these to the rest. If you agree, please send me a copy of them, for I have none. If you say no, I admire your strength of character.

There's a dreadful row going on here because one of the women employed in the place was discovered indulging in the act of love with a male colleague, which gave rise to considerable scandal.

[1] These were: 'Mattino' (Morning), written between 15th and 18th August 1940; 'Estate' (Summer), between 3rd and 10th September 1940; and 'Notturno' (Nocturne), on 19th October 1940. They were included in the second edition of *Lavorare stanca* and will be found in English in the collection *A Mania for Solitude* (Peter Owen, 1969).

We've all been brought into it, and cleared of any involvement, apart from threats of blackmail.

In our digs, shared by five of us, three men and two women (all employed at Einaudi's office in Rome and sent here from Turin), we live an ideal life, occupied with domestic duties and congenial studies, getting on so well together that I'd never want to change it for matrimony, if only I had not already promised my hand. It's true enough that sex is the ruination of life, but it's also a great consolation. Don't underrate sex, Fernanda. It is the inspiration of literature and art, and inspires town-dwellers to love their country. Appreciate it. Write and tell me you do.

Your
Pavese

To Fernanda Pivano, Mondovi Breo

[Rome] Tuesday 25th [May 1943]

Dear Fernanda,

I've always known you are naughty and egotistical, but I'm not joking and am willing to run the risk.

Speaking of higher things, have you made up your mind to continue your studies or not? Nobody can get on in Rome without knowing another language. So-and-so did, if you remember, and she's stupid, but she has a husband who makes her keep on with translating. You have not.

I called in to see Cecchi, who was very complimentary about your translation of *Spoon River*. It's sure to be a success and you'll be quite celebrated.

Who are the smart young fellows you say are trying to scrape acquaintance with you? I want to know. I've never run after any girls. That's why none of them would have anything to do with me. When I'm seventy they'll be chasing me and I'll tell them with gusto: 'You should have made your mind up when you first had a chance.'

Dear Fernanda, when you refused to marry me, you at least took the trouble to make up for it by continuing your cultural studies and our friendship. You cannot understand as I can (now I'm pushing on towards fifty),[2] what it meant to me to have my arm around

[2] Pavese (b. 9th September 1908) was not yet thirty-five years old at this time.

my first love. Now my arms, empty and powerless, fall back against my breast. Don't think you can read a book when you're in your dotage. The fact that you're a would-be writer of elegant poetry will do nothing at all to attract young men then. Oh, marry that stationmaster of yours quickly and forget all about it.

Here there's been another call-up and we're all sitting around with our feet up. We've received permission to go ahead with *Farewell to Arms*, but we'll leave all the fuss and bother to Diderot.

We don't get much to eat in this place. Three out of the five of us are down with whooping-cough. Probably I'll catch it too. Wouldn't it be nice if we both had it in a little house by the sea, patting each other on the back and whooping in unison!

Your
Cesarino

To Fernanda Pivano, Mondovi Breo

[Rome] Sunday 30th [May 1943]

Dear Fern,

Your letter upset me very much. If only I could, I'd rush over to prove it's not true that you're 'surrounded by coldness and hostility'. I cannot understand why you are finding life so hard, now you have a steady nine hours a day job and can keep yourself. Haven't you always dreamed of being independent? Perhaps you're finding, like everyone else, that once you've gained independence you don't know what to do with it. I've always urged you to cultivate an inner life of your own, a life of study, affection and human interests, not to 'get anywhere' but simply to enjoy living. You'll find that life gains a new significance.

I can't get away just now because we've had police-officers in the place for days. Now one of the women working here has been arrested. Imagine the commotion!

Dear Fern, there is only one cure for feeling lonely. You must go out and about and mix with people, learning to give instead of receiving. It's a problem of ethics rather than a social one. Learn to work and live, not just for yourself but for somebody else, everybody else. Once anyone says 'I'm on my own, I'm left out in the cold, people just ignore me', he will at once feel worse. *No one is alone unless he chooses to be.* To live a full, rich life you must feel drawn towards other people, humble yourself and serve them. That's all there is to it.

Here our position is precarious. Every now and then our boss talks of moving the office to Piedmont. I wouldn't mind that at all. Meanwhile I'm simply doing nothing and feeling fed up.

Chin up! See you soon,
Pavese

To Fernanda Pivano, Mondovi Breo

[Rome] 24th June [1943]

Dear Fern,

The other day the police came for me. I'd been expecting them a week earlier and was now taken by surprise. I'd instructed the secretary to tell them: 'Pavese isn't here. He's probably in the army.' Then Carlo Muscetta came in and they chattered away for ages.

We're in an awful muddle here. The woman who's supposed to look after us has gone to help bring in the harvest, so I take my turn with the others to cook and wash up. I make my own bed, too, and am bored sick with it all.

I hope that by now you've finished with those exam papers and can now get on with something more sensible. When will you push on with translating *Farewell to Arms*? One fine day we'll take the job away from you on the score of incompetence!

Pavese

To Fernanda Pivano, Mondovi Breo

[Rome] 21st July [1943]

Dear Fern,

It's been decided that we're to move our office to Turin. It'll take a week to remove and sort out the files. This changes everything, and I think we'll all be happier there. (I shall, anyway.) I hope the move goes well. I'm writing to you at one o'clock in the afternoon and I haven't eaten anything today, so far, and am beginning to feel quite faint. We're in a state of fear and upheaval.

As for my feelings towards you, I will say this: in '40 it was an aesthetic delight, hence my poetry. Then, naturally enough, it developed into an affinity of mind, so I wrote my little romance, *La spiaggia.* Now what occupies my mind and fills my dreams is not your beauty but your mental apathy. It is essential for your own peace of mind and inner well-being to retain your gay attitude to life. On this score there is much to be desired. That's why I'm preaching at you. You must get rid of your usual egotism (that's all it is) and rid yourself of certain habits that may, for all I know, have stood you in good stead on other occasions but are now worse than ridiculous—they are tragic.

I love you well, believe me, but I would repulse you with horror and disgust unless you changed first. That's all.

Let's meet again soon. I give your elbow an affectionate squeeze.

Your Pavese

To the Director of the Trevisio Boarding School, Casale Monferrato

Serralunga di Crea, January [?] 1944

Reverend Father,

The intense cold, the impossible state of the roads, and my own ill-health have prevented me from carrying out my duty this past week. I'm counting on being able to start my private lessons again in February, but a new difficulty has arisen. As from 1st February, no one is allowed to leave the place where he lives unless he has a very special authorisation from the German in command of the area. All previous permits are cancelled.

Thus I am compelled to give up my work with you. I cannot tell you how sorry I am about it, particularly since this must create an embarrassment to you and to the college to which I owe so much. I hope, however, that you will have no difficulty in finding a substitute for me in some young Italian living in your area. I hope, in any case, that I may yet have an opportunity of visiting the college, if, in time, the present severe restriction is relaxed. I want to thank you and all the other Rev. Fathers who, in these hard times, have helped me with such Christian charity. I beg you, remember me in your prayers.

Yours

To Giuseppe Vaudagna, Turin

[Serralunga di Crea] 18th December 1944

Dear Giuseppe,

Your reviews have kept me happy all day. As things are now, the resurrection of an old friend is enough to move us to our very roots. I'd had no news of you for ages, except that you were in the field of action. Now you're living a normal life, having taken that step into matrimony that formerly you were afraid of. You must have confidence in life.

I have little or no news to tell you, but millions of things to talk about. I'm in the country with the rest of my unit, slaving away in the neighbouring city by day. But, as in literature, mere facts don't count for anything. What really counts is the inner tension alternating with periods of slackness, both fighting furiously to gain the upper-hand. If I could still recall those days, the memories would accentuate my present torments. It's a terrible thing to be caught up in the talons of history.

So you've written a romance? These things do happen, and I certainly won't judge it too harshly. I'll be glad to look it over, if only to breathe again the air we knew when we were young.

The news you have of our friends must be pretty well the same as mine, brought through by Pinelli. I heard him say he's been shot twice by heaven alone knows which group of partisans. I fancy he's out of danger now. I compliment you on reading history books. They'll effectively cure you of any liking for practical jokes.

I take it that your family are all well. I hope soon to make the acquaintance of the new Vaudagna baby not yet born. Give your wife my kind regards and good wishes. Her head must be full of very different matters just now. One fine day she must resign herself to hearing all about the peccadilloes of her 'lord and master'.

So long,
Cesare

1945

To Giuseppe Vaudagna, Turin

Serralunga di Crea, 21st January 1945

Dear Giuseppe,

What torments me is not a literary problem, and all the more lacerating for that. I mourn for the fate of the world and of myself. It's extremely hard to get any pages out, even in rough, except reports of a case of neurosis or a fine funeral. You call such things 'experiences'. I call them head-blows, nightmares.

I've read your *Liubiza*. For goodness' sake change the title. That 'Slavonic lover' sounds like comic opera and has nothing to do with the story. Make it the tale of an ordinary girl, not of a fascinating Slav. You are not making a study (even fatally superficial) of exotic things or even exotic experiences, but of the eternal feminine.

That, I think, fixes the limits of your work. There are vivid pages when *Liubiza* is on the scene, emphasised by factual touches about nomadism, and a wandering life. When she is not, your pages are dull, halting and vague. It's all very well to describe Liubiza as 'an unending and lovely mystery'. Here is your other main motive : amorous intimacy, the battle of the sexes presented as a means of social advancement, with all the nostalgic, languorous aspects of love. The language of your story is indifferent, good enough when dealing with Liubiza, but for the rest a mere approximation. It's not easy to explain my meaning, but you must either make it even more sombre, or wholly colourful. In short, you must learn how to cope with variations so that you value the word for what it is, a living reality and not a mere symbol. D'Annunzio, with all his faults, taught us that and we can no longer forget it.

I did not know of your father's death and the news has depressed me very much. I remember seeing him several times on my return from Brancaleone. Once, talking about the death of your younger brother, George, he said : 'This is a prison that never ends.' Remember me to your mother and give her my respectful condolences.

A friendly handshake to you both,

Cesare

To Piero Jahier, Bologna

Turin, 11th May 1945

Dear Jahier,

The publishing house of Einaudi has weathered the storm. All our scattered editors are coming back and our collaborators are springing to life again. I expect you've already heard of our irreparable loss through the deaths of Leone Ginzburg and Giaime Pintor. A dreadful blow to the house of Einaudi. We must all work that much harder in the future, and you are one of those who can help us. Give us some information about your city, what's been happening there, naturally mentioning what you're working on now: translations of Conrad, Molière, Arden of Faversham, Ben Jonson and so on. We're especially keen on Conrad. Hoping to have good news of you,

Cordially yours,
Pavese

To Ernesto De Martino, Bari

Turin, 30th May 1945

Dear Professor,

Doubtless you've already heard that this publishing office was invaded by the police in December 1943, but we all got away. They put one of their own men in charge and printed all sorts of rubbish, but that's all over now and we're left in peace.

Those of us here in Turin still do not know whether our Rome office, where Giulio Einaudi is, has been able to renew contact with you. We don't even know whether you've got off scot-free during the last couple of years. I, personally, would like to be reassured above all about your own state of affairs and the books we discussed with you in Rome. We're still counting on Cassirer and the work on *Magismo*,[1] but I should like to resume our discussion on that exciting series dealing with ethnology. Also *Kulturkunde*, which I've thought about a good deal. I consider you could make something very intelligent out of it.

Yours

To Aldo Camerino, Venice

Rome, 26th July 1945

Dear Camerino,

By now you will have received the contract for Stevie Crane's *Red Badge of Courage* and I hope you've already started work on it. I'd like to know whether you can take on any other translation just now. As for the *Diavolo Zoppo*, no one knows anything about it. It may well have been lost when we were getting rid of manuscripts at the time of police investigations and arrests.

I'm told that works by Stevenson and Hardy cannot be sent to me because of postal restrictions.

As you see, I'm in Rome too. It can be taken for granted that neither Einaudi nor Muscetta can answer for your MS., great men though they are. I've done practically nothing these last few years, apart from a little libretto due out soon, to keep my name in the public eye.

Here's to our next meeting

[1] De Martino had been commissioned by Messrs Einaudi to translate *Das mythische Denken*, by Ernst Cassirer. He was also writing a book, *Mondo magico, prolegomeni a una storia del magismo* (The World of Magic, etc.), which came out in 1948.

To Ernesto De Martino, Rome

Rome, 30th July 1945

Dear De Martino,

I have discussed with Einaudi your series on ethnology and your accompanying suggestions. He considers it unwise, at least for now, to publish such a specific series, though if you were to translate the volumes one by one we may be able to insert them into one of the series already running, *Saggi, Biblioteca di cultura storica* and *Corrente* [Essays, Library of Historical Culture and Current Affairs].

He suggests an arrangement on the following lines: you would busy yourself with translating the various volumes one by one in accordance with our views and send in your MS. quickly to be stamped. For your work as curator Einaudi offers you 6000 lire per volume, quite apart from your salary as translator, which Einaudi will pay direct to you. In special cases one may even review your pay for a particular volume.

If you could manage to produce six volumes a year, your salary would amount to 36,000 lire, paid monthly. Naturally any translations requested by the firm would be paid for separately. As for the copyright, that can be discussed with Einaudi when it is decided which book to do next. Do you feel you can accept this?

Personally I quite agree with all the adjustments you made to my former list, intended to be a reminder, nothing more. As for the various books on the *History of Christianity*, they were left in by mistake and can be discussed again, one by one.

Hoping to see you soon in Rome,
Cordially your

To an unnamed girl-friend

Turin, 25th November 1945

. . . I know now what is wrong with me. It is called pride, and can be conquered. I'm not sensual or miserly, only proud. You are somewhat responsible for my outbursts of pride, because you have never humiliated me in the past and have always praised me personally for my intelligence, my importance. Only last night, as it happened, you were in this sense a friend to me. You told me flatly that I'm a twister, even that I lay traps for you. You said there was nothing between us worth the trouble of saving. I kept turning this phrase over in my heart all night until finally it has made me write.

I tried to determine whether this phrase is so terrible to me because it wounds my pride, and indeed that comes into it, but chiefly I find it intolerable because it is not true, because it tears down everything unnecessarily. Leaving on one side myself and my stories, you too are part of this 'togetherness', bringing with you values that are something more than passion. No one knows better than I do how sterile and empty a passion may be. (That's why I asked you yesterday to try reading my diary. When you refused, I confess I felt an author's chagrin.) But hitherto this has been my instinctive way of coming to grips with a woman and her affairs, as a drowning man clutches another by the neck. I have always looked beyond passion. Passion has always been merely a *condition* imposed by my pride, but my intention was rather different, an objective valuation, a good thing. I gave it a new and arrogant expression in my ideas of 'flesh and blood', monogamy, the Absolute. Substantially it meant the choice of another woman, her material quality, her reality as a person, the first step towards respecting her. It has always been warped love, not absence of love.

I have sometimes said jokingly that I'm a Catholic. Well then, the duty of a Catholic (or a Christian if you like) is to believe in other people's souls and to respect them. I have violated, murdered, exploited and tricked the souls of others, but I always knew I was doing wrong. I mean to do so no more.

I am determined not to drink so dramatically and not to be so headstrong. In this respect, what happened last night was a victory for me. I did not mean to tell you I was thinking of going to Turin. I meant to slip away quietly, to impress you. Instead, I told you.

If we don't count those sweet (too sweet) days when we first began to know each other (that idyllic period), yesterday was in a way our first day of 'togetherness'. Think about it. What happened was that I talked to you without pride. I started off with half a mind to be tough and laconic. Instead, you made me look my own soul in the face. Why? Because we had managed to kid ourselves there was something between us, even before we lost all sense of shame. You said yourself, a little while ago, that we must know everything about each other. Only then could love mean anything. If so, the hasty intimacy we have known since then should be reason enough for breaking off everything between us. Or have we discovered we are poles apart?

I have a deep conviction that we sought each other out *because* we differ. It took us a month to clarify this difference of ours. Last night was the crisis of our mutual reaction to contact (we seethed like a couple of acids). Can it end like that, after all there has been between us? I believe now is the time to readjust ourselves and rediscover a real togetherness. It may not be erotic (and I could weep for us), it may not even work out. Will it settle down to exchanging letters? Shall we be as brother and sister? I don't know.

I resisted the temptation to slam the door when I left you, a thing I've always done in the past. But somehow, with you, slamming the door means nothing. We both suddenly feel stupidly proud and resentful. One day I told you: 'In your presence I will never do anything to be ashamed of.' Today I believe it would be shameful if I broke with you solely for fear of burning my wings or making you suffer. I shall *not* burn my wings or cause you to suffer anything more from me.

Don't you love me at all? I've been wondering all night whether it is true that I'm totally incapable of love, as you told me last night, and as I have found. My sister—I do love my sister because she never chatters, because she is better-looking than I am, because I know she is disappointed and hurt by the very things that lie closest to her heart, her home, her children and life itself. Her hands are work-worn. She gets up every morning at dawn and goes to church, not that she's a believer, but once she gives herself up to it for a moment it becomes an inflexible rule, the right and proper thing to do. I really do love her, and when I think of her I feel an urge to send her money, write her all the things we don't know how to say to each other, to comfort her.

Can you believe me? In the old days, if I found you in tears I felt for you the same dull annoyance I feel for Maria when I see her obstinately set (as she can well be) on fretting herself sick over something or other. I feel the same helplessness I have suffered before, the need to send you money, write to you, find out what has upset you and give you my very heart's blood. Do you want the meek, submissive blood I shall henceforth strive to find as a monk? To conquer my pride I will enter a close religious order where I can learn to control my thoughts. The only proud thought I will retain is my hope of succeeding in this. You may be right when you say I shall never be a man of flesh and blood, but you are wrong to say I could never become what you'd like me to be.

I must become so, for I *will not* let our story be like the others that have burned themselves out. Tell me what to do and I'll obey it like a commandment, no matter what it may cost me.

Cesare

Now I will confess to you other things I'm ashamed of :

I still hope to marry you—
When I used to show myself to you in despair, it was just to impress you—
The most delirious pleasure I know is to be pitied—
I have to make a great effort to 'feel' politics—
With everyone I put on an air of not putting on airs—
When I told you 'every man has his own phthisis', I thought the phrase would impress you more than any other—
There was a shameful interruption in the 'five years of knightly chastity' I boasted about—
In telling you so, I was flattering myself that to confess *one* interlude would be more effective than to say there were none at all. I was simply telling a lie—
I'm ashamed of my tobacconist cousin—
At one time I used to masturbate a lot

To Aldo Camerino, Venice

Rome, 17th December 1945

Dear Camerino,

It seems the decision has gone against James. Instead, I've been given the job of suggesting to you a big volume of Mark Twain's *Tales of the West*. There's some talk of translating his *Tom Sawyer*, *Huckleberry Finn*, *Life on the Mississippi* and all those short stories with a Western atmosphere such as 'The Celebrated Jumping Frog of Calaveras' and 'Roaring Camp'. If you have any ideas on this, let us know.

Your remuneration could be fixed at a rate payable according to the various sections—so much for *Tom* (20,000?), so much for *Huckleberry* (40,000?) so much for *Mississippi* (20,000?)—and a figure to be agreed for the short stories.

What do you say?

1946

To Bianca Garufi[1]

Rome, 21st February 1946

Dear Bianca,

I've received three letters from you, all with an air of having come from the Elysian Fields. So it happens to you too, that moving to another place, another house, makes you feel you're a little girl again, larking about like a clown. Now you're studying astrology and the world before man was created. I well remember that book by Flammarion.[2] I read it in the public library when I was fifteen, the *first* real book I read. I learned about the Silurian and Jurassic periods and realised that the adventure stories I read as a boy were very much like them. I remember that towards the end there is an engraving of Truth (or Science or Humanity) flying stark naked towards the light of the future. I thought what a fine thing it would be if nude women could symbolise Truth and the future. I took long notes from this book and knew it almost by heart.

In short, we're returning to our adolescent years, living in paradise. How can you say you feel limp and exhausted? Feelings of that sort are all very well when one works in an office, not now when you're on holiday and writing. . . . What are you writing? And how is it that you only have Sunday off? Surely you need some rest, even working in a surgery?

You're ruthless, Bianca, quite ruthless, to waste your time translating treatises on astrology. There will be other things claiming your attention if you're not translating. There is always time for translating and you will always be capable of doing it.

I've sent you a dialogue and Chapter 6 of our joint venture, so

[1] Bianca Garufi was a contemporary Italian novelist and a friend of Pavese's. As an experiment they agreed to collaborate in writing a novel, each doing alternate chapters, presenting the reactions of a young man in love and a woman who has already had some sexual experiences but lacks the courage to confess them. The story was to end in her suicide. Pavese's contribution to this joint venture ended with his own suicide and the novel was laid aside. It was eventually published in 1959 under the title *Fuoco grande* (see p. 210 *n.* 4).

[2] *Le monde avant l'apparition de l'homme,* by Camille Flammarion.

you can get on with Chapter 7. It should be going ahead now. Here I'm alone and happy. Nothing is nicer than to have someone at a distance who remembers us kindly. It's even better than having her close at hand, but that absence shouldn't last too long. Yet to curtail that absence is almost a sin. . . .

To Bianca Garufi

[Rome, end of February 1946]

Dear Bianca,

At last I've received Chapter 7 and your sad letter. I've skipped through the chapter and don't see why you should belittle it. Your style is more forceful than in anything else you have hammered out to date. In planning Chapter 8, it seems to me that Sylvia and the baby must die, somehow or other, but so far I can't work out how to justify Giovanni's vicious streak.

At the moment I'm obsessed by the personal disclosures in your chapter, and the acts of violence I shall have to introduce to conform to Sylvia's stolid ferocity. I was well aware, when I started this book, that we should each drain into it all our own bitterness and gall, but I know also that your words express some subconscious conviction that has had, and still has for us, a significance not entirely literary. . . .

To Sanford J. Greenburger,[3] *New York**

Rome, 22nd March 1946

Dear Mr Greenburger,

Yours of 5th, 6th, 7th, 9th and 11th March to hand. I am glad you are meeting and working with Kamenetzki.[4] His idea to include New York in the network of our secretariats is good. Of course

[3] Sanford J. Greenburger was Einaudi's agent in New York.

[4] Mischa Kamenetzki served the same New York agency as Greenburger, as a consultant.

decisions must come from Giulio Einaudi himself, at present in Milan, and we shall write to you soon about them.

I thank you very much for your suggestion as to copyright our books and for the copy of the U.S. Law which will be exceedingly useful.

At last I read *Three Essays on America* (Dutton) by Van Wyck Brooks. They are very good and can interest our Italian readers. Instead of *The Age of Washington Irving*, would it be possible to translate and publish these three essays? I chanced to read *American Renaissanc*e by F. O. Matthiessen, and think this work, as a study of that literary age, immensely superior to all the Flowerings and Indian Summers Van Wyck Brooks ever wrote. I am planning to translate it as soon as our reading market will be ready to absorb it, that is in a year or two. Can you obtain us an option on this book? The exact title is: *American Renaissance* by F. O. Matthiessen, Oxford University Press, New York 1941. I am now reviewing it and the effect will be that many other publishers will want to get hold of the book.

Methinks there is nothing else waiting for immediate discussion. Our secretariat is sending you immense lists of new requests for options, copies and rights. Please remember that my concern is literary things and don't starve me. With best wishes and thanks.

1947

To Carlo Musso, Rome

Turin, 8th January 1947

Dear Musso,

I can understand your disappointment and am sorry it all came about while I was away. Hence the delay. Your MS. was not read until today, when the decision was made to reject it.

If it's any consolation to you, I assure you that every volume of stories is now being rejected by Einaudi on principle. They simply do not sell. It's hard enough to get the public to buy a novel, even a short romance.

I read your MS. myself and agree for the most part with Natalia Ginzburg's opinion. She was very much struck by the polished style and precision of many pages of your work, and she is a woman incapable of being wrong in a matter of taste.

I myself like 'Teresio' ['Terence'] best. It is the only really worthy example of your style, and to me it seems very promising. Teresio emerges as symbolic of a whole way of life, an epoch. Your 'Notte di Roma' ['Roman Nights'] is a close second, and contains several beautiful passages, but it is a bit too whimsical, almost 'impertinent', though a complete novel in the same vein might well be a success. Your 'Polifemo' ['Polyphemus'], taking into account the time it was written, is really an experiment in style, rather than a convincing story. The same comment applies to 'Pietro' ['Peter'], a simple period piece. Your 'I gibli' aims high, but in my view it falls short of the light-hearted gaiety of your prose in 'Teresio' or 'Notte'. There is something contrived about it, something cold. It lacks the sensitive, sustained inventiveness of detail I enjoyed elsewhere in your work.

By and large, I suggest you look for an editor who publishes collections of stories and send him 'Polifemo' by itself. You're already a literary character who will make critics and suchlike sweat. The public, on the other hand, expects from you something with a different atmosphere, something I expect you are already working on. Take heart and keep trying.

Your 'Rome as Seen by a Visitor from Piedmont' is good. Actually, last November and December I too was working on a book on Rome, as seen through the eyes of someone from Piedmont.[1] What odd things happen!

To Fabrizio Onofri,[2] *Rome*

Turin, 9th September 1947

Dear Onofri,

I think I must be the person least qualified to reply to your request. You already know why. I never see anybody. Besides, Turin is surely the city least disturbed by movements, organisations and reforms. As for Piedmont, the least said the better. I know a few people living there, that's all.

While I was living in Rome ('45-'46), there was a flourishing Cultural Union, built up by a lawyer, Zanetti, and the painter Menzio. At first it was definitely inclined to leftist views, but took no part in demonstrations or discussions in that sense. They contented themselves with organising concerts and recitals, exhibitions, conferences and lantern lectures, etc. More than anything else it was a group of artists and fashionable literary figures, supported chiefly by painters to display their works. At the end of '46 the presidency passed to Franco Antonicelli, an ex-liberal, a republican with strong leanings towards socialism. Everyone said 'the party of the right has won' (thinking of the drawing-room in Antonicelli's house, frequented by wealthy people and certain questionable members). Instead, Antonicelli limited himself to slowing down the activities of the Union. He himself is one of the most significant cultural types in Turin. I knew him at one time and can confirm that he is a man of integrity, sincerely democratic, plucky (he has

[1] Pavese is referring to his novel *Il compagno*, published later in 1947, and in English under the title *The Comrade*, trans W. J. Strachan (Peter Owen, 1959).

[2] Fabrizio Onofri, an official of the Italian Communist Party, had asked Pavese (in a letter dated 5th September) to prepare a report on cultural developments in his area, with particular reference to the attitude towards the Communist Party.

been President of the Committee of the CLM in Piedmont),[3] with nothing against him except perhaps a certain international air about the way he lives. He has received Salvemini in his home, breaking his journey from Turin, and introduced him to several socialist members of the PdA. He seems to me a typical member of the Christian Democrats. But he is also, and primarily, a fine humanist, a director of the printing firm De Silva, a pre-war organisation similar to Einaudi Editore.

In much the same position as Antonicelli (except for the drawing-room) is Massimo Mila, ex-partisan, member of the PdA, an outstanding philosopher, by profession a musicologist, a pupil of Augusto Monti, the PdA federalist. Associated with the Cultural Union are, or were, the painter Casorati; the classical philologist Ciaffi, and Alberto Rossi, formerly a journalist for *Stampa.*

All these could be brought together and unified (?) in one way only, to create a great series such as 'Pan' or 'Pegaso', sufficiently well known to the public, cultural, with leftish tendencies if you like, popular enough in some quarters, but not prophetic and erratic like *Politecnico*. Actually they are all scraping a living as best they can, finding the cultural level of *Unità* detestable. There's no point in saying that the review must be paying them well, or they wouldn't be willing to do it, and even more pointless to say that the initiative couldn't have come from the unqualified and low-class *Unità.*

I don't know of anyone else, or at least I haven't followed their careers to the extent of being able to express any useful opinion. I know there are, as everywhere else, religious-political fanatics among them; I know that painters and artists work in a group, but nothing more. We others are often approached, individually, to collaborate with independent periodicals. This means we count for something and I wonder whether it would not be extremely useful in the end to talk to certain groups about accepting (cautiously, of course) these proposals.

But I think all I'm saying is biased, that middle-class intellectuals include three or four notorious names. Any true penetration must come about through the herd of cultural hangers-on (teachers, technical specialists, professional men). Then the problem will no longer be whether or not to produce some stupid review, but to convince them that we are representing their own interests. Are we intellectuals capable of solving this problem? It would be enough if we managed to enable them to live together, intellectuals

[3] The Comitato di Liberazione Nazionale—organisers of the resistance movement during the war.

and proletariat, without repugnance and mutual suspicion, giving certain intellectual groups a taste for mixing with a crowd of workers. From my own personal experience, such contacts in most cases inspire fresh literary discoveries. In short, the only thing missing is common ground for discussion on mutual concerns. Nowadays it's purely a question of interests, and all propaganda in my opinion is directed to that end. Furthermore, since we need them more than they need us, we ought to make concessions, keeping in mind that people of that class are more terrified by an uproar in the piazza than by the most hazardous political manifesto.

In short, we must be careful not to confuse two different aims: one, making the average middle-class intellectuals link up with one another; two, the construction of a new culture. Now and then it seems to me that the two things are involved with one another, trying to convince the great with propaganda more suitable for accountants, or accountants with propaganda more suitable for writers.

1948

To Enrico Cederna, Milan

[Turin] 17th January [1948]

Dear Mr Cederna,

I have received the little book and your kind letters. Any translator would jump for joy at such a stroke of good luck. But I'm an old fox and I know that Joyce has never been translated in sufficient depth. I'll tell you in confidence that certain verses of his poems are quite incomprehensible to me.

It is a great responsibility to translate such a delicate little flower, but don't despair. I've talked with Alberto Rossi, who will be pleased to do it. You will know that Rossi wrote the preface to my *Daedalus* and has translated the first chapters of *Ulysses.* He has been in touch with Joyce by letter and is a friend of Linati. In temperament he is the ideal choice. If I were to translate these poems myself I should feel ashamed to meet Alberto.

He himself asked me to put the proposition up to you, and is disposed to treat with you on the basis of 10,000 lire, more or less. In the last few days Rossi has just finished, for Einaudi, Shakespeare's sonnets, a miracle of precision and scrupulous accuracy.

If you agree, write to him. I'm keeping Linati's libretto. Tell me what to do. Am I to send it back to you or pass it to Rossi for translation?

Cordially yours,
Cesare Pavese

To Carlo Musso, Rome

[Turin] 15th March 1948

Dear Musso,

I've been thinking again about our discussion, and of how much you told me. People in Rome will be able to feast their eyes on a whole series of regional films. We ought to involve ourselves in doing something for Piedmont, even though, as you know, it's my rule in life not to be involved in anything. A few ideas have occurred to me for a film and I'm sending you a summary of the plot, well worked out and sound.[1] Do you like it? Do you think it can be cut at all? Think it over and write me some of the news from down there.

So long,
Yours sincerely,
Pavese

*To Sanford J. Greenburger, New York**

Turin, 20th March 1948

Dear Sir,

I got yours of 11th March about *The Ox-bow Incident* and *The Cross and the Arrow*. You are right, quite right, but these two books turn out to be a *plague*. *The Oxbow* was rejected by two translators and now we are frantically trying to get back our copy.

The Cross was two years in the hands of a translator who disappeared without giving notice. So we are in a position to ask for new copies of both and beg to be granted another year to issue them. You can say that *The Cross* could not be published by any other firm.

Have you noticed that things are no more as they were, and people are working less hard than before? I think it's a consequence of the war psychosis which is sweeping all around us. What do you think over there?

Yours sincerely

[1] Pavese enclosed an involved scenario, amounting to approximately 1,250 words. He did not give it a title, and I have found no evidence that it was ever filmed.

*To Sanford J. Greenburger, New York**

Turin, 3rd April 1948

Dear Greenburger,

The City of Trembling Leaves by Tilburg Clark is just now beginning to print. I got Leiber's letter on Maltz, but I want also the book.

Scherrer says that a month ago he shipped seventy *Cristoes* and other titles. More were shipped afterwards. You'll have begun to get them by now.

About Gramsci, I know only *Letters from Prison* and *History of Materialism,* which are published. The other copybooks containing some more essays are in the hands of the editor and nobody knows anything as yet. But I don't think democratic America will allow the translations of these pages. They were written in a fascist jail by a fighter who, were he alive today, would, for instance, be forbidden entrance to the U.S.A.

Yours

To Giuseppe Cocchiara, Palermo

Turin, 7th June 1948

Dear Cocchiara,

I am gratified by your invitation and your letter. I have read your *Buon selvaggio* which, followed as it is by other essays, becomes a real and accurate history of ethnology, an Italian rival to the manual of Schmidt, a mine of information and attractions whether scientific or editorial. For instance, would it be possible for you to send me, for examination, Frazer's *Man, God and Immortality*; *Sex and Repression* by Malinowski; and the book by Spencer and Gillen? It's most difficult to get hold of them for editorial purposes; Turin is not rich in libraries, so how can I form an opinion? I haven't forgotten your earlier proposal to do some translating, but to translate one must first have the original text. Einaudi thanks you for using our books and is interested in your forthcoming work, *Storia del folklore* [History of Folk-lore].

It is difficult for me to come to Sicily, an area that, at best, could summon me to a conference, and I never attend conferences.

Cordially yours,
Pavese

To Giuseppe Cocchiara, Palermo

Turin, 7th July 1948

Dear Cocchiara,

I have received the four volumes but not the initial translation of Frazer that you promised me. The best of the four, editorially and humanistically, is without doubt *Sex and Repression* by Malinowski. We will at once write to Kegan Paul for the translation rights and a copy in English, then we can set about getting permission to translate. Frazer's *Psyche* seems very old-fashioned to me. It has an air of a conference and illustrations that I do not much like. I hoped for something better from his *Man, God,* etc.

The other thing by Malinowski and Rivers seems too specialised, almost like monographs. Actually I haven't read it yet.

Let me thank you again for your generous invitation. As soon as possible you shall have everything back. I very much hope that the Frazer will be suitable and that you can translate it.

In a few days now, you'll be plunging into the festivities for the centenary.[2] I still envy you, and only wish I could be there, but when one is involved in a publishing business one is no longer one's own master.

Cordially,
Pavese

[2] Celebrating the 'Five Days of Revolution' that led to the Peace of Villafranca (11th July 1948) and the declaration of the Italian Republic.

*To Sanford J. Greenburger, New York**

Turin, 23rd September 1948

Dear Mr Greenburger,

I read *Nobody's Fool,* by Yale,[3] and thank you. But it doesn't fit. Such pamphletistic subject-matter is not for us. It's written very badly in that would-be witty style also used by movie-scenarists and radio-announcers. Last but not least, as you already saw, it's too steeped in American technicalities and gossip. I think that as yet we are not agreed on what an Einaudi book is. How is that?

At last I read yesterday *The Ides of March* by Th. Wilder and found it the very thing. I cabled to Longmans to send over a contract. How comes you let it slip?

Best wishes

PS. I hear today that Mondadori has got Wilder. Giulio is mad.

[3] Charles Yale Harrison.

1949

To Innocenzo Monti, Milan

Turin, 4th January 1949

Dear Monti,

Does it seem to you that, whatever we may say, what really concerns us is the verdict of non-literary people. We already know all the little peccadilloes of the literary world (take our own for a start). But to succeed in moving someone who lives a very different life from ours and judges the world by standards probably more sound than our own, that is a great triumph.

Because of this, your letter gave me rare pleasure. For the rest, I see you have divided the work between you. Lalla has written me about the technical aspect, and you yourself the human angle.[1] I thank you both and hope you will not be disappointed in the future, about the promise made to your descendants.

Don't you come to Turin any more? I'd be happy to see you.

Greetings and good wishes to you both,

Yours,
Pavese

To Giuseppe Cocchiara, Palermo

Turin, 11th January 1949

Dear Cocchiara,

Thanks for the apples of the Hesperides. We are hardly prepared for such proof of the grace of God.

We are still negotiating for the Cassirer. I've been waiting for the three books you told me about, but so far they haven't come.

[1] Innocenzo Monti, the husband of Lalla Romano, had written to Pavese about his impressions in *Prima che il gallo canti,* a book comprising two novels, published 1948.

Bad news of De Martino. He writes that he's in hospital with a pulmonary lesion. It's a great shame, because his work is his whole life. Perhaps he may feel freer now, but perhaps not. We must just wait. Write him something courteous and kind.

The proofs from Propp should be reaching you soon. I'm not sending them for you to correct, but so that you can judge the book and write a preface for it.

We're sending you, just to amuse you, Einaudi's booklist for '48.

Thanks again,
Yours,
Pavese

*To Sanford J. Greenburger, New York**

Turin, January 18th 1949

Dear Mr Greenburger,

Since some days I'm beaming and whoso ask me why is answered: 'I got *Criticism*.' It's a wonderful book and a mine of precious information and sheer delight. Thanks also for *The Ordeal of M.T.* and for the *Macmillan Literary History*. This last one we examined for translation. Have you already secured an option?

But today I want to forget all the publishing rubbish and lose myself in contemplation of the three titles. Why are not all American books like these?

Dear Sanford, I thank you very very much. Is there anything I can do in return?

Best wishes

To Giuseppe Cocchiara, Palermo

Turin, 27th January 1949

Dear Cocchiara,

I am taking advantage of your kindness and sending you *The White Goddess* by Robert Graves, the author of *I, Claudius*. That, as you will see, is a book of staggering erudition. Would you glance through it and consider whether it's possible to do it? *Then send it back by return of post,* unless you have a translator over there (for whom you must take all responsibility).

If you approve of the volume (but I don't think you will), you will need to negotiate for the rights before getting involved. The Frazer is practically out now.

Cordially,
Pavese

*To Sanford J. Greenburger, New York**

Turin, 17th February 1949

Dear Mr Greenburger,

Our 'gentlemen'[2] are: Natalia Ginzburg, in charge of Italian and French fiction, translator of *Black Boy,* by Wright; Felice Balbo, in charge of philosophical and political matters; Giulio Einaudi, the Boss; Cesare Pavese, in charge of ethnology and anthropology; Antonio Giolitti, in charge of historical and economical books. Other signatures are small fry.

Best regards,

To Luigi Berti, Milan

Turin, 2nd March 1949

Dear Berti,

I've been expecting, not another postponement but Lowry's MS. ready for printing. Since it has not reached us, your contract with Einaudi is cancelled. The translation has already been given to

[2] In a letter to Pavese (dated 1st February) Greenburger complained that in his correspondence with Einaudi, 'The gentlemen now writing letters to me all have illegible signatures. Please give me their names, and a list of Who's Who in the firm of Einaudi.'

someone else. Send the text back to us at once. Generally we write to the Editors for another copy, apologising for the delay.

It still remains understood that Einaudi is awaiting your work on Poe. We repeat that the due date is Easter, this year. After that date this contract, too, will be cancelled.

To Enzo Giachino, Milan

Turin, 21st May 1949

Dear Giachino,

At last I am sending you the first volume of the *Life of Studs Lonigan*, by James T. Farrell (translated by Serini).[3] I have glanced through it and am not discouraged. I was afraid it might be worse. The Italian reads very well. It will be enough if you regularise the names and find better equivalents for slang terms. (For instance, on your first page 'dump' is translated as *'rottura di scatole'—a pile of broken boxes.*)

No need to add that we're pushed for time. We insist on having *Huck* and *Tom* by 15th May, and all the Farrell between 30th May and 20th June. Please don't forget it.

Translator's Note: Pavese wrote many other letters during this year, most of them very short, all dealing with business matters arising out of his work as an editor employed by Einaudi. During this period he was writing about his personal affairs in some detail in his diary, *Il mestiere di vivere* (This Business of Living).

[3] Maria Livia Serini was one of Pavese's office colleagues at Einaudi's at that time.

1950

To Augusto Monti, Turin

[Turin] 18th January 1950

Dear Monti,

When I read about my being compared with Pastonchi, 'the other admirer of D'Annunzio', I said 'He's gone mad, that's all there is to it.' Whether a story can be considered as belonging to this or that school, in the past or the future, is a question to be settled by good taste and by good reading, things that cannot be discussed.

But a judgment on 'positive ethics' is another matter and can be discussed. It seems to me that the two stories under discussion (*Il diavolo sulle colline* and *Tra donne sole*—I'm not talking of the first, a tale of virginity defending itself)[1] are distinguished by the level of humanity and its working background, in which everything is useful for something. People who do not work and are no use to anyone, fall a prey to gangrene and rot away. What is this story you attribute to me, of hatred for one's neighbour? *Il diavolo* is a young man's hymn of discovery as he comes to realise nature and society. To the three lads everything seems beautiful. It is only little by little that each in his own way comes to realise how sordid, how futile, the world is, a certain suburban world that does nothing, believes in nothing, a world they do not see because a veil is drawn over it. Much the same can be said of *Tra donne sole*. Here there are no young lads, no song of discovery, just the harsh experience of a working girl who comes into contact with the ordinary world and sees how rotten it is, how intent upon self-destruction.

I have a dawning suspicion that you are so sentimentally attached to the upper-class world that it annoys you to hear anything said against it, so bound up with the world of workers that you expect a book to give you the vague, abstract optimism so typically militant. In that case, it's obvious we can never understand each other.

So long,
Pavese

[1] The first mentioned novel was published in English under the title *The Devil in the Hills,* trans D. D. Paige (Peter Owen, 1961); the second (winner of the Strega Prize) under the title *Among Women Only,* trans D. D. Paige (Peter Owen, 1953).

To Constance Dowling,[2] *Rome*

[Turin] 17th March 1950

Dear Connie,

I wanted to play the strong man and not write to you at once, but what's the good of that? It would be only a pose.

Did I ever tell you that when I was a boy I had a superstition about 'good deeds'? When I had to face danger—get through an exam, for example—I was very careful for days not to do anything wrong, not to offend anyone, not to raise my voice, not to entertain unkind thoughts. All that so as not to drive away my good luck. Well, what happened was that in those days I became a boy again, facing a real danger, enduring a terrible exam, because I realised I didn't dare to be naughty, offend people or think wrong thoughts. The thought of you is quite incompatible with any unkind thought. I love you. Dear Connie, I know the full weight of that word, the dread and wonderment of it, yet I say it to you almost serenely. I have used it so little in my life and so badly that it's like a new word to me.

Now I'm alone with my work, with Turin and with Ciccio and Dada.[3] Neither of them has said a word to me. So much the better. I don't know how I've managed to resist the impulse to tell them and betray myself like a greenhorn. They're a little less gay than they usually are, that's all. Yesterday I sent them the records and today I've posted to you the books you selected.

My love, the thought that when you read this letter you'll be in Rome—with all the discomfort and confusion of the journey safely over—moves me as if you were my sister. But you are *not* my sister. You are sweeter and more terrifying. The very thought of you makes my pulses tremble.

Dear, I'm working for you, as fast as I can.

[2] Constance Dowling, an American film star, met Pavese at the home of some friends, Giovanni Rubino and his wife Alda Grimaldi, with whom Pavese stayed during the New Year holiday in Rome. Later he met Doris Dowling, the sister of Constance, also a film star. Pavese's letters to Constance of 17th and 19th March were written in Italian. Those written in English are indicated by an asterisk.

[3] 'Ciccio' and 'Dada'—nicknames for Giovanni Rubino and his wife Alda.

To Constance Dowling, Rome

19th March [1950]

Dear Connie,

Here's my suggestion for *The Two Sisters* (the title does not matter). It's only in rough, just an idea. If you think it worth-while we'll go on working at it. If it doesn't, I'll do another. In the end we'll find something good. Life is many days.

To me it seems that I've taken into account the characteristics and possibilities of you both. I have given you a greater depth and significance. Something really fine may come of it, something tender and wonderful in the most moving and important scenes. Naturally all the dialogue and research, the setting and typecasting, are still to be done, but that won't be any difficulty. As for the dialogue, I am a recognised master of the subject (!). I know nothing about cinematograph technicalities, but with goodwill one can master it all. Life has already taught me to become a translator, a poet, a literary critic, an author, a proof-reader, a teacher, an editorial consultant, all things I knew nothing whatever about when I was twenty. I can learn this too. You'll have just as much to do: learning your lines, dancing, posing, speaking Italian. Until now, Italian-American collaboration has produced nothing worth-while.

At this point, Doris goes off. Good-bye, Doris. I want to take my leave of Connie when the two of us are alone together.

You dappled smile, you wind of March. . . .

To Rino Dal Sasso, Rome

20th March 1950

Dear Dal Sasso,

Thank you for your letter. You have written for me a statement forecasting the literature of the future. But I disagree with some of your views. My beliefs are:

(a) No code of morality is better than another, unless it is understood and put into practice.

(b) For the artist, all intellectual systems generally accepted in his own times are valid for him. They are life itself.

(c) The 'morality of discovery' is no more conventional than that of an unbeliever, it is merely harder to confute.

(d) Tragedy does not necessarily demand a confrontation of good and bad. It would be possible to write a tragedy in which one of the characters is laughing all the time. That is what happens with the three young fellows and to Clelia. It represents a verdict on a certain phase of middle-class society, simply because the flower of that social group (juvenile brashness, actual stoicism) are definitely unhappy if only because of their (apparent) nothingness. But note that all their experience, their inner life, is in my opinion positive and has a value.

This is the substance of my thoughts on reading your dignified and exhaustive letter, but you are fatally biased against Corrado. In short, I wanted to present a hesitant and solitary man who, because of (or in spite of) his low status finds (or knows by intuition) there are new values (an awareness of death, humility, an understanding of others). If you tell me that I haven't had much success on those lines, you may be right, indeed I know you are. If you say that there's no need to introduce such subjects, I can only shrug my shoulders. The world is wide and there's room for everyone. If in my poetry there is any risk of my writing an opera about the devil, you run much the same risk. I don't say that's what you aim at, but it happens, it really does happen. Art should discover new human values, not fresh institutions. Taking it all in all, is it worth the trouble? Let us therefore translate all the old, educational stories into a progressive language, and that's all there is to it.

Pavese

To Constance Dowling, Rome [?]*

Rome [?] April [?] 1950

I cannot give you jewels—you are worth many of them—but in old times they said that the rarest jewel was a true heart. *Depend upon it.* I'm yours, I envy your N.Y.

I wrote this before our last dinner together. Something has changed now. You'll come back perhaps, and I thank for it, 'whatever gods may be' dear.

Cesare

1

*To Constance Dowling**

[Turin] 17th April [1950]

Dearest,

I am no more in a mood to write poems. They came with you and go with you. This one was written some afternoons ago, during the long hours in the hotel I was waiting and hesitating to call you up. Forgive its sadness, but I was *also* sad with you.

You see, I began with an English poem and end with another. In them is the whole range of what I experienced in this month—the terror and the marvel of it.

Dearest, don't be cross if I am always speaking of feelings you cannot share. At least you can understand them. I want you to know that I thank you with all my heart. The few days of wonder I snatched from your life were almost too much for me. Well, they are past, now horror begins, bare horror, and I'm ready for it. The prison door has banged again.

Dearest, you'll never come back to me, even if you set foot again in Italy. We both have something to do in life that makes it improbable for us to meet again, let alone to be married, as I desperately hoped. But happiness is a thing called Joe, Harry or Johnny—not Pavese.

Will you believe—now that you can no more suspect that I'm 'acting' in order to entrap you some way—that last night I wept like a child, thinking on my lot and also on yours, poor strong clever desperate woman fighting for your life?

If I've ever said or done anything you could not approve of, forgive me, dearest. I forgive you all this pain gnawing at my heart, yes, I welcome it. It's you, it's the true horror and wonder of you. My vision of spring, good-bye. I wish you a big luck in all your days and a happy marriage.

You'll get in time *La luna e i falò*.[4] Perhaps it will be waiting for you before you get there. I'm so glad your name is on it. Remember that I wrote this book, the whole of it, before meeting you, and yet somehow I felt in it you were to come. Wasn't it wonderful?

My vision of spring, I used to love all of you, not only your beauty, which is easy enough, but also your ugliness, your bad moment, your *tache noire*, your *viso chiuso*, and I pity you too. Don't forget it.

Cesare

[4] This novel was published in English under the title *The Moon and the Bonfire,* trans L. Sinclair (John Lehmann, 1952).

*To Doris Dowling, Rome**

[Turin] 29th April [1950]

Dear Doris,

This is the first draft of my suggestions for your film with Chevalier. Excuse me if I didn't write it in English, but I wanted you to have it at once. When Elio is in Turin, we'll speak about this and if necessary I'll retouch the draft, of which I have a copy. Cable me something. Meanwhile I'll think about Gabin, you and C. It's wonderful how I enjoy working for you both.

Love,
Cesare

*To Doris Dowling, Rome**

[Turin] 1st May [1950]

Dear Doris,

I wonder about Gabin and the D. sisters. Say, give me some directions about the possible or the impossible background (country life? underworld, high life? etc.), in order not to start on a blind path. Explain also what do you mean when you say: 'too many characters', etc.

Now I send an important afterthought on *La vita bella*. It struck me that in my first draft Luigi is not leading, but led. Perhaps it's better to have him turn out a naughty boy, to have him doing things and going under, just when his girl begins to be really in love with him and to want to save him. So their roles almost interchange, till to break the spell Linda kills herself. It's only a hunch. I put it down hurriedly and didn't as yet find out the gags, the facts, to materialise this idea, but should you approve of it, nothing could be easier.

Remember that I kept the whole subject on a dingy background of cafés, boarding-houses, stores, city streets, and bourgeois interiors, in order to give De Sica his whole scope. He *must* see in this film his chance to sing his new-old song. He must rediscover in it the humble horrid-tender 'real thing' he is always after. The leitmotiv of the lavabos could be a contribution.

So long

*To Doris Dowling, Rome**

[Turin] 4th May 1950

It's little comfort, Doris, being a genius:[5] 'twere better for me to be a cat in N.Y., a swallow in Maine, a little ant under the slabs of a certain house in California. An ass certainly I am.

Our present problem is only to pull the right strings, in order to have our puppets do the right faces. I'll be glad if the story of Linda will startle our puppets but it's not sure, it's never sure. So I'm ready, at a wink, to begin again.

Your lovely letter caught while typing the second draft, the Gabin one. So I couldn't keep your advice to set the story in Rome, but should the draft suit you it'ld be easy to change the setting to a cheaper place.

This Gabin story is the more Gabinesque he ever acted in. But it's also very Italian and, I hope, full of suspense. You are of course Alda and C. is Bianca. While typing it struck me that perhaps we are silly to humour so our big French stars: I think Gabin could turn out wonderful in light comedy, where nothing would be funnier than his 'murderous' eyes and you girls both leading a merry dance around him, a high-style imbroglio. You also, Doris (with your murderous eyes!) could make havoc. I think the story speaks by itself.

I sent for you and Harry a booklet of mine which is just out.[6]

Love me as I love your blood.

[5] In a letter dated 2nd May, Doris Dowling wrote to thank Pavese for his help and added: 'This is just a note to tell you what a great man I think you are. . . . I'm not a genius like you are so before I go into any lengthy comments I'll have to re-read it a few times and think it over.'

[6] This must have been *La luna e i falò* (The Moon and the Bonfire), which was dedicated (in English) 'To D. and H., children of the gods, this tale of wistful, priest-ridden, desperate Italy from a conservative C. P. Pavese', followed by an Italian rendering of the same dedication. Pavese called himself 'conservative' as a joke, because his initials, C.P., also served to identify the Partito Communista, the Communist Party.

*To Doris Dowling, Rome**

[Turin] 13th May [1950]

Dear Doris,

When receiving your *éclaircissements* about the Johnson censorship (it sounds fantastic).[7] I've seen a whole row of American pictures where characters gain money by immoral means: crooks, gangsters, politicians, gamblers, demi-reps and so on. I expect to be taught also about what you mean by 'terms of cinema'. Not, of course, that I don't know that in the movies all must be action and thoroughly explained—what I'm asking for is the form I must give to my script. Am I to tell my tale in simple descriptive prose, like a short story, or to try a real scenario? Here is a difficulty: I don't know the movie jargon; I don't quite know what's a *campolungo,* a *carrellata,* a *dissolvenza,* etc. My idea is to write simply as a writer, a story-teller. You state how many pages this second script must be. Then, should the tale satisfy those guys, we will discuss who will be in a position to turn out a *sceneggiatura.*

Here enclosed is another Gabin story, where you girls are real sisters. Funny thing is that I started from the very idea you declared 'awful', days ago. But there's a different point to *Amore amaro*: the two sisters (you are Cloti, C. is Natalia) are not in love with the same man. Cloti of course is in love with Claudio, but Natalia is choking with the bitterness of her own past life, and only decides to betray Claudio out of horror for what she knows will be the lot of her younger sister. And then the whole meaning of this picture (if it has any) is in the nightmarish days and nights the trio spends in Natalia's appartment. Here Gabin will have full scope to be a shrugging, hard-eyed, blood-sweating fallen angel. He will smokes thousands of cigarettes. He will slap and stare about, etc.

[7] Pavese is replying to a letter from Doris (dated 9th May) in which she said: 'A rather important point comes to my mind. In America there exists a form of censorship known as the Johnson Office that prohibits portraying any character gaining money by immoral means. That would seem to indicate great difficulties in doing a story where your leading lady is a whore. Maybe you had better hold off on your work till I find out how far we can go.'

Dear D., I thank you for the few words you say about C.[8] I think they come from your concern, not hers. I thank you the same for them, nay more.

*To Constance Dowling, New York**

19th May [1950]

Dearest Connie,

Let's speak of hate. I hate the Atlantic. I'm so glad with your speaking of being back soon, but I don't like your disaffection [*sic*] with the picture. I'm contact with Doris and tried my hand in some other scripts. One of them was a success with her, and I hope something good for you both will come out of all this. *La luna e i falò* is already in Hollywood waiting for you. It's a good book and you the fittest patron for it. Remember me in old N.Y. I loved it with all my heart already, when I didn't know you were a little girl in it.

Can I send you my love?

Ces

*To Doris Dowling, Rome**

[Turin] 8th June [1950]

Poor Doris,

I understand you have a hell of a time trying to get something from these horrid men. The silence of De Sica is really ominous. I was on an advertising tour with my boss these days (that's why I

[8] Pavese is referring to the closing phrases of Doris Dowling's letter of 30th April, in which she says: 'I hear from Connie now and then and she always asks how you are. She has started the picture and doesn't seem too pleased with it, but that is nothing new for Connie. She mostly talks about wishing she were back in Italy, so I think it is safe to assume she'll be back as soon as she can.'

opened your letter only this morning). Zavattini told me that by August the Milan picture will be finished. Afterwards they'll spend four or five months on another one about a poor old *pensionato* (the underdog note again). In February they will cross over to United States on an Italo-American production plan, and mean to turn out a picture on how America looks like to Italian eyes. Zavattini will ferret and daydream in Broadway, Bronx and what not, De Sica will follow him with gaping camera. Looks like they are laying it over a little too thick, don't you think?

It's a pity we lose Chevalier. As for Cervi, I fear he will give your picture a provincial outlook. Perhaps Spadaro or De Filippo or any bright young man made up like an elderly well-to-do bourgeois will do the job. But you are wiser than I can boast of in such things.

No, I didn't think any more about the light comedy for you both and Gabin. I thought the idea didn't appeal to you, as you didn't take my hint then. Now I'll try and do my best. Meanwhile I thought of another subject for the sisters, a gruesome one, and will send it tomorrow, as today is a holiday and the post office closed. Its theme is 'suicide' seen as a contemporary way of life.

I start immediately on the development of *La vita bella.* A sainted power certainly there is who can make of me 'something rich and strange'—but she is not in Heaven. She is almost that far.

Love,
C.

About the last week of June I'll probably be in Rome to be awarded a literary prize. Could I meet you there to talk things over I'd be delighted.

So long,
C.

*To Doris Dowling, Rome**

[Turin] 11th June [1950]

Dear Doris,

Here's *La vita bella.* I was four days busy at it, but keep in mind that I had to write and type it afterwards, as I get ideas only with a pen in my hands.

Now the long day's task is done and I have immortal longings in me. 'Tis lousy to feel like a caged eagle, but feel we must.

Always ready at your sweet pleasure, Milady,

Love

*To Doris Dowling, Rome**

[Turin] 6th July [1950]

Dear Doris,

Well, I got a merry and reassuring card from Connie, in New Mexico (27th June), and I was very sad, knowing, as I know, that she'll never come back. I felt like a man deviously told that he's got cancer. It's a long time I realised that my lot is to hug shadows.

Rome was great, but would it have been anything without your loveliness and concern?[9] You made me feel at peace with you and my lot. You were a real friend, a fond sister, something I didn't know. Why can't one always feel so? Why must there be wars, threats, love, sex, oceans and cancer?

I hope something will turn up that will make you stick a little more to Italy. Working for the sisters is all that's left to me now. Don't laugh about this, I'm almost an old man.

They (I mean the whole [of] Turin and Italy) are treating me like a little Caesar and I'm behaving as prettily as I can. The trouble about these things is that they always come when one is already through with them and running after strange, different gods.

Love

[9] On 24th June Pavese was given the Strega Prize, a coveted literary award. Doris Dowling went with him to the celebrations.

*To Doris Dowling, Rome**

[Turin] 19th July [1950]

Dear Doris,

I hope your quarrel with Harry is by now patched up and another started and so on. Anyway this is better than looking at clouds and dreaming about their future shape when they'll have sufficiently progressed westward.

You speak no more about your production plans. Has the whole thing gone with the wind? Don't give up. You (let alone C.) are too clever to be satisfied with working for others. After all, neither marriage nor easy living nor anything of that sort can suffice: once I told you I was a caged eagle—well, you also and C. are.

The news about you staying and C. coming back started a dynamo in my system. But, you know, my only problem when as a boy, I ate ice-cream was 'How long is it going to last?' My rendezvous is going to be such an ice-cream.

Meanwhile Turin without you is like a tale told by an idiot. Don't say tomorrow and tomorrow and tomorrow, but come at once. You'll die of heat, but at least your corpse will be taken good care of. We'll offer you a suite at the Principi di Piedmonte and a place in Italian literature.

Regards to all concerned,
Love

To a girl, Bocca di Magra

[Sarzana (?) August 1950]

Dear Pierina,

When I came home last night I saw myself in the mirror. I didn't know I'd reached such a stage. You've been very good not to have told me this before.

I must have said and done many strange and wicked things last night. I notice that always happens when I see you dancing with other people. But to become detached, isolate myself, remain alone, would be a sin.

I wanted to go by myself to Sarzana for a rest, but then I hadn't the courage to come to Bocca. In short, I acted exactly as Poli did in my *Il diavolo sulle colline*, the fellow student in love with Gabriella.

'Why all this?' You will say, and may write to me about it. You see, when writing of me and you my hands are tied. Our states of mind are so different, so out of proportion, that my own words come back to me and wound me.

I simply must manage to overcome this reaction. I think it may be the music to which you are dancing that makes me feel hollow inside, curdles my blood and gives me the look of a maniac (the fierce, wild look of a suicide). There are moments when the most banal tunes seize me by the throat and make me weep.

So I'm writing to you this morning, master of myself and full of mortification. I will go to Bocca, not for this evening's dance, and will hope to see you on Monday. I beg you, Pierina, don't disappear—I love you.

Pav.

To the same girl

[Bocca di Magra, August 1950]

Dear Pierina,

I've ceased causing you this displeasure, but I couldn't do anything else. My immediate motive is that, while you are dancing and being guided by someone else, I am always out of it, but there is another, truer, reason. My candle has almost burnt out. Pierina, I wish I were your brother, primarily because there would then be a true bond between us, you could listen to me and believe what I tell you in all good faith. If I'm in love with you it is not only because (as they say) I desire you, but because our minds are akin. You move and talk as I had hoped, as a boy, I should do when I grew up to be a man. Instead of learning how to write, I should have spent time learning to take my place in the world.

But you, for all your dryness and cynicism, are not at the end of your candle, as I am. You are young, incredibly young, much as I was at eighteen, when I resolved to kill myself over some delusion or other, but did not do so. I was curious to know what tomorrow might bring, curious about my inner self. Life seemed horrible to me, but I was still interested in myself. Now the opposite is true. I know that life is a tremendous thing, but that I cannot shape it to my own liking. This is a futile tragedy, like having diabetes or lung-cancer.

I can tell you, love, that I've never woken up with a woman of my own beside me; that no one I have loved has ever taken me seriously; that I know nothing of the look of recognition a woman can give to a man. Remember that, by means of the work I've done, my nerves have always been under tension, my fancies swift and precise, my taste for other people's confidences. I've been in the world for forty-two years. One cannot burn the candle at both ends. In my case I have burned it all from one end only and the ashes are the books I have written.

It is not to arouse your pity that I've told you this—I know what pity amounts to in such cases—but for the sake of clarity, so that you won't believe that I've had bronchitis for fun, or to make me more interesting. I've finished with politics. Love is like the gift of God. Shrewdness is not enough. As for me, I love you Pierina, a fierce bonfire of love. Let's call it the final flicker of the candle.

I don't know whether we shall see one another again—at bottom there's nothing I want beyond that, but I often wonder what advice I would give you if I were your brother.

Love,
Pav.

To his sister Maria, Santo Stefano Belbo

[Turin] 17th August [1950]

Dear Maria,

I have the key now. All's well, except that my light isn't working. I spend most of my time at the local tavern, which costs me very little and I sleep well there. My clothes get filthy, but I am rich. For one short novel I've been paid 30,000 lire. Thank Federica for her note and tell her that, if God has made me great gifts, he has also given cancer to others. I don't see how those 'great gifts' are any help to me, but then I don't understand anything.

Keep well. I'm well, like a fish in ice. Remember me to Guglielmo.

So long,
Cesare

To Mario Motta, Rome

[Turin] 26th August [1950]

Dear Motta,

I've nothing to say. I trust your proof-sheets. Fortini will probably publish it. I have no intention of replying.

Who has 'returned'? the American girl? I've something else to think of now.

So long,
Pavese.

Index of Letters

Note: Letters to unknown and/or anonymous persons are listed under *Miscellaneous*